Major Religions

in India

Hinduism

Islam

Christianity

Sikhism

Buddhism

Jainism

K.S. Bhalla

Bhalla, Kartar Singh:
MAJOR RELIGIONS IN INDIA
Star, New Delhi (2005)

© **K. S. Bhalla**
ISBN 81-7650-164-6

First Edition: 2005
Price: Rs. 450/-
        (in U.K. £ 15.95)

Published in India by
STAR PUBLICATIONS PVT. LTD.
4/5-B, Asaf Ali Road
New Delhi-110 002 (INDIA)
(E-mail: starpub@satyam.net.in)

Distributors in the U.K.:
INDIAN BOOK SHELF
55, Warren Street, London W1T 5NW (U.K.)
(E-mail: indbooks@spduk.fsnet.co.uk)

Cover Design and Layout
Deepa Mukherjee

ACKNOWLEDGMENT
The author and the publishers gratefully acknowledge the co-operation
and help received from various friends and other sources from
where the material and the pictures included in this book were collected.
Errors, if any, are inadvertent.

Major Religions in India

CONTENTS

*****

Major Religions in India

India is the home of Philosophy, Religion and Spirituality. It is the birthplace of some of the most renowned religions of the world. It has produced spiritual masters of exceptionally high order who proclaimed that all religions were true, if followed in the right spirit. This was explicitly demonstrated by the great master Sri Ramakrishna (1836-1886) in his life. He took up spiritual paths of Hinduism like Vaishnavism, Shaaktha, Advaitism, and dived deep into Christianity and Islam, one after the other, one at a time, and followed them in full earnest and showed that they all lead to the same goal.

The most dominant religion in India today is Hinduism. It is also the most ancient of living religions of the world having its origin in pre-historic times. About 80.5 % of Indians are Hindus. Around 500 BC two other religions developed in India, namely, Buddhism and Jainism. Today about 0.40% of Indians are Jains and about 0.76% are Buddhist. Buddhism spread not only within the Indian sub-continent but also to kingdoms east and south of India. One comparatively new religion in India is Sikhism which was established in the 15th century. About 1.84 % of Indians are Sikhs.

A few non-Indian religions entered India at various points of time. Among them are Islam, Christianity, Zoroastrianism, Bahaism and Judaism. The largest non-Indian religion is Islam. Its followers are about 13.4% of India's population. It first came into India in 711 A.D. when an Arab general conquered Sindh and incorporated it into Umayyad Caliphate. From 1000 A.D. onwards, there was a series of Muslim invasions. Most of the Muslims who came with invading armies settled down here permanently and with them Islam spread in India.

Christians are about 2.33 %.of Indian population. Though first Christians came to India almost 2000 years ago, Christianity spread when Christian missionaries arrived in India with the European powers in 15th century.

Two other religions that arrived in India because of religious persecutions in the country of their origin, were Zoroastrianism (7th century) and Bahaism (20th century).

"Major Religions in India" gives a concise account of the origin, growth, tenets, beliefs, scriptures, shrines, traditions and practices of six major religions, namely,

Hinduism: The religion of infinite adaptability and diversity

Islam: The religion of submission to God

Christianity: The religion of the fatherhood of God and the brotherhood of man

Sikhism: The religion of divine grace, harmony and sacrifice

Buddhism: The religion of peaceful, ethical self-culture

Jainism: The religion of asceticism

The book is informative. It brings out positive aspects of these religions with a view to promoting among their followers and others a respect for and an understanding of each other's faith.

To guard against any factual error , texts were shown to scholars of respective religions before these were finalised for publication.

— K S Bhalla

Hinduism

THE RELIGION OF INFINITE ADAPTABILITY AND DIVERSITY

Table of Contents

ORIGIN

Hinduism is the oldest and perhaps the most complex of all the living world religions. It is the name given to a family of religions and cultures that began in India thousands of years ago and is as vigorous today as ever. It is the sum and substance of the life, history, growth and philosophy of the original Aryan settlers in Indus Valley from time immemorial up to the present. It reflects a continuous thought process of a country whose inhabitants aimed at finding out the meaning of life and death and what could have been the motivating force in the very creation of world. It is a spiritual history of Indian race.

Hinduism is not merely a religion. It is more than a religion in the Western sense. It encompasses an entire civilization. It is a way of life and culture of the people of India as a whole. Based on the teachings of ancient sages and scriptures like the Vedas and the Upanishads, it is a set of beliefs and traditions of many schools of philosophy and theology, many popular cults, and a large pantheon symbolizing the many attributes of a single God.

The word Hindu or Hinduism has not occurred even once in any book revered by Hindus. The word "Hindu" is derived from the name of River Indus, which flows through northern region of Indian sub-continent. In ancient times the river was called the 'Sindhu', but the Persians who migrated to India called the river 'Hindu', the land 'Hindustan' and its inhabitants 'Hindus'. Thus the religion followed by the Hindus came to be known as Hinduism.

Originally known as the Vedic Religion, i.e. the Religion of the Vedas (Scriptures) and Sanatan Dharma, i.e. the everlasting faith or eternal religion, it does not have a starting point in history, does not have a founder, and has no Church, as such. As a religion, it has no common creed, no fixed doctrine, and no binding rules. A Hindu can believe in several gods, one God, or no God at all.

DATING HINDUISM

The origin of Hinduism is looked at by different people in different perspectives. Some hold that it dates back to pre-history and that it started from the time of the creation of the universe 2.8 billion years ago. Some others stretch it to

Mohenjo-daro, Sindh: This view shows the high western mound made up of a massive mud brick platform and brick houses of the Harappan period (2600 to 1900 B. C.).

the origin of human race 1.34 million years ago. One school of thought says that it is 50,000 years old. Most Indian historians hold that it is about 10,000 years old. According to some other historians, including theologist like Max Mueller of Germany, it was practised by the "Aryan settlers" of Indus Valley and the local community, some 6000 years back. Archeological evidence found at Indus valley civilization at Mohanjodaro and Harappa appears to date Hinduism to 6000-7000 years Before Christ. The importance attached to the

River Saraswati and the numerous references to it in the Rigveda indicate that the Rigveda was being composed well before 6500 B.C. The first vernal equinox recorded in the Rigveda is that of the star Ashwini, which is now known to have occurred around 10000 B.C.

HINDU SCRIPTURES

The authorities for the Hindu way of life and beliefs and attitudes are its scriptures which fall in two main categories, namely, Shruti and Smriti..

■ Shruti means 'what was heard'. This refers to that philosophy which is thought to have been handed down to ancient sages directly from the gods. It includes the earliest of the Hindu scriptures, the Vedas and the Upanishads.

■ Smriti means 'what was written down and remembered'. This is the literature which is said to have been remembered and handed down by tradition. It includes all scriptures other than Vedas and Upanishads.

Vedas

The Vedas are based on older oral versions and are written in Sanskrit. They stem from the inner spiritual experiences of the ancient seers and constitute the highest religious authority in Hindu religion. Hindus believe that the Vedas are divine, timeless and eternal. There are four Vedas, namely Rig, Sama, Yajur, and Atharva Veda. Each Veda consists of sections namely *Samhita* (containing the hymns) and *Brahmana* (significance of the hymns), *Aranyakas* (interpretations), and *Vedanta* (Upanishhads which are metaphysical dialogues).

■ Rig Veda is the most important of the Vedas .It is a collection of 1,028 hymns written in praise of the most important gods of the Vedic period - such as Agni (god of fire), Indra (the storm god), and Varuna (the god of rain). These hymns were probably used during ancient sacrificial worship.

■ The Sama Veda is a samhita (collection of hymns) taken from the Rig Veda and arranged for use during worship.

■ The Yajur Veda is a collection of instructions to be followed by the Brahmin when making sacrifices.

■ The Atharva (or Brahma) Veda was the last of the four to be written down. It contains the knowledge given by Sage Atharvana. It contains magical charms and incantations

Upanishads

Upanishad means receiving knowledge while sitting near the teacher. These are conversations between self - realized souls and their students on the subject matter of Absolute Truth. They are concerned with learning about *Brahman* (the all-pervading life-force) and the relationship between *Brahman* and the universe. In these teachings the ideas of *karma, samsara* and *moksha* are introduced for the first time. Almost all the Upanishads are concerned with the relationship between *atman* (the individual soul) and *Brahman* (the universal soul). Upanishads are called Vedanta, because they expound on the spiritual essence of Vedas and they are found at the end of the Vedas. The Upanishads are texts, while Vedanta is a philosophy. There are 108 extant Upanishads

Smritis

Smriti scriptures include five distinct groups of writings :

Itihāsas (Epics): It comprises the two epics: Ramayana and Mahabharata, which contain detailed accounts of the lives and philosophies of two incarnations of Lord Vishnu, namely, Rama and Krishna, respectively. Ramayana was first written by Valmiki while Mahabharata by sage Vyasa. The Bhagavad-gita is the epitome of Hindu philosophy and is found in the Mahabharata. It contains some of the most brilliant theological lessons about the nature of God and of life ever written

Purãnas (Mythology): Puranas are called Vedas of common folk and are written in question & answer form. There are eighteen major Puranas. Each is a long book consisting of various stories of gods and goddesses, hymns, an outline of ancient history, cosmology, rules of life, rituals, instructions on spiritual knowledge. They consist of religious stories which make common people understand the higher truths of life.

Dharma Shãstras (Law Codes): Dharma Shastras are law codes based on Vedic teachings written by sages like Manu, Yatnavalka, Parasara and Gauthama.. These are the backbones of ethics and morality of Hinduism. The earliest Dharma Shastra is called "Code of Manu" and is popularly known as Manusmriti.

Ãgamas & Tantras Sectarian Scriptures : These are a group of literature which deals with worship of God in many forms and they lay down their own set of rules and regulations for their devotees. These provide guidelines as to the ways in which the worship of God can be performed, temples built etc. They have great amount of details on yoga also. The Agamas gave rise to 3 branches of Hinduism -

    a.   Vaishnavism

    b.   Shaivism

    c.   Shaktism

Darshana Sutras : The Darshanas are manuals of philosophy. These are explanatory texts of Vedas for the learned authors. They explain the Vedic teachings and philosophy for daily practice and understanding.

There are six Darshana Sutras :

Brahma Sûtra	Vedãnta philosophy of Sage Vyãsa
Mîmãmsã Sûtra	Philosophy of rites and rituals of sage Jaimini
Nyãya Sûtra	Logical analysis of sage Gautama (not Gautam Buddhã)
Vaisheshika Sûtra	Atomic school of philosophy of sage Kanãda
Sãnkhya Sûtras	Sãnkhya philosophy of sage Kapila
Yoga Sûtras	Yoga philosophy of sage Patãnjali

Period of Hindu scriptures

It is very difficult to give a date to any of the Hindu scriptures as most of them have a long oral tradition. They also have a history of being composed over a number of years by different writers.

The Vedas are as old as the Hinduism which many scholars believe to have originated about 6000 -10000 years Before Christ. But these were composed and written much later in point of time. The Rig Veda, the oldest of the four Vedas, is believed to have been composed around 1500 B.C. and written down about 600 B.C. According to a school of thought which believes in astronomical dating, the Rig Veda was composed between 4500 B.C. - 6500 B.C..

The Upanishads which are a continuation of the Vedic philosophy are believed to have been written between 800 B.C.- 400 B.C.

The Ramayana and Mahabharata , the national epics of India, describe events relating to Lord Rama and Lord Krishna. Different historians have dated Ramayana differently: Around 1000 B.C. - 4000 B.C. Based on astronomical dating Dr P V Vartak holds that Lord Rama lived around 7600 B.C. Guru Valmiki (the author of Ramayana) is referred to in the Taittiriya Brahmana (around 4600 B.C.) and therefore Ramayana is believed to have been written before that period. Some hold that Ramayana existed in oral tradition around 1500 B.C. and that it was composed around 400 B.C.

Mahabharata era is placed around 5561 B.C according to astronomical dating and around 5000 B.C according to some others. Some place Mahabharata era around 1200 B.C. It is said to have been composed between 1000 B.C. - 300 B.C. Bhagavad Gita , a part of the Mahabharata, is believed to have composed between 400 B.C.-200 B.C.

The Puranas are dated between 200 A.D. - 1,000 A.D The Sutras are placed between 7th and 2nd century B.C. Āgamas & Tantras scriptures are believed to have been composed between 650 A.D -1000 A.D.:.

PRINCIPAL HINDU BELIEFS

1. **Divinity of Vedas**:- Hindus believe in the divinity of the Vedas, the world's most ancient scriptures, and venerate the Agamas as equally revealed. These primordial hymns are God's word and the bedrock of Sanatana Dharma, the eternal religion which has neither beginning nor end

2. **Brahman** - *The God*:- Hindus believe in a one, all-pervasive Supreme Being, the God, who is both immanent and transcendent, both Creator and Unmanifest Reality. *Brahman* is not God in the Western concept of God. *Brahman* is the universal, cosmic soul. *Brahman* is everything and everything is *Brahman*. It is not personal and is seen more as the great energy that pervades everything. The fundamental concept in Hinduism is that God is one but He has many attributes and many functions and is called by many different names. Hinduism allows Hindus to believe that God is formless and also allows them to worship Him in diverse forms.

3. **Cycles of creation:-** Hindus believe that the universe undergoes cycles of creation, preservation and dissolution.. From the destruction of a previous universe, Lord Brahma arises to create a new universe; Lord Vishnu sustains it through a cycle of birth, growth and decline; Lord Shiva destroys the universe and the cycle begins again. Starting from *Satya Yuga* (when justice, truth and virtue reigned supreme), world has passed through *Treta* and *Dwapara Yugas* (when there was progressive downfall of values) . It is currently in *Kali Yuga*, the age of decline. The world will eventually be destroyed, only for a new world to appear in the distant future.

4. **Doctrine of 'Karma':-** Hindus believe in Karma, the law of cause and effect, by which each individual creates his own destiny by his thoughts, words and deeds; the law that good begets good, and bad begets bad. Every action, thought, or decision one makes has consequences - good or bad - that will return to each person in the present life, or in one yet to come.

5. **Re-incarnation**:- Also known as "transmigration of souls". Hindus believe that the soul reincarnates, evolving through many births until all *Karmas* have been resolved, and *moksha*, spiritual knowledge and liberation from the cycle of

rebirth, is attained. This is a journey on the cycle of life, where each person goes through a series of physical births, deaths, and rebirths. With good *Karma,* a person can be reborn into a higher physical form. Bad *Karma* can relegate one to a lower physical form.

6. **'Ahimsa'**:- *'Ahimsa'* means non-violence, non-injury (in thought, word and deed). Hindus believe that all forms of life are different manifestations of God ; that all life is sacred, to be loved and revered, and therefore not to be subjected to suffering, pain or injury.

7. **Many paths lead to God:-** Hindus believe that no particular religion teaches the only way to salvation above all others. It believes that all genuine religious paths are facets of God's pure Love and Light, deserving tolerance, regard and understanding. This doctrine lays foundation for the Hindu ideal of universal harmony.

8. *Nirvana* (**salvation**) :- *Nirvana* is the release of the soul from the seemingly endless cycle of rebirths. Hindus believe *Nirvana* to be the ultimate goal of their life.

9. *Avatars* (**Incarnation**):- Hindus believe that God incarnates on earth to uphold righteousness and destroy evil whenever there is decline of virtue.

HINDU GODS AND GODDESSES
BRAHMAN, the one true reality

For Hindus, the entire universe is part of the *Brahman. Brahman* is God but not God of just one world or a few worlds. It represents all the universes - the past, the present and the future . "God", for Hindus, is present in everything.

BRAHMAN, the 'impersonal' God and the universal soul (*Mahan Atma*)., is the Absolute Truth. It is the spiritual essence underlying all reality, is the only reality. All gods and the world

are only aspects of *BRAHMAN,* only an illusion in comparison to the one reality. *Brahman* is both the unmanifest and the manifest, the formless and the one with form. He is here and beyond. He is limitless, indefinable, without qualities, eternal, unchanging, inactive (complete in itself thus no need to act).

Hindus acknowledge and worship various gods, but these are all aspects of the one supreme "God".

BRAHMAN has multiple roles to play: To create; to maintain; to destroy. This can be viewed as the origin of the Trinity of Hindu gods:

Bramha [the creator]
Vishnu [the preserver]
Shiva [the destroyer]

Each god in the Trinity has his consort. Brahma's - Saraswati, the goddess of knowledge.

Vishnu's - Lakshmi, the goddess of wealth. Shiva's - Kali (Parvati), the goddess of power. The three goddesses are often worshipped in their own right as well as along with their spouses.

There are four similar sounding words, each different from the other: *'Brahman'* is the impersonal God and the world soul. *'Brahmanas'* are the appendices to Upanishad where the sacrificial rituals are carefully delineated. *'Brahma',* the Creator, is one of the three gods of the Hindu Trinity. *'Brahmin'* is one of the four castes among Hindus.

GODS AND GODDESSES

While Hindus believe in the existence of one and only one Supreme being, they worship Him in various forms known as deities or gods. The Hindu worship of many deities is not polytheism, but monotheistic polytheism. The monotheistic Hindu pantheon is an affirmation that the Supreme Being can be known in many ways and worshipped in many forms.

There are two distinct classes of gods. There are **Vedic gods** and **Brahmanic gods.**

The **Vedic gods** are the gods of the agricultural people of earliest times. Some of them are : *Dyaus*, the god of bright sky; *Varuna*, the god of rain; *Indra*, the god of sky and clouds; *Surya*, the god of light; *Savitar*, another personification of the sun; *Soma*, the god of light and dark; *Agni*, the god of fire; *Vayu*, the god of winds (air); *Yama*, the god of death; *Kuber*, the god of material wealth; Som, the god of moon.

Brahmanic gods
(Their physical characteristics are based on symbolism.)

Brahma

Lord Brahma , the first of the Trinity, is the god of creation, assisted in this process by his consort Saraswati, who is the possessor of ulti-

mate knowledge. Together, they are believed to have introduced soul into the cycle of life. He has four heads (originally five), representing the four Vedas which are said to have sprung from his heads. His four heads are also said to represent the four *yugas*. He is bearded & his eyes are closed in meditation. He sits on a lotus & his *vahana* (vehicle) is the swan. In his four arms he holds the Vedas, the *kamandalam* (water pot), *suruva* (sacrificial spoon) & a *mala* (rosary). He is a serene soul and is the provider of all sources of knowledge & wisdom.

Vishnu

Lord Vishnu, the second of the three gods of the Trinity, is the protector and preserver of the world and restorer of *dharma* (moral order). He is shown with four hands. One holds a conch shell (*sankha*) indicating spread of the divine sound "Om"; the second holds a discus (*chakra*), a reminder of the wheel of time, and to lead a good life; the third holds a lotus (*Padma*) which is an example of glorious existence and the fourth hands holds a mace (*gada*) indicating the power and the punishing capacity of the Lord.

His vehicle is the swift-flying bird *Garuda*.. He rests on the bed of the powerful, coiled serpent, *Seshanag* who represents the sleeping universe. He is believed to have appeared on earth in physical form to fight the evil elements whenever '*dharma*' (moral order) is disturbed. The forms in which he has appeared so far are: *Matsya* (fish), *Kurma* (tortoise), *Varaha* (boar), *Nara-simha* (man-lion), *Vamana* (dwarf), *Parashurama* (a powerful warrior), Rama (the Divine warrior and upholder of righteousness) , Krishna (the Divine lover and destroyer of evil), Buddha (the Divine sage) - according to some , it is Balaram. The tenth form in which he is yet to appear is that of *Kalki* (the saviour).

Shiva

Lord Shiva, the third god of the Trinity, appears in a meditating but ever-happy posture. He has matted hair which holds the flowing Ganges river and a crescent moon, a serpent coiled around his neck, a trident (*trishul*) in his one hand and ashes all over his body. Shiva's attributes represent his victory over the demonic

activity and the calmness of human nature. He is known as the "giver" god. His vehicle is a bull (symbol of happiness and strength) named Nandi. Shiva temples have *Shiva-Linga* as the main deity. He is also known as Mahadeva , Mahesh and Nataraj (the Lord of Cosmic Dance). His wives include Parvati and Sati and his sons are Ganesh (elephant-headed) and Skanda (many-headed).

Satyanarayana

Lord Satyanarayana is another form of Lord Vishnu who is commonly worshipped by Hindus in their homes . He has four hands like Lord Vishnu. However, his fourth hand does not hold a lotus; it is extended upward to bless people.

Rama

Rama, the central character of the epic Ramayana, is the seventh and most renowned incarnation of Lord Vishnu. Hindus believe that Rama lived in the *Treta Yug* . He is also called *Maryada Purusottama*, the most exalted and perfect human being. He was an ideal son, an ideal brother, an ideal king and, with his wife Sita, is held to be an ideal couple. Rama, the perfect *avatar* of the Supreme Protector Vishnu, is an all-time favourite among Hindu deities. He is the most popular symbol of chivalry and virtue and is held to be the embodiment of truth and morality. He respected the learned and the elderly. People adored him and he loved them. He was eloquent, handsome, and master of situations. He was courageous, brave and unconquerable. He is most often represented as a standing figure, with an arrow in his right hand, a bow in his left and a quiver on his back. He is depicted in princely adornments with a *"tilak"* or mark on the forehead, and as having a dark, almost bluish complexion, which shows his affinity with Vishnu. Although Rama and Krishna, both incarnations of Vishnu, are almost equally popular among Hindu devotees, Rama is seen as an archetype of righteousness. The prefix "Shri" to Rama indicates that Rama is always associated with *"Shri"* - the essence of four Vedas. Uttering his name (*"Ram! Ram!"*) while greeting a friend, and invoking Rama at the time of death by chanting *"Ram Naam Satya Hai!"*, show the profound respect he commands among Hindus..

Krishna

One of the most widely revered and most popular of all Indian divinities is Krishna who appeared in *Dwapara Yuga* and is worshipped as the eighth incarnation (*avatar*) of Lord Vishnu. His incarnation brought about a profound influence upon Indian thought and life. He plays a very important part in the Hindu epic Mahabharata, where he is a friend, philosopher and guide to Arjun. The most profound philosophy of Krishna and his teachings have been embodied in the Bhagavad Gita. He is also known for destroying evil powers throughout his life. Lord Krishna is shown as blue in colour and wears yellow clothes. The blue colour is always associated with infinity and the yellow colour represents earth. The blue form of Krishna clothed in yellow suggests the Infinite Reality reduced to a finite human being. He is usually shown with his pet cow, playing flute which symbolizes the spread of melody of love to the people. Lord Krishna performed many divine sports (*leela*) as a child. Along with Radha, his childhood devotee, the pair is worshipped as Radha-Krishna. This association symbolizes the eternal love between people and God . Of all the Vishnu *avatars* he is the most loved and one of the closest to the hearts of the masses who consider him their leader, hero, protector, philosopher, teacher and friend, all rolled into one.. He has influenced not only the religion and philosophy of India , but also its mysticism and literature, painting and sculpture, dance and music, and all aspects of Indian folklore. Krishna is the embodiment of love and divine joy that destroys all pain and sin..

Venkateshwer

Lord Venkateshwer is another form of Lord Vishnu.. He is also known as Balaji or Bithala. He has dark complexion and four hands. In his two upper hands he holds a discus (a symbol of power) and a conch shell (a symbol of existence). With his lower hands extended downward he asks devotees to have faith and surrender to him for protection. The famous temple at Tirupati (South India) is dedicated to him.

Hanumana

Hanumana is a monkey god. He is a great devotee of Lord Rama.. He is a symbol of courage, hope, knowledge, intellect and devotion. He is pictured as a robust monkey holding a mace (*gada*) which is a sign of strength and having a picture of Lord Rama tattooed on his chest which is a sign of his devotion to Lord Rama. He is also called *Mahaveera* (the great hero) or *Pavan-putra* (son of the wind). He is also known as '*Sankat-mochan*' (the remover of difficulties) and '*Bajrangbali*' (the strong).

Ganesha (Ganapati)

Ganesha , the elder son of Lord Shiva, is one of Hinduism's most popular deities. He is called *Vinayak* (kowledgeable) and *Vighneshwer* (remover of obstacles). He is also patron of letters and of learning; he is the legendary scribe who, using his broken tusk, which he often holds, wrote down parts of the Mahabharata epic. He is worshipped at the commencement of an auspicious function and new project for blessings and suc-

cess.. He has four hands, elephant's head and a big belly. His vehicle is a tiny mouse. In his hands he carries a rope (to carry devotees to the truth), an axe (to cut devotees' attachments), and a sweet dessert ball -*laddoo*- (to reward devotees for spiritual activity). His fourth hand's palm is always extended to bless people. A unique combination of his elephant-like head and a quick moving tiny mouse vehicle represents tremendous wisdom, intelligence, and presence of mind.

He is the Destroyer of obstacles -
'Vighna Vinashaka'
The harbringer of happiness and joy -
'Sukha Kartha'
The absorber of sorrow and misfortune -
'Dukha Hartha'
He makes wishes come true -
'Siddhi Vinayaka'

In Hindu mythology, there are differing accounts of how Ganesh acquired the head of an elephant. One account of his birth is that Parvati formed him from the rubbings of her body so that he might stand guard at the door while she bathed. When Shiva approached, unaware that this was his son, he was enraged at being kept away from his wife and proceeded to lop off the head of Ganesha. To ease Parvati's grief, Shiva promised to cut off the head of the first living thing he would see and attach it to the Ganesha's body. That creature was an elephant. Ganesha was thus restored to life and rewarded for his courage by being made lord of new beginnings and guardian of entrances. A prayer to Ganesha is invariably accompanied by smashing a coconut, symbolic of smashing the undesirable forces inherent in oneself.

Parvati / Durga

Goddess Parvati is the wife of Lord Shiva and exists in various divine forms. Two of her fierce but very powerful forms are Durga (goddess of power) and Kali (goddess of destruction). Both have eight hands and great power and energy (*Shakti*). Durga rides on a tiger and Kali rides on a corpse of a demon. Parvati was called *Sati* in her previous divine incarnation. The family of Lord Shiva, Parvati and their sons Ganesha and Kartikeya is an ideal example of family unity and love. She has a charming personality. She is adored by married women for a happy married life.

Lakshmi

Goddess Lakshmi is the wife of Lord Vishnu and is the goddess of wealth , purity, chastity and generosity. Her four hands represent four spiritual virtues. She sits on a fully blossomed lotus, a seat of divine truth. An aura of divine happiness, mental and spiritual satisfaction, and prosperity always exist around her. Her palm is always extended to bless people. She is worshipped especially during the festival of Diwali.

Saraswati

Goddess Saraswati is the wife of Lord Brahma and possesses power of speech, wisdom and learning. She has four hands representing four aspects of human personality in learning; mind, intellect, alertness and ego. She has sacred scriptures in one hand and a lotus (a symbol of true knowledge) in the second. With her other two hands she plays the music of love and life on violin (*veena*). She is dressed in white (sign of purity) and rides on a white goose (swan). She is given credit for inventing the language of Sanskrit and the Devanagari script in which it is written.

Vaishno Devi

Goddess Vaishnavi Devi , commonly known as Mata Vaishno Devi, is the manifestation of the collective spiritual strengths of Kali (goddess of power and destruction), Lakshmi (goddess of Wealth) and Saraswati (goddess of Learning). According to Hindu mythology, Vaishnavi, a devotee of Lord Vishnu, used to pray to Lord Rama and had taken a vow of celibacy. Bhairon Nath (demon god) tried to behold her and once, while she walked towards the Trikuta mountains, started chasing her. The long hike made Vaishnavi thirsty and she shot an arrow into the earth from where water gushed out. Charan Paduka is where she stopped and rested and is marked by the imprints of her feet. While she stopped to meditate in the cave at Adhkawari, it was nine months before Bhairon found her. Vaishnavi escaped by blasting an opening at the other end of the cave with her trident. On arriving at the Holy Cave at Darbar, she assumed the form of Kali and beheaded Bhairon. His head was flung up the mountain by the force of the blow and fell at the place where the Bhairon Temple is now located. Beheaded Bhairon prayed to Mata for mercy and was granted divine forgiveness before he died The boulder at the mouth of the Holy Cave is believed to be his torso. Thereafter, Vaishnavi decided to abandon her human form and assumed the face of a rock and immersed herself forever into meditation.

The shrine of Mata Vaishno Devi was discovered at an altitude of 5,200 ft in the Trikuta mountains forming a part of the lower Himalayas in Jammu and Kashmir. The belief is that anybody who walks the Himalayan trail to her abode to ask for a boon rarely goes back disappointed. The incredible and miraculous powers of Vaishno Devi draw devotees from far and wide. Devotees get divine motivation by chanting Jai Mata Di as they make the climb.

Gods/goddesses and their characteristics at a glance

God/Goddess	Characteristic
Brahma	Creator
Vishnu	Sustainer
Shiva	Destroyer
Saraswati	Knowledge
Lakshmi	Prosperity
Durga/Parvati	Shakti/Family
Venkateswara	Form of Vishnu
Satyanarayana	Vishnu - Protection
Rama	Ideal king - Ideal man
Krishna	Love, destruction of evil
Kartikeya	Perfection
Ganesh	Knowledge - Remover of obstacles
Hanuman	Courage
Gayatri	Vedas
Indra	King and warrior

RAMAYANA

The Ramayana is one of the two great Indian epics .It is about Rama who was born in a royal family of Raja Dasrath and was supposed to be the king, but because of his step- mother, he was forced to exile from his kingdom for fourteen years. During this period his consort Sita was kidnapped by Ravan, who was the Raja of Lanka. Rama with the help of his brother, Lakshman, and an army under the leadership of Hanumana, rescued Sita.

But the Ramayana is not only about Lord Rama and his attempt to rescue his wife Sita. Ramayana is also about devotion, loyalty, respect to elders and *Dharma* of a son, brother, husband and Raja. It is also about Ravan who terrorized religious-minded people and prevented them from performing religious rituals, to destroy whom Lord Vishnu incarnated in the form of Rama, eldest of the four sons of Raja Dasrath of Kosala. Prince Rama was to become Raja after his father retired . His stepmother, however, wanted to see her own son Bharata become Raja. Remembering that Raja Dasrath had once promised to grant her any two wishes she desired, she demanded that Rama be banished for fourteen years and Bharata be crowned Raja. The Raja had to keep his word to his wife and ordered Rama's exile. Rama accepted the decree unquestioningly

Rama's wife Sita and his brother Lakshman accompanied Rama in exile. Bharat was not happy at all this. Raja Dasrath could not bear the grief of his son Rama's exile and died. After his father's death, Bharat went to Rama in the forest and tried to convince him to return. Rama refused and insisted that father's wishes would be respected. Having failed to bring his brother back, Bharat brought with him Rama's wooden slippers and placed them on the throne and ruled in the name of Rama till Rama's return from the exile . In the forest, a female demon, Surpanakha , tried to seduce Rama but failed. On her persistence in her designs, Lakshman cut Surpanakha's nose. She was the sister of Raja Ravan, whom she told of the disgrace that she suffered at the hands of Rama and Lakshman. Ravan decided to avenge this humiliation. He kidnapped Sita and took her to his kingdom Lanka.

During their travels in the forest, Rama helped Sugreeva overthrow his brother Bali out of Kishkindha and become the Raja. In return, Rama got the entire army of Sugreeva including his commander Hanumana to help him out in the search for Sita..

Having failed to rescue Sita peacefully from the clutches of Ravan, Rama declared war on Ravan. In the war, Rama killed Ravan and was re-united with Sita. Meanwhile, the period of exile had ended. Rama, accompanied by Sita and Lakshman returned to Ayudhya and ascended the throne.

But the Ramayana did not end here. The fact that Sita had lived in another man's palace caused some murmurs about her chastity. She was required to take a fire test in which she sat in a fire . She came out unharmed and thus established her purity. Later, Rama abandoned her in deference to public opinion . The pregnant Sita went away to the forest and lived in the ashram of sage Valmiki and gave birth to Rama's twin sons, Lava and Kush. After 12 years, the separated family reunited with Raja Rama. Sita approached Rama and said, "Let me prove my innocence before you once and for all.". Sita took a step back and said, "Mother earth, if I have been faithful to my husband, take me home." It is said that the earth rumbled; the ground opened and took Sita in .

MAHABHARATA

Mahabharata is the longest epic poem in the world, almost 100,000 couplets long, originally written in Sanskrit, the ancient language of India. It is a timeless saga woven around two branches of a royal family divided on the issue of inheritance. The most important segment of the poem is the Bhagavad-Gita, a dialogue between Krishna, the eighth incarnation of Lord Vishnu, and the Pandava hero Arjuna on the meaning of life. The conflict begins when because of his blindness, Dhritarastra, the elder of two princes, is passed over as king on his father's death in favour of his brother Pandu. Dhritarastra later assumes power when Pandu renounces the kingship to become a religious hermit. The sons of

Pandu, the five Pandava brothers (Yudhisthira, Bhima, Arjuna, Nakula, and Sahadeva), grow up in the court along with their cousins, the Kauravas - one hundred sons of Dhritarastra, the eldest being Duryodhana. Because of the enmity and jealousy that develops between the cousins, the Pandavas are forced to leave the kingdom at the time of their father's death. All of them loved and worshipped their mother Kunti. During their exile, Kunti asked them to marry Draupadi, daughter of Kind Drupada. The Pandavas obeyed their mother. They return to experience some years of prosperity in a divided kingdom but are again forced to retire to the forest for 12 years when the eldest brother, Yudhisthira, loses everything in a game of dice to the eldest of the Kauravas. The feud between the Kauravas and Pandavas culminates in a great war on the field of Kurukashetra (north of modern Delhi, in Haryana State)..

The most dramatic figure of the entire Mahabharata is Krishna Vasudeva who was the supreme god Vishnu himself, descended to earth in human form to rescue law, good deeds, right, and virtue (all of these words refer to different aspects of "*Dharma*"). Krishna Vasudeva was the cousin of both parties, but he was a friend and advisor to the Pandavas, became the brother-in-law of Arjuna Pandava, and served as Arjuna's mentor and charioteer in the great war. All the Kauravas are annihilated, and, on the victorious side, only the five Pandava brothers and Krishna survive. Krishna dies at the hands of a hunter who mistakes him for a deer. The five Pandava brothers, along with Draupadi and a dog who joins them (*Dharma*, the god of justice, in disguise), set out for Indira's heaven. One by one they fall on the way, and Yudhisthira alone reaches the gate of heaven. After further tests of his faithfulness and

constancy, he is finally reunited with his brothers and Draupadi to enjoy perpetual bliss.

BHAGAVAD GITA

The Bhagavad Gita, the Song of the Lord, is one of the most revered of Indian scriptures. It is the epitome of Hindu philosophy, the essence of India's Vedic wisdom . Gita, a part of the Indian epic Mahabharata, recounts the greatest philosophical and religious discourse given by Lord

Krishna (the 8th incarnation of Lord Vishnu) to Arjuna at the time of the great war of Mahabharta . As the battle lines are drawn, Arjuna throws down his bow and arrow, and confesses his inability to kill his own cousins , kinsmen and those

revered teachers who had been the common teachers of the Kauravas and Pandavas. Lord Krishna exhorts him to realize that, truly speaking, we do not have it within power to kill anyone, nor can we be killed by anyone; and if Arjuna should imagine that he has such power, he has failed to understand the nature of the Divine. Lord Krishna then urges Arjuna to perform his duty, to be the warrior that he is. It is these teachings which brought Arjuna to proper mental poise, and enabled him to face the life and situation in a befitting manner. It imparts the knowledge of Self and answers two universal questions: who am I and how can I lead a happy and peaceful life in the world of dualities.

Some of the key teachings of the Gita are:

■ "The truly wise grieve not for the dead, nor for the living. Never have I (divine) not been, never hast thou not been, nor shall we ever cease to be hereafter."

■ "Just as a person lays aside worn-out clothes and puts on new ones, so too the embodied Self leaves its worn-out body to enter others that are new."

■ Weapons cannot cleave it; fire cannot burn it; water cannot wet it; winds cannot dry it. Beyond the powers of all these, the Soul remains everlasting, all-pervading, motionless, ancient."

■ To that which is born, the coming of death is certain; to that which is dead, certain is the coming of a new birth. Therefore, grieve not over the inevitable."

■ Thy right is to thy work, but not to its results. Let not the fruit of action be thy motive; nor be attached to inaction. "

■ Let the wise work, without attachment, wishing for the welfare of all the world."

■ Forsaking arrogance and lust, greed and anger, free from ego and the notion of "mine", one is beyond grief and desire. He treats alike all beings and attains supreme devotion to divine."

- all quotations from Bhagavad Gita.

Fundamentally, the Gita preaches three things:

First - do your duty to the best of your ability without expectation of results;

Second - believe that God is present equally in all human beings; and

Third - the ultimate aim of all mortals is to attain salvation, self realisation . A realised person lives in a spirit of love, forgiveness, strength and compassion.

The Gita is compiled in 18 chapters and has 700 Shlokas (stanzas).

Bhagvad Gita lays down three paths to moksha (salvation): Jnana Yoga, Karma Yoga and Bhakti Yoga. There is also a fourth path, Raja Yoga which is derived from the Yoga Sutra.

YOGA - PATH TO SALVATION

Yoga is a systematic discipline which includes a technique for the mastery of bodily organism and for rendering it healthy and various methods or techniques of mind- training for the sake of gaining the final knowledge and liberation. "Yoga is the cessation of agitation of the consciousness with the objective of creating a silence of the mind which is the prerequisite for the mind to be able to accurately reflect objective reality without its own subjective distortions. Yoga is the science and praxis of obtaining liberation (*moksha*) from the material world. The practice of yoga may lead to the union of the human with the divine - all within the self.

Yoga

- unites body, mind, and soul.
- unites the individual self (atman) with the universal Self (Brahman).
- unites individual people together in a community.

In Hinduism, there are four main ways to reach towards the divine reality, whether the ultimate goal is a better life, union with the divine, or a release from cycle of life. These ways are called yoga. They are:

Jnana-yoga - **the path of knowledge:** It is a system of reaching enlightenment by adopting the path of knowledge or Hindu philosophy. The basic premise of the way of knowledge is that the cause of our bondage to the cycle of rebirths in this world is ignorance. According to the predominant view among those committed to this way, our ignorance consists of the mistaken belief that we are individual selves, and not one with the ultimate divine reality -Brahman. It is this same ignorance that gives rise to our bad actions, which result in bad Karma. Salvation is achieved through attaining a state of consciousness in which we realize our identity with Brahman. This is achieved through deep meditation, often as a part of the discipline of yoga,

Karma-yoga - **the path of action:** It is a system of attaining liberation through selfless actions. Our actions shape our present and future. This is the path of doing acts free from the desire for selfish gain and dedicating everything one does to God. It lays emphasis on the idea that liberation may be obtained by fulfilling one's familial and social duties thereby overcoming the weight of bad *Karma* one has accrued.

Bhakti-yoga - **the path of devotion:** It is dedication, total surrender to God. This process involves total dissolution of "I" or "Ego". This path is God-centered, where a person's actions are performed for God and not for oneself.. This is the way most favored by the common man. It satisfies the longing for a more emotional and personal approach to religion. It involves the self-surrender to one of the many personal gods and goddesses of Hinduism. Such devotion is expressed through acts of worship, temple rituals, and pilgrimages. Some Hindus conceive of ultimate salvation as absorption into the one divine reality, with all loss of individual existence. Others conceive of it as heavenly existence in adoration of the personal God.

Raja yoga - **the path of meditation**, suited to the quiet and reflective personality (the spiritual side of human nature) . *Raja Yoga* is known as the 'royal' yoga. This is essentially the path of meditation, that is, of being able to remove one's own consciousness from its awareness of this world of *maya* and to focus only on the ultimate reality of the cosmos' unity. It is a very scientific path of God Realization. In this the individual practises self control and thought control of his body and mind.

These are all spiritual approaches to understanding the divine world. What is generally termed "Yoga" in the west are forms of physical exercises and control of the body and is properly known as *Hatha yoga*. It has no spiritual impact.

THE CYCLE OF CREATION AND DESTRUCTION

Hindus believe that time can be separated into 4 Yugas or periods. Together these four *Yugas* are called the Great Cycle of Time. They are: *Satya Yuga, Treta Yug, Dwapara Yuga* and *Kali Yuga*. In the *Satya Yuga*, truth, justice and virtue reigned supreme. These characteristics declined progressively in the subsequent eras . The world is now believed to be in the fourth and most degenerate stage, the *Kali Yuga,* which started in 3102 BC. Throughout these 4 Yugas, Lord Vishnu is believed to have already incarnated nine (9) times to fight against evil and to uphold righteousness. At the end of *Kali Yuga,* Lord Vishnu, it is believed, would appear in his 10th incarnation as Kalki - like a Messiah - on a white horse to punish the wicked and usher in a new age of happiness.

STRUCTURE OF HINDU SOCIETY

Caste system

There are four major divisions of traditional and orthodox Hindu society:

(1) the Brahmin (priestly and learned class); (2) the Kshatriya (military, professional, ruling, and governing occupations); (3) the Vaishya (landowners, merchants, and business occupations); and (4) the Sudra (labourers, manual workers).

The caste system started in the Vedic age but then it was not very rigid . It was in a rudimentary form in which a person's caste depended not upon his birth but upon his profession as is evident from some of the hymns of the Rigveda (9.112.3). But during the later Vedic period it became very rigid. In the name of religion, the caste system was then exploited by those in positions of power and authority to perpetrate the dominance of the priestly class and reduce competition to the ruling class in matters of political dominance.

True Hinduism does not support caste system. The focus of Hinduism is on the individual and his salvation, not on his caste or its privileges. Lord Krishna, who is one of the most revered gods of Hindus, was neither a Brahmin nor a Kshatriya, but belonged to a pastoral community

Caste System has been the bane of Hindu society for centuries. It has done much greater harm to human progress and suffering for a much longer period to a great many people than the slave system of the western world. Today 'untouchability' is a serious crime. But the idea of caste system still lingers in the minds of many Hindus and the caste is still considered important in determining a Hindu's place in society.

Ashramas - stages of life

As well as the social division of society into classes, the life of an individual was divided into stages, called *Ashramas* .In the Upanishads there are four stages of life which are suggested for the devout male Hindu.

1. **The Brahmacharya ashrama** - the student age. This *ashrama* lasts until the age of 25. The *dharma* of a student includes being obedient, respectful, celibate, and non-violent. His motto is : "The teacher is God."

2. **The Grihastha ashrama** - the householder. This *ashrama* begins when a person gets married, has a family, earns a living and serves others. It lasts until around the age of 50.

3. **The Vanprastha ashrama** - the stage of retirement from active life. The person spends time in prayer and distances himself from mundane involvements.. In earlier times, a man was expected to leave his home and live in forest, *(vana)*

4.. **The Sanyasa ashrama** - total dissociation from worldly involvements. . In this ashrama, the man totally devotes his life to God. He has no home or any other attachments. All worldly ties are broken, and the sole concern is *moksha* - liberation.

These stages of life were ideal but not rigidly enforced. Very few Hindu men ever became *sadhus* - holy men - as is contemplated in the fourth *ashrama* .

GOALS OF A HINDU

There are 4 legitimate goals in life *(purusharthas)* :

- *Dharma* (righteous living),
- *Artha* (pursuit of material gains by lawful means)
- *Kama* (delight of the senses),
- *Moksha* (salvation).

HINDU SYMBOLS

Hinduism employs the art of symbolism with amazing effect. No religion is so replete with symbols as this ancient religion. And all Hindus are touched by this all-pervasive symbolism all through the life in some way or the other.

OM

Om or Aum is of paramount importance in Hinduism . This symbol is a sacred syllable representing Brahman, the impersonal Absolute - omnipotent, omnipresent, and the source of all manifest existence. *Om* is not a word but rather an intonation, which, like music, transcends the barriers of age, race and culture . *Om,* is perhaps

the only word that phonetically and logically signifies the primordial sound. It is said that all the Vedas dissolve into the *Gayatri* and the *Gayatri* itself dissolves into *Om*. It is perhaps for this reason that almost all Vedic *Shlokas* (verses) begin with the word *Om*. The most revered symbol in Hinduism, it occurs in every prayer and invocation to most deities begins with it. As the symbol of piety, *Om* is often found at the head of letters, pendants, enshrined in every Hindu temple and family shrines. A newly born child of a devout Hindu is ushered into the world with this holy sign written on his/her tongue with honey.

Swastika

Second in importance only to the *Om,* the *Swastika* holds a great religious significance for the Hindus. *Swastika* is not a syllable or a letter, but a pictorial character in the shape of a cross with branches bent at right angles and facing in a clockwise direction. A must for all religious celebrations and festivals, *Swastika* symbolizes the eternal nature of the *Brahman,* for it points in all directions, thus representing the omnipresence of the Absolute.

Swastika is Ganesha's primary symbol. It is regarded as the sign of good-luck. It is used by housewives to symbolically guard thresholds and doors, by priests to sanctify ceremonies and offerings, and by businessmen to bless the opening pages of their account books. No ceremony or sacrifice is considered complete without this symbol of Lord Ganesha who is believed to ward off all types of misfortunes and obstacles.

The term '*Swastika*' is believed to be a fusion of two Sanskrit words '*Su*' (good) and '*Asati*' (to exist), which when combined means 'May Good Prevail'.

Hindu *Swastika* is not the same as Nazi *Swastika*. Hindu *Swastika* is a religious and a sacred symbol which is as ancient as Hinduism itself - over 6000 years. It is a symbol of godliness, not a symbol of hatred.

The Saffron Colour

If there is any colour that can symbolize all aspects of Hinduism, it is saffron - the colour of *Agni* or fire, which symbolizes the Supreme

Being. The saffron colour is considered auspicious by Hindus. It signifies the temple, the house of God, purity, devotion and godliness. Triangular saffron coloured flags are seen flying atop Hindu temples and clothes of this colour are worn by sages and monks as a mark of renunciation of material life.

The Lotus

The holiest of flowers for Hindus, the beautiful lotus is symbolic of the true soul of an individual. It represents the being, which lives in turbid waters yet rises up and blossoms to the point of enlightenment. Mythologically speaking, lotus is also a symbol of creation, since Brahma, the creator, came forth from the lotus that blooms from the navel of Vishnu.

Tilak

Tilak is a mark of auspiciousness. It is put on the forehead with sandal paste, sacred ashes or *kumkum* (red turmeric). It is applied at the *Ajna Chakra,* the space between the two eyebrows. Shaivites apply three horizontal lines with the sacred ashes. The vaishnavas apply three vertical lines *(Tripundra)* with sandal paste *(chandan)*. Some Vaishnavas apply only one vertical line. The worshippers of Devi or Shakti apply *Kumkum,* a red turmeric powder. Only the method and material of application differ, but the significance is the same.

Nandi

This is the Holy Bull (Nandi) - the vehicle and the flag of Lord Shiva. This is the emblem of Shaivites. On the wall of the Shaivite temples, in the flags, in the message headers and many other articles this emblem could be found. According to Shaivite scriptures bull represents the *dharma* (justice). *Nandi* is white which signifies purity of heart

leading to purity of thought, word and deed.

Trishul (trident):

The tri -headed spear is one of the renowned weapons of Lord Shiva. This is the second important emblem of Shaivites after *Nandi*. As the goddess Shakti also holds this trident, this is the symbol that is held high by the devotees of Shakti as well.

Tulsi

Tulsi plants are kept in the front yard of the house and are worshipped daily. *Tulsi* brings auspicious atmosphere and the leaves have medicinal value as well

Deep (Jyoti)

Every auspicious function is started by lightning a *deep* (lamp). Light represents knowledge, hope and all that is noble. It is lit in every temple and in the prayer room in Hindu homes.

Nataraj

Nataraj symbolizes Shiva, the Lord of Cosmic Dance. The circle around Shiva is a circle of fire, representing samsara, the endless cycle of death and re-birth. Shiva has four hands. In one, he holds a two-sided drum, symbolic of creation and the life-pulse of the universe. The opposite hand holds fire, signifying destruction. These balanced upper arms represent the balance of creation and destruction. The lower right hand displays the mudra of fearlessness. Shiva's lower left hand points outward, indicating his compassion and promise of release. Shiva's raised left foot indicates ascension to a higher level, a stepping out, or release, from the cycle of death and re-birth..

Shiva's right foot rests on a dwarf, symbolising the crushing of immaturity, ignorance and blindness towards the truth. Despite the chaotic and almost violent appearance of his dance, Shiva maintains a tranquil expression, lips closed together. The eye in the centre of Shiva's forehead indicates that he has a higher level of vision or insight into the universe, a deeper understanding of it. As an indication of the speed of his movement, strands of Shiva's long, matted hair extend outward in wild waves. These waves represent the flow of the sacred Ganges River. Shiva wears two symbols near the top of his head. The image of the skull represents death and Shiva's ability to escape or conquer it. The crescent moon represents illumination or consciousness.

HINDU RITES AND CEREMONIES

"*Godbhari*" and other ceremonies may be performed during pregnancy to ensure the health of the mother and the child-to-be-born.

At birth, before the umbilical cord is severed, the father may touch the baby's lips with a gold spoon or ring dipped in honey, curd, and ghee. The word *vak* (speech) is whispered three times into the right ear, and mantras are chanted to ensure a long life.

Namakarana, the ceremony of giving the child a name, takes place at the earliest convenience of the newborn baby's family. A sacrificial fire is lit and scriptural rites performed. A gold object such as a ring is placed around the child's neck. The child is then given a name that has previously been selected by parents in consultation with the priest or the astrologer or the elder members of the family.

During infancy, a number of rituals for the infant such as the first visit outside the house, preferably to a temple and the first feeding with solid food (usually cooked rice) are held in some Hindu families.

Karna-vedha or ear-piercing ceremony, now mainly restricted to girls, is held when the parents think they are ready but it is normally held quite early in life. The ear is pierced by a goldsmith who uses a gold, silver, copper or iron needle.

Mundan (tonsure) At a special ceremony, called *Mundan* ceremony, the first hair-cut, is held some time between the first and seventh year of life. This entails the shaving of a boy's head. As *mantras* are chanted, the father cuts the first tuft of his hair. The barber completes the job with a razor .

Upanayana (Sacred thread ceremony) A crucial event in the life of orthodox Hindu male is an initiation ceremony, called *upanayana* ceremony, which takes place for young males between the ages of six and twelve to mark the transition to awareness and adult religious responsibilities. At the ceremony , the family priest invests the boy with a sacred thread to be worn always over the left shoulder and under the right arm, and the parents instruct him in chanting the *Gayatri Mantra*.

Vivah (Wedding): The next important transition in life is marriage. For most people in India, wedding is preceded by a formal engagement ceremony . The exact date and time of the wedding are matters decided by the parents, usually, in consultation with astrologers. On the day of wedding, the groom, decked in all his finery, often travels to the wedding site on a caparisoned white horse or in an open limousine, accompanied by a procession of relatives and friends,

On arrival at the brides's place, preliminary rituals follow : *Jai Mala, Ganesh Pooja, Var Pooja, Kanya Daan, Paani Grahan, Gathbandhan,* etc. The bride and groom go through all the rituals with the help of a priest . And finally, amidst chanting of *mantras* before holy fire, the bridegroom and bride walk around the fire seven times and make vows of loyalty and sharing. In the first four rounds, the groom leads and in the next three rounds, the bride leads. On the completion of the seventh round, the marriage is deemed to have been solemnized and the parents of the bride give her away to the bridegroom who pledges to take full care of the bride The priest and elder members of the two families bless the couple . The bridegroom applies vermillion *(Sindur)* to the head of the bride and ties a *Mangal Sutra* (a special type of necklace of black beads) around the girl's neck .

Death: For most Hindus, cremation is the ideal method for dealing with the dead, although some groups practice burial instead. Infants are buried rather than cremated. At the funeral site , the closest relative of the deceased (usually the eldest son) takes charge of the final rites and, if it is cremation, lights the funeral pyre. Two or more days after cremation, ashes and fragments of bones are collected and eventually immersed in a holy river. Readings from holy books may take place for a few days following the death. The mourning period concludes with the holding of a ceremony, a memorial service, at which priests chant *mantras* from holy books and recite hymns; relatives and friends pray for the peace of the departed soul and offer him tributes; and the deceased family gives donations and gifts to religious institutions and charities.

REFORM MOVEMENTS

Arya Samaj

Swami Dayananda Saraswati (born in Gujarat into a rich Brahmin family) founded the Arya Samaj in 1875 as a reform movement within Hinduism. Arya Samaj aims at re-establishing the Vedas as the primary scriptural source, disavowing Puranic Hinduism in favour of Vedic Hinduism. It believes that the Vedas are eternal, infallible and a complete revelation of God. It expects every Hindu to know them and to expound them for the benefits of others. It advocates worship of God through study of the Vedas and holding of *havans* accompanied by recitations from the Vedas and observance of *Dharma* (moral duty and action) as prescribed in the Vedas. It believes in the Law of *Karma* and reincarnation of soul. It rejects caste system based on birth and believes that the depressed classes and Dalits are entitled to be invested with the sacred thread and given equal status with other Hindus. Arya Samaj is opposed to idol worship, non-Vedic literature such as the Puranas, animal sacrifice, discrimination against women, pilgrimage, ritual bathing , polytheism and complex temple rituals. It condemns child marriages and segregation of women.

Brahmo Samaj

In 1828, Raja Ram Mohan Roy founded the Brahmo Samaj (Society of Brahma) in an attempt to reform Hindu religious beliefs and practices. He was born into a Brahmin family in Bengal and experienced the orthodox practices of Hinduism in his youth. He studied the Quran, Buddhism and the New Testament. He disliked idol worship and hated the practice of *Sati*, after seeing his brother's widow burnt alive on her husband's funeral fire. He fought to abolish polytheism, idol worship, the caste system, child marriage, animal sacrifice and *Sati* .At the centre of the Brahmo Samaj are the beliefs that there is one God, who is omnipresent , omniscient, eternal and blissful, the creator, and the saviour of this world; that the human soul is immortal and is responsible to God for its doings; that man's happiness in this and the next world consists in worshipping God in spirit and in truth; that loving God, holding communion with Him, and carrying out His will in all the concerns of life, constitute true worship ; that no created object is to be worshipped as God, and God alone is to be considered as infallible and that the true way of serving God is to do good to man.

Sri Ramakrishna Mission

Sri Ramakrishna Paramhamsa, a great devotee and mystic, had a broad outlook of universalism. Ramakrishna brought old truths to light. He was an embodiment of the past religious thought of India. Ramakrishna preached that realization is the essence of religion and that all religions are paths leading to the same goal.

Under the inspiration of Sri Ramakrishna, Swami Vivekananda , the most outstanding of his followers founded a great and worldwide organization called the Ramakrishna Mission, which has worked for the spiritual welfare and multiform amelioration of the living conditions of the people of India and other countries. The Mission has dedicated itself to the service of those who were starving, depressed, or beyond the social pale. It highlights that the religion of the Hindus is centred on self-realizalion. Idols, temples, churches and books are aids and nothing more. It exhorts people to go to the root of religion, the God, and not merely talk of Him.. Ramakrishna Missions advocates tolerance and brotherly feelings among followers of all religions. According to it, the habit of prayer is good but if this is not accompanied by a corresponding improvement in one's nature, it is not worth much.

ISKCON- INTERNATIONAL SOCIETY FOR KRISHNA CONSCIOUSNESS

Sri Krishna Chaitanya Mahaprabhu introduced the chanting of Hare Krishna, Hare Krishna, Hare Rama ,Hare Rama, as a great vehicle for spreading love of God. He swept aside the restrictions of the hereditary caste system and made it possible for people of all ranks to achieve the highest platform of spiritual enlightenment. Prabhupada Swamy elaborated the *Mantra* and took it to all the corners of the world in 1965. "HARE " is the form of addressing the energy and the names Rama and Krishna are forms of addressing the Lord Himself. The three words Hare, Rama, Krishna are the transcendental seeds of the *Mahamantra*. The chanting is a spiritual call for the Lord and His energy to give protection to our soul. Hare Krishna movement's mission is to present Krishna's teachings as they are, without watering them down or compromising to suit popular fashion. All initiated devotees of the Hare Krishna movement vow to follow four rules: (1) No gambling; 2) No intoxicants : (3) No meat-eating: (4) No illicit sex:_

Sathya Sai Baba Mission

At the age of 14, Sathya Sai Baba declared to his parents that he had come to this world with a mission to re-establish the principle of Righteousness, to motivate love for God and service to fellow human beings. Since then, he has consistently called on all mankind to Love All, Serve All and has repeatedly asserted that the essence of all scriptures is Help Ever, Hurt Never!

Sathya Sai Baba urges mankind to:

- Believe in God --for there is only ONE GOD for all mankind, though He may be called by many names.
- Follow sincerely your respective religions and live your daily lives in consonance with the teachings of good behaviour and morality.
- Respect all other religions --for no religion advocates the negative and lower qualities of man.
- Perform selfless service to the poor, the sick, and the needy without thought of reward or fame.
- Cultivate in your lives the values of truth, divine love, right conduct, peace, and non-violence and promote these values among all.
- Be patriotic and respect the laws of the country in which you live.

Radhasoami Satsang

The Radhasoami Satsang was founded in Agra in 1861 by a banker named Shiv Dayal Sahib (1818-1878) when he publicly proclaimed his doctrine. He was the first Guru and was later known as Soamiji Maharaj. Radhasoami Faith is a gospel of love. Love towards the holy feet of Radhasoami Dayal, love towards the Guru of the time and love with all the human beings, is its cardinal message. The basic tenets of the Radhasoami tradition are: (1). The practice of *surat shabd yoga* (daily meditation). (2). Obedience to the living master who initiates the disciple into the path. (3). A pure moral life which includes abstinence from meat, fish, eggs, alcohol, drugs, and sex outside of marriage. (4). The firm conviction that *jivan mukti* (liberation or enlightenment while living) is possible under the guidance of a realized saint or mystic. The teachings of the Radhasoami Faith are similar to those of the faith known as the Religion of the Saints or *Sant Mat* as taught by Guru Nanak , Kabir Sahab and other saints. It is said that one can be a Hindu, Sikh, Muslim, Christian or of any faith and still be a Radhasoami. Prayer and work to help others is a necessary part of daily life. The Radhasoami movement has splintered into groups. Each group has its own main centre. Radhasoami Satsang (Soamibagh) and Radhasoami Satsang (Dayalbagh) are in Agra. Radhasoami Satsang (Beas) is at the Dera Ashram, Beas, Punjab. In the U.S., Sant Bani Ashram is in New Hampshire.

PROMINENT HINDU SAINTS

Adi Shankaracharya: Adi Shankaracharya was born in the early 9th century AD at Kaladi in Kerala. This was the time when Hinduism was divided into various sects and Buddhism held somewhat of a sway in India. Shankaracharya was a child prodigy who mastered the Vedic scriptures at a very early age and renounced the worldly life at the age of eight. He lived a very short life of 32 years but in that brief span of life he changed the outlook of the country and its people by revamping the vast Hindu literature into simple, easy to understand language , revived Hinduism and strengthened its base . Acclaimed as one of the greatest philosophers and savants of Bharat, he established four spiritual centres in the four corners of the country, thus upholding the underlying unity of the holy land of Bharat.

Anandamayi Ma (1896-1983): Was born to Bengali parents in a small village of Kheora in Tripura(now in Bangladesh) . After her marriage at an early of age of 12, she passed through difficult times, but carried herself with aplomb. During this period she developed intense devotion to Lord Krishna and underwent gradual inner transformation, which led to her self realization at the age of 26. As time went by, her popularity grew and people from far and wide

started visiting her to seek her blessings..

Aurobindo, Sri(1872-1950): Born in Calcutta , Sri Aurobindo was sent to England for education at the age of seven. Back in India in 1893. he worked in the Baroda State Service when he developed deep love and reverence for Indian culture, nationalism and *Yoga*. He translated some Upanishads, the Gita, the two epics, the works of Kalidasa, Bhavabhuti and some other prominent ancient writers. At that stage, he chose to join the revolutionary indepenence movement. Returning to Calcutta In 1906 he joined the National College as its Principal and turned increasingly to the practice of *yoga* and meditation. Due to his revolutionary activities, he was sentenced to one year imprisonment. While serving the jail term, he experienced the universal presence of Lord Krishna. After his release, he shifted his residence to Pondicherry, where he spent the rest of his life exploring the various levels of consciousness and trying to bring the supramental consciousness into earth consciousness. In his efforts, he was assisted greatly by the Mother who came originally from France. His mission was continued by the Mother till she passed away in the seventies.

Chaitanya Mahaprabhu (1486- 1533) : . Born in Mayapur, West Bengal, Sri Krishna Chaitanya Mahaprabhu was the tenth child of his parents, Jagannath Misra and Sachi Devi. The first eight- all daughters- had died soon after their birth. Gauranga as he was originally called, was kind and compassionate, pure and gentle, sweet and loving. In 1509, Gauranga went on a pilgrimage to Gaya, where he took Isvar Puri, a Sanyasin of the order of Madhvacharya, as his Guru and became a devotee of Lord Krishna. At the age of twenty-four, Gauranga got himself initiated by Swami Keshava Bharati under the name of 'Krishna Chaitanya'. Gauranga preached Vaishnavism wherever he went and held *Sankirtan* attracting thousands of people. At last, Gauranga returned to Puri and settled there. Disciples and admirers from Bengal, Brindavan and various other places came to Puri to pay their respects to Gauranga. Gauranga held *Kirtan* and religious discourses daily. When in communion with his Lord, he danced in ecstasy. When he was in an ecstatic mood, he did not eat or drink. He spread the *Yuga-dharma* and the process of *Harinam Sankirtan* - the congregational chanting of the Holy Names of the Lord - Hare Krishna Hare Krishna Krishna Krishna Hare Hare . Hare Rama Hare Rama Rama Rama Hare Hare.

His last words were: The chanting of Krishna's Name is the chief means of attaining Krishna's feet in the *Kali Yuga. Sankirtan* of the Name is the supreme healer in the Iron Age. *Sankirtan* tantamounts to Vedic sacrifice. Sankirtan destroys sins and purifies the heart and creates *Bhakti*. Chant the name while sitting, standing, walking, eating, in bed and everywhere. The Name is omnipotent. You can repeat the Name at any place, at any time.

Dayanand Saraswati, Swami: Swami Dayanand (1824-1883), born in Tankara in the state of Gujarat, India, was the founder of the Hindu reform organization Arya Samaj, which he established on April 7th 1875, in Bombay . His original name was Mool Shankar. Throughout his life, his main message was " Back to the Vedas ". By this, Swami Dayanand meant that Hindus should stop practising beliefs such as idol worship, caste, polytheism, pantheism, untouchability, child marriages, forced wid-

owhood, and many other practices which he felt were wrong. To spread awareness of his movement and to revitalize Vedic knowledge, Swami Dayanand published many religious books. These include; Satyartha Prakash (The light of Truth), the Rig-Vedaadi, Bhasyya- Bhoomika, and Sanskar Vidhi.. His relentless campaign against Hindu orthodoxy earned him the wrath of orthodox Hindus. There were 14 attempts at poisoning Dayanand. The 14th attempt proved fatal. He was a great sage and a fearless reformer who worked all his life for restoration to Hinduism its natural radiance and wisdom

J. Krishnamurthy (1895-1986): J.Krishnamurthy was born at Madnapalle in Andhra Pradesh. At the age of 14, when he was in Madras (now Chennai), he happened to come into contact with Annie Besant, who recognized his spiritual evolution and adopted him. Three years later she took him to England for his education. . Annie Besant and Lead Beater wanted to groom J.Krishanmurthy as a future Messiah. They were fully convinced of his spiritual greatness and his role in the spiritual evolution of the world. To prepare him and his close associates for his future role, they set up the Order of the Star. But while in England, Krishnamurthy developed a new vision of his own which prompted him in 1929 to disband the Order of the Star and distance himself from the activities of the Theosophical Society. From then on till his death , Krishnamurthy travelled to several parts of the world, holding public as well as private conversations with various people. J. Krishnamurthy is undoubtedly one of the greatest original thinkers of the modern world. His teachings are transcendental and incomprehensible to minds that are caught in the mire of conformity and conditioning.

Mirabai: Mirabai is the most famous of the women *bhakta* poets of north India. There are differences about the precise details of her life. According to one version, she was born in 1504 and was the only daughter of a Rajput chieftain ,Ratan Singh. Her mother died when Mirabai was only four or five years old.. Mirabai is said to have been devoted to Lord Krishna from a very early age. She was married to Bhoja Raj, the heir apparent to the throne of the famous warrior Rana Sanga of the House of Sisodiya. There were no children from this marriage, and in the event Mirabai took no interest in her earthly spouse, since she believed herself to be married to Krishna. By 1527 A.D. she lost her father, her husband and her father-in-law . Mira, who had dedicated her life to Lord Krishna, accepted these bereavements stoically. It is said that her relatives expected her to commit *sati* (self-immolation), after the death of her husband . But Mira did not. She wrote: *"sati na hosyan girdhar gansyan mhara man moho ghananami",* "I will not commit *sati*. I will sing the songs of Girdhar Krishna." Then onwards, Mira began to devote most of her time in prayer and worship and, when things became too uncomfortable for her in the palace, she left the palace for good and went to the pilgrimage of Mathura, Vrindavana and finally to Dwarika. Mira composed hundreds of poems in praise of her God, Lord Krishna. They are full of vivacity and feelings. Her poems have gained a unique popularity and are sung by the rich and the poor alike, even to this day. She spent her life dancing in trance and singing the attributes of her Beloved Krishna till she left this mortal world in 1550.

Morari Bapu, Sant: (1946-) Sant Morari Bapu was born in 1946, in Gujarat in a large family of six brothers and two sisters. He was a child prodigy who started learning the great epic Ramayana at the early age of five from his grandfather. By the age of 12 he mastered the entire Ramacharit manas and was able to recite it by heart. His discourses on Ramayana have won him fame in all parts of India as well as outside.

Ramakrishna, Sri (1836-1886): Born at Kamarpukur near Calcutta, in Bengal, and originally named as Gadadhar Chatterjee , Sri Ramakrishna , was destined to return to Hinduism the glory it had enjoyed before the foreign rule. He was described by Romain Rolland as "the perfection of two thousand years of the spiritual life of three hundred million people". Sri Ramakrishna showed wonderful qualities of purity and love. He was initiated into Vedantic meditation by Totapuri, a reputed monk who attained oneness with God after forty years of penance. Such was the devotion of Sri Ramakrishna that, to the amazement of his Guru, he attained in one day, what the Guru took forty years to achieve. He explored each of the world's great religions, Islam, Christianity and Buddhism, and found that he could have the vision of God by following any one of their paths. He could neither read nor write, yet he soon knew the basic teachings of all the sects of Hinduism. A great part of Sri Ramakrishna's life was spent in training his disciples, among whom Swami Vivekananda stood foremost. His spiritual impact on India and the world has been tremendous

Ramanujacharya, Sri: (1017-1137): Born at Sri Perambadur in Southern India and named Ilaya Perumal by his parents.,.Sri Ramanujacharya was one of the foremost exponents of the Vishishtadwaita (qualified dualism) philosophy, which was based on the premise that

God and soul were separate entities as opposed to Shankara's philosophy of Advaita (Non duality). Young Perumal grew up at Kanchipuram and mastered all the Vedas by the age of 16.. He renounced the worldly life at the age of 30 and got a new name as Ramanuja Muni. After being initiated into the secrets of Vaishnavism, he decided to help the people with the knowledge he gained. Soon his popularity grew. He traveled to various parts of India spreading the message of Vishishtadvaita and winning many people to his path. After his death, his body was said to have been preserved within the temple precincts, at Sri Rangam, in a sitting posture.

Rama Tirtha, Swami (1873-1906) : Gossain Tirtha Rama was born in a small village in the district of Gujranwala (now in Pakistan). From an early child hood he was inclined to listening to recitations from the holy scriptures. After completing his college education he worked for a while as a Professor of Mathematics. A few years later he resigned from his job, renounced the worldly life and went to the Himalayas. After returning from the Himalayas, Swami Ramathirtha spent the rest of his life, spreading the Vedanta. He visited Japan and then USA, where he attracted attention and made a mark.. After an eventful life, the Swami t left behind him a large following and a great legacy.

Tukaram, Sant: Sant Tukaram was born in 1608 in village Dehu on the banks of the river Indrayani into a Sudra family. In mid-twenties, Tukaram turned to poetic compositions (*abhangs*). He is said to have been visited in a dream by Namdeo, a great poet-saint of the thirteenth century, and the family deity Lord Vitthal , who inspired him to compose *abhangs*. In doing so, Tukaram incurred the wrath of the Brahmins. Taunted by the local Brahmins to throw his compositions into river Indrayani and recover them if he were a true devotee, Tukaram threw them into the river, went on a fast-unto-death, and after thirteen days of his fast, the manuscripts of Tukaram's poems reappeared. This turned his detractors into his followers and over the few remaining years of his life, Tukaram acquired a reputation and following of a great saint. In the forty-eighth year of his life, in 1649, Tukaram disappeared. His followers believed that Lord Vitthal himself carried Tukaram away. Most of his hymns are devoted to Lord Krishna. His love for beggars and the poor, whom he gave away money and his possessions, was boundless.

Tulsi Das, Goswami (1532- 1623): He was born in a Saryuparin Brahmin family of Gonda district, western U.P. The various traditions about him affirm that he was deeply in love with his wife Ratnawali and could not bear separation even for a short while. On one occasion due to her sarcastic reproach: "My body is but a network of flesh and bones. If you would develop for Lord Rama even half the love that you have for my filthy body, you would certainly cross the ocean of *Samsara* and attain immortality and eternal bliss". These words touched Tulsidas deeply. He left his wife and home and became an ascetic. He spent fourteen years in visiting the various sacred places of pilgrimage .He is believed to have started his magnum opus, the Ram Charit Manas (in Avadhi dialect) in A.D. 1574, at the age of 42, on the sacred banks of Ganges in Banaras and completed it in A.D. 1584. He spent most of his later life in Banaras, engaged in his literary career. Tulsi Das wrote a number of other poems , namely, Dohawali, , Kavita Ramayan, Gitawali, Vinay Patrika .. His smaller works include Ram Lala Nahachhu, Parvati Mangal, Janaki Mangal and Barvai Ramayan. Tulsi Das was not merely a poet of great excellence but a spiritual teacher. His name has become a household word and his memory is worshipped by millions.

Shirdi Sai Baba: Born in a an obscure village of Maharashtra nearly a hundred years ago, he is regarded as one of the greatest saints of the 20th Century. Through his life and activities he proved to the world that religion is not a barrier to the goal of universal brotherhood. During his life time, on many occasions he exhibited wondrous miraculous powers and through the purity of his character and love of his heart he won the hearts and souls of millions of people from diverse backgrounds. His greatness lay in his simplicity and his unconditional love for his followers. He passed away on October 15, 1918.

Vallabhacharya (1479-1531): Son of a Telugu Brahmin and a contemporary of Sri Chaitanya Mahaprabhu, he was the founder of the Vaishnavite cult of Rajasthan and Gujarat and was regarded as an *Avatara* of *Agni*. In his twelfth year, he completed the study of the Vedas, the six Darshanas and the eighteen Puranas at Varanasi.. For his genius and learning, Raja Krishna Deva at Vijayanagar invested him with the title of '*Vaishnavacharya*'. On cmpletion of his life's mission, he went one day to bathe in the Ganges at Hanuman Ghat. when a brilliant light was seen ascending to the sky and he had disappeared.. Vallabhacharya was the exponent of pure Monism or the *Shuddhadvaita* school of philosophy. He laid great stress on *Pushti* (grace) and *Bhakti* (devotion). He regarded *Maha Pushti* as the highest grace or *Anugraha*

which helps the aspirant attain God-vision.

Vivekananda, Swami (1863-1902): Born in Calcutta and named Narendranath Datta, he was very generous, loving and devoted, with a strange attraction for wandering *Sadhus*. He enjoyed doing worship of Lord Rama and Lord Krishna with his mother. He came into contact with Sri Ramakrishna in a function in his college when on hearing him sing devotional songs, Sri Ramakrishna fell into a state of ecstasy. Narendra yearned intensely for God and began to follow the Master for realisation. Narendra, now known as Swami Vivekananda, founded an Ashram near Calcutta, in order to organise better the Master's mission. This was the beginning of the Ramakrishna Mission. In 1893, Swami Vivekananda went to America to attend the World Parliament of Religions in Chicago. His powerful speech on Hinduism, which he described as the mother of all religions, brought him instant fame and he was acclaimed as the most ideal interpreter of India's wisdom. As a true Sanyasin he refused to sell religion for the sake of amassing money. While turning down an offer from Harvard to teach Indian religions and philosophy, he preached the gospel of unity of faiths and stressed the need for service to the poor and the sick. He believed that no religion was higher than 'service to the mankind'. After his stay of two years in America he toured England and Europe for three months. His aim was to awaken the masses by reviving Vedic religion, and to clean it of the dross and impurity that had clung to it for so many centuries. In 1902 Swami Vivekananda entered *Mahasamadhi*. Six years of discipleship under Sri Ramakrishna had taken him to the realms of God-vision. Swami Vivekananda's gospel was one of hope, faith and strength. His clarion call to the nation was: "Awake, arise, and stop not till the goal is reached."

WORSHIP

Hindu worship, or *puja,* involves images or icons *(murtis)* and prayers *(mantras)* . Worship may be performed at home or in the temple. Hindu worship is primarily an individual act rather than a community one. Worshippers repeat the names of their favourite gods and goddesses or/and repeat *mantras.* Water, fruit, flowers and incense are offered to god during worship. A large segment of Hindu homes have a separate exclusive place where deities are installed and prayers are said and offerings are made. At a Hindu temple, a priest may read, or more usually recite, from the Vedas and other scriptures to the assembled worshippers. Hindu worship may be classified into three categories: *Nitya* (every day); *Naimittika* (at certain times during the year, such as celebration of festivals etc); and *Kamya* (optional but desirable such as pilgrimage).

Gayatri Mantra

Gayatri Mantra is the most revered and the most widely known mantra of Hindus. It is recited almost every day during celebrations and ceremonies and on other occasions .

It is the universal prayer enshrined in the Vedas. It is the essence of the Vedas. Lord Krishna says in the Bhagavad Gita: " Amongst the *Mantras,* I am the Gayatri". It is believed that by chanting the *Gayatri mantra* and firmly establishing it in the mind, if one carries on one's life and does the work that is ordained, one's life will be full of happiness. It reads as follows **(in Sanskrit):-**

Om Bhoor Bhuvah Svah
Tat Savitur Varenyam
Bhargo Devasya Dheemahi
Dhiyo Yonah Prachodayaat.

It means:
We meditate on the glory of the Creator;
Who has created the Universe;
Who is worthy of Worship;
Who is the embodiment of Knowledge and Light;
Who is the remover of all Sin and Ignorance;
May He enlighten our Intellect.

Aarti - Jai Jagdeesh Hare

In temples and households in the north India, the following *'Aarti'* - devotional song - is sung in the morning and in the evening .The *Aarti* is performed with a small deep placed on a plate which is rotated in circle in front of the deity accompanied by ringing of bells.

Om Jaya Jagadeesha harey Swaami Jaya Jagadeesha harey
Bhakta janon key sankata, daas jano key sankata, Kshana mein door Karey - Om Jaya Jagadeesha harey .
Salutation to Thee, O Lord of the universe,
Thou, who, in an instant, removest the sorrows and problems, of those who love Thee!
Salutations unto Thee!

Jo Dhyaavey Phala Paavey Dukha Vinasey Mana kaa
Sukha Sampati Ghara Aavey, Kashta Mitey Tana kaa -
Om Jaya Jagadeesha harey…
Thou rewardest Thy devotees, who singest Thy praise, by removing their mental afflictions. Joy, prosperity and health enter the homes of those who pray to Thee!

Maat Pitaa Tum Merey Sharana Gahoon kiski Tum Bin Aur na Doojaa Aash karoon Jiski - Om Jaya…

Thou art my Mother and Father, whose refuge I seek, There is no one else beside Thee, who I could really count on!

Tuma Purana Paramaatmaa Tuma Antaryaami
Par-Brahma Parameshvara Tuma Sabake Swami - Om Jay…

Thou art Complete and Perfect! There is nothing hidden from Thee!
Thou art Perfect, Eternal, Absolute. The Lord of all Creation!

Tuma Karunaa Ke Saagar Tuma Paalana Kartaa
Mai moorakh khal-kaami
Mai Sevaka Tum Swami Kripaa Karo Bharataa - Om Jay….

Thou art an Ocean of Compassion, Thou art the Protector of all, I am ignorant, O Lord! I am but your Servant, while Thou art my Master!
Do Have Mercy on me!

Tum Ho Ek Agochara Sabkey Praanapati
Kisa Vidhi Miloon Dayaamaya Tuma ko main kumati - Om Jay..

Thou art the One. The Real Essence. The Life of all lives. How do we unite?
I, who am so ignorant, and Thou who art All Merciful?

Deena Bandhu Dukha Harataa Thaakur Tum merey Swaami Rakshaka tum Mere
Apney haath uthaao, apney charan lagaao, Dwaar para main terey, Om Jay……

Thou, art the Succour of the oppressed, and the Remover of pain and sorrow. Thou art my Protecting Force! I beseech Thee to Raise Thy hand, so that I surrender to Thee!

Vishaya Vikaar Mitaao Paap Haro Devaa
Shraddhaa Bhakti Badhaao Santan Ki Sevaa - Om Jay…..

Help me to get rid of my imperfections and vices, Bless me with increasing faith, and spirit of service to the devout!

Tan Man sab tera, sab kuchh hai tera,
Tera tujhko arpan, kyaa laagey mera. Om Jay…

All that I possess belongs to Thee, I offer Thee what in reality is Thine, As nothing is truly mine!

IMPORTANT HINDU FESTIVALS

Hindu festivals are based on the lunar calendar. Some of the important festivals are:

Deepavali (Diwali)

It is also called the Festival of Lights and comes in the month of Kartika [Oct./Nov.]. Many mythological stories prevail for Deepavali; the major two being the return of Lord Rama to Ayodhya after killing Ravana and the second being the death of Titan of Hell, Narakasura by Lord Krishna. Both the events signify victory of good over evil. People light candles and earthen lamps in their houses, worship Laxmi [Goddess of Wealth] and exchange gifts and distribute sweets .

Dussehra

Ten days of celebration during September-October in honour of Durga or Kali to celebrate the triumph of good over evil. In north India, it is celebrated particularly to mark the victory of

Lord Rama over demon king Ravan by burning his effigies .

Holi

A spring festival also called Festival of Colours. It is celebrated in the month of February/March. The mythological story behind Holi is of Prahlada, Holika and Hiranayakshyup which signifies Holika burning to ashes and Prahlada emerging as great worshipper of Lord Vishnu and defeater of demon Hiranayakshyup. People celebrate Holi by throwing coloured water and bright powders on each other A very exuberant festival marked by dancing, singing and merry-making when distinctions of caste, class, age, and gender are suspended .

Onam

Celebrated in Kerala to mark the end of summer monsoons. It has a mythological story of welcoming demon King Mahabali to his lost kingdom.

Pongal

Celebrated in Tamil Naidu during the months of Januray/Feburary. It is celebrated at the time of rice harvest.

Raksha Bandhan

Celebrated in the months of July/August. Sisters tie Rakhi [sacred thread] to the wrists of their brothers who in turn give them presents and renew commitment to protect them against any harm.

Rama Navami

Held in March/April to celebrate the birthday of Lord Rama, the 7th incarnation of Lord Vishnu.

Ganesh Chaturthi

Celebrated in August/September to mark the birthday of Lord Ganesha.

Navratri

Festival of Nights; lasts for 9 days with 3 days each devoted to worship of Goddess Durga [Goddess of Valour], Lakshmi [Goddess of Wealth] and Saraswati [Goddess of Knowledge].

Saraswati Puja

A festival honouring Goddess of Knowledge.

Shivaratri

Celebrated (January/February) as the birthday of Lord Shiva.

Krishna Janamashtami

Celebrated as the birthday of Lord Krishna. in August/September

Kumbh Mela

It is a religious bathing festival of enormous size where millions of monks, pilgrims, and religious devotees come for a historical ritual bathing at river sites considered sacred. The significance is spiritual purification and spiritual elevation of the pilgrims. Bathing in the sacred rivers is believed to purify and wash of the sins of the pilgrims. The bathing is followed a ceremony which secures them the blessings of the deity.

Kumbh Melas are held at various intervals:

Maha Kumbh Mela: This is an extraordinary, once-in-a-life-time festival held at Allahabad , occurring every 144 years.

Purna Kumbh Mela: Takes place after every twelve years and the last one took place in January 2001. It is held at the confluence of three rivers Ganga , Yamuna and the mythical river, Saraswati in Allahabad (U.P.)

Ardh Kumbh: Held in the 6th year after Kumbh Mela, i.e. it falls between two Puran Kumbh Melas. It has the same religious value and the same main bathing days as in Kumbh Mela.

Kumbh Mela: The mela is held every three years, rotating through the four cities of Prayag/Allahabad (in U.P. at the confluence of three rivers Ganga , Yamuna and the mythical river, Saraswati,) , Nasik (in Maharashtra on the banks of Godavari river), Haridwar (in U.P. where the river Ganga enters the plains from Himalayas) and Ujjain (in Madhya Pradesh on the banks of Shipra river) .

Magh Mela: The Annual Mini Kumbh is held every year except the years of Kumbh Mela and Ardh Kumbh Mela. Magh Mela is held in the month of Magh (Jan-Feb); hence the name.

HOLY PLACES AND PILGRIMAGE CENTRES

Pilgrimage is an important aspect of Hinduism. It's an undertaking to see and be seen by the deity. Popular pilgrimage places are rivers, but temples, mountains, and other sacred sites in India are also destinations for pilgrimages as these are the sites where the gods are believed to have appeared or become manifest in the world. Some of the prominent pilgrimages are:

Varanasi (also known as Benares and Kashi) , on the banks of the holy river Ganges in Uttar Pradesh, associated with Lord Vishwanatha (Shiva) - considered to be the holiest of holy places.

Rameshwaram at the southern tip of India is the southern counterpart of Kashi.

The river Ganges is the holiest river for Hindus.

Char Dham (Four pilgrimages): Badrinath [North]; Puri [East]; Rameshwaram [south]; Dwarka [West]

Char dham circuit of Garhwal and Kumaon: Kedarnath, Badrinath, Gangotri and Yamunotri.

Char dham circuit of Shankaracharya maths : Kancheepuram, Puri, Dwarka and Varanasi

Other pilgrimage centres

Amarnath	J & K	Lord Shiva
Ayodhya.	Uttar Pradesh	Sri Rama (birth place)
Dakshineshwar	West Bengal	Kali
Dwaraka.	Gujarat	Lord Krishna
Gokarna.	Karnataka	Shiva
Hardwar	Uttaranchal	Holy Ganges
Kanchi.	Tamilnad	Kamakshi
Kanyakumari	Kerala	Kanyakumari (Parvati)
Kurukshetra.	Haryana.	Hindu Dharma Kshetra
Madurai.	Tamilnad.	Meenakshi
Mathura.	Uttar Pradesh.	Sri Krishna (birth place)
Melukote.	Karnataka	Cheluvanarayana (Krishna)
Nasik	Maharashtra	Kumbh (Godavri river)
Nanjanagudu.	Karnataka	Srikanteshwara
Pandharpur.	Maharashtra	Panduranga
Prayag.	Uttar Pradesh.	Confluence of Sacred rivers
Puri.	Orissa.	Lord Jagannath
Sabarimalai.	Kerala.	Ayyappa
Srirangam.	Tamilnad.	Ranganatha

Sringeri.	Karnataka	Sharadamba/ Shankaracharya
Tirupathi.	Andhra Pradesh	Venkateshwara (Vishnu)
Tiruvanatapuram.	Kerala.	Anantha Padmanabha
Vaishnodevi.	Kashmir	Durga

FOOD INJUNCTIONS

Most devout Hindus are vegetarian. Some may eat fish and eggs. Occasionally westernized Hindus may eat meat. But Beef is taboo because the cow is sacred. Devout Hindus may avoid alcoholic beverages while westernized Hindus often drink alcohol. Some sections of Hindus avoid onions, garlic, turnips, and mushrooms. Some even avoid red foods (tomatoes) because of association with the colour of blood.

HINDU (INDIAN NATIONAL) CALENDAR

The Indian National Calendar, called the Saka era, is based on both lunar and solar years. The start of the Indian National Calendar year coincides with March 22, except in a leap year, when it coincides with March 21. The year is counted from the first year of the Saka era, in A.D. 78. The Gregorian year 2004 translates to Saka era 1925-1926.

Month	Days	Begins
1. Chaitra	30 / 31*	March 22 / 21*
2. Vaisakha	31	April 21
3. Jyaistha	31	May 22
4. Asadha	31	June 22
5. Shravana	31	July 23
6. Bhadra	31	August 23
7. Asvina	30	September 23
8. Kartika	30	October 23
9. Agrahayana	30	November 22
10. Pausa	30	December 22
11. Magha	30	January 21
12. Phalguna	30	February 20
* leap year		

The traditional Hindu calendar is called the Vikrami Samvat which started 57 years before the Gregorian era . It is based on a year of 12 lunar months; i.e., 12 full cycles of phases of the Moon. The discrepancy between this lunar year of about 354 days and the solar year of about 365 days is partially resolved by addition of an extra month every 30 months. Gregorian year 2004 translates into Vikrami Samvat era 2060-2061.

HINDU POPULATION

According to one view, the highest figure for Hinduism , world-wise, is 1.4 billion

(Clarke, Peter B., editor, The Religions of the World: Understanding the Living Faiths, Marshall Editions Limited: USA (1993); pg. 125.). According to another view, World Hinduism adherent figures may be between 850 million and one billion.

Top 10 Largest National Hindu Populations

Country	Percent	Number
India	80.5	827 Million (2001 Census Report)
Nepal	89	17,380,000
Bangladesh	11	12,630,000
Indonesia	2.5	4,000,000
Sri Lanka	15	2,800,000
Pakistan	1.5	2,120,000
Malaysia	6	1,400,000
USA	0.2	910,000
Mauritius	52	570,000

South Africa	1.5	420,000
United Kingdom	1	410,000

Source: Ash, Russell. The Top 10 of Everything, DK Publishing, Inc.: New York (1997), pg. 160-161; Adherents.com.

Figures are approximate.

HINDU SAYINGS

The one who remains the same towards friend or foe, in honour or disgrace, in heat or cold, in pleasure or pain; who is free from attachment; who is indifferent to censure or praise; who is quiet, and content with whatever he or she has; unattached to a place, a country, or a house; who is cool and composed, and full of devotion--that person is dear to Me." ~ **Bhagavad Gita**

"Let noble thoughts come to us from everywhere."—**The Vedas**

Treating pleasure and pain, gain and loss, and victory and defeat alike engage yourself in your duty. By doing your duty this way you will not incur any sin. (2.38) —**Bhagavad Gita**

As leaving aside worn-out garments, a man takes other, new ones. So leaving aside worn-out bodies, to other, new ones goes the embodied (soul). —**Bhagvad Gita**

Neither the study of Vedas, nor excessive charity, neither Yajnas nor any vows and austerities can ever yield rewards for a man whose heart is tainted." **Manu 2.97**

A man who is sinful, whose wealth is begotten by evil means, who is ever engrossed in violence—such a man will never attain happiness in this life. **Manu 4.170**

The sinner might achieve success in the short run, he might even amass a fortune and might then conquer his enemies. But soon, his sins visit him and he is destroyed branch and root. **Manu 4.174**

For all the sins created by his students, the Guru is morally responsible . **Neethi Sastram**

Whenever there is decline of righteousness, O Arjuna, and rise of unrighteousness, then I manifest Myself. (IV.7) For the protection of the good, for the destruction of the wicked, and for the establishment of righteousness, I manifest Myself in every age. (IV.8) - **Bhagavad Gita**

He that does everything for Me, whose supreme object I am, who worships Me, being free from attachment and without hatred to any creature, this man, Arjuna!, comes to Me.- **Bhagavad Gita 11:55**

He who hates no single being, is friendly and compassionate, free from self-regard and vanity, the same in good and evil, patient; contented, ever devout, subdued in soul, firm in purpose, fixed on Me in heart and mind, and who worships Me, is dear to Me. - **Bhagavad Gita 12:13-14**

Honour thy teacher as God - **Upanishads**

Lead me from the unreal to the real.

Lead me from the darkness to light.

Lead me from death to immortality.- **Upanishads**

GLOSSARY OF HINDU TERMS

Agni: The Hindu god of fire

Ahimsa: "noninjury." It is the principle that a person should do no harm to any living being

Ashram: A stage in the life of a Hindu. Life of a Hindu is divided in four stages - Brahmacharya Ashram, Grihastha Ashram, Vanprastha Ashram and Sanyasa Ashram.

Atman: An individual's soul or self..

Aum: See om .

Avatar: An incarnation of God ; Lord Vishnu has ten avataras.

Bhagavad Gita: A Hindu holy book of Hindus

Bhakti: Worship of or devotion to God.

Bhakti yoga: - the path of devotion., dedication, total surrender to God.

Brahma: One of the three gods of Hindu Trinity. The Creator

Brahman: The spiritual essence underlying all reality, the only reality, limitless, impersonal, indefinable, eternal, unchanging; all-pervasive Supreme Being who is both immanent and transcendent, both Creator and Unmanifest Reality.

Brahmin: The highest of the four main Hindu castes. It is the priestly caste.

Caste System: Division of Hindu society into four castes, namely, Brahmin (the priests); Kshatriya (warriors); Vaishya (artisans, farmers and traders); and Sudra.(manual workers).

Deva/Devi: Hindu terms for god and goddess.

Dharma: Code of righteous living. Proper social behavior; virtuous behavior; social duty; acting in prescribed ways;

Durga: One of the wives of Lord Shiva. The goddess who defeats the forces of evil in order to protect the world

Ganesha: Son of Shiva and Parvati . The elephant-headed god of wisdom, good luck and remover of obstacles .. Also known as Ganapati.

Garbha-griha: Ihe innermost sanctuary of a temple

Guru: A spiritual master or teacher.

Jnana yoga (pronounced as Gyana Yoga): A system of reaching enlightenment through the path of knowledge.

Kali: A goddess - wife of Shiva.

Karma: The moral law of cause and effect by which one reaps what one sows.

Karma yoga: A path to liberation through following a code whereby one acts without desiring the fruits of one's actions..

Kshatriya: The second of the four main Hindu castes, warriors, leaders, and administrators.

Lakshmi: Wife of Lord Vishnu, the goddess of wealth , purity, chastity and generosity.

Linga/m: An oblong, upright stone that is a symbol of Shiva.

Mantra: A verse from Hindu scriptures.

Moksha: Liberation or release from the cycle of death and rebirth.

Om (Aum): The most sacred syllable representing Brahman, the impersonal Absolute. The most revered symbol in Hinduism . An intonation with which every prayer begins.

Parvati: Shiva's wife ; .mother of Lord Ganesha

Prasad: Food or some other offering given to a deity and then returned by the priest to a devotee as a blessing.

Puja: Worship, usually of a deity or the image of a deity. . An offering (usually flowers, food, adoration, music, etc.) to a god or goddess.

Puranas: Hindu mythology. Religious stories to make common people understand the higher truths of life.

Rama: The central character of the epic Ramayana. The seventh and most renowned incarnation of Lord Vishnu.

Reincarnation: The cycle of death and rebirth. The transmigration of an individual soul to a new body after death.

Rig-Veda: The oldest sacred book of Hindus

Sadhu: A Hindu holy man who renounces life and everything that goes with it and becomes a wandering hermit

Samsara: The cycle of death and rebirth

Sanatana Dharma: The 'Eternal religion'; Hinduism.

Sannyasin: A Hindu who has dissociated himself from worldly involvements and entered Sanyasa Ashram.

Shaivism: The worship of Shiva, including beliefs and rituals.

Shiva/Siva: One of the three gods of Hindu Trinity. The Destroyer

Shudra: The fourth group in the Hindu caste system (menial workers).

Transmigration: Notion that after death, a person's soul is born again into another individual (human, animal, etc.).

Upanishads: Scriptures which expound the spiritual essence of Vedas and are parts of the Vedas. These are texts of conversations between self-realized souls and their students on the subject matter of Absolute Truth.

Vaishya: The third group in the Hindu caste system (merchants, traders, farmers and craftsmen.)

Vaishnavism: The worship of Vishnu, often in the form of one of his avatars, Rama and Krishna.

Varna: The term for caste, a social division into which a person in Hindu society is born. There are four major castes in Hindu society: Brahmin, kshatriya, vaishya, and shudra..

Vedas: The oldest of Hindu scriptures. They are four in number .

Vishnu: One of three gods in Hindu Trinity, the Preserver.

Islam

THE RELIGION OF SUBMISSION TO GOD

Table of Contents

BEFORE ISLAM

Before the birth of Islam, there was no political unity in the Arabian peninsula. The nomadic tribes of the region subscribed to a primitive religion of naturism, whereby they attributed spirits to inanimate objects such as stones and trees. They had no formal priesthood but, when in need of advice, consulted soothsayers who would respond with brief, enigmatic oracular utterances.

Within Mecca itself tribes worshipped idols placed around and over the Ka'aba. As the trade routes of the Arabian peninsula grew in importance in the fourth century AD, towns developed, especially along the west and east coasts. Among these towns was Mecca made up of a number of tribal groups, the most important of which was the Quraish tribe. It was from the Quraish that the Prophet Muhammad (peace be upon him - pbuh) was believed to have descended.

BIRTH OF ISLAM

Islam, the second largest religion in the world today, was founded by Prophet Muhammad (pbuh) in Arabia in the early 7th cent. AD. The word ' islam' means "submission"-specifically, submission to the will of the one God, called Allah in Arabic. The word Islam comes from the same root word as "salam"which means peace The very name of the religion, AL ISLAM in Arabic, means at once submission and peace, for it is in submitting to God's Will that human beings gain peace in their lives in this world and in the hereafter.

The word "Muslim"means one who submits to the will of God regardless of ethnic background, nationality, or race. Being Muslim is living according to the Prophet 's message, willful submission, and active obedience to God.

Prophet Muhammad (pbuh) was born in 570 CE in Mecca to a merchant family of the Hashemite clan of the Quaraishi tribe. His father, Abdullah, died several weeks before his birth. His mother died when he was six years old. He was raised by his paternal grandfather 'Abd al Muttalib until the age of eight, and after his grandfather's

death, by Abu Talib, his paternal uncle.. Under the guardianship of Abu Talib, Muhammad (pbuh) began to earn a living as a businessman and a trader. Muhammad (pbuh) was popularly known as 'al-Ameen' for his unimpeachable character by the people of Mecca and the visitors alike. The title Al-Ameen means the Honest, the

Reliable and the Trustworthy, and it signified the highest standard of moral and public life. Upon hearing of Muhammad (pbuh)'s impressive credentials, Khadijah, a rich merchant widow, asked Muhammad (pbuh) to take some merchandise for trade to Syria. Soon after this trip, when he was twenty-five, Khadijah proposed marriage to Muhammad (pbuh) through a relative. Muhammad (pbuh) accepted the proposal.

Living and working in the city he was born in, Muhammad (pbuh) was unhappy and disturbed by the selfishness and lack of compassion of the elite of the city. He started going to hills to meditate in the solitude of the desert. He frequently visited a cave called Hira just outside Mecca. During one of his meditations in the month of Ramadan - he was forty years at that time - he received the first revelation from God through the Archangel Gabriel. Gabriel appeared to him and said: "Rise, for thou art the Prophet of God. Go forth and preach in the name of thy Lord. Your God is merciful."A voice was heard - the voice of the Lord - addressed to the Prophet.

When he returned from the cave, Mohammed (pbuh) was filled with divine majesty. On informing his wife of the vision he had, she said, "You are faithful and never utter an untruth. Therefore, you may obey the call and follow the voice." Khadija was the first disciple to profess faith in the Prophet. She became his disciple and the first follower of Islam.

Gabriel visited the Prophet as commanded by Allah revealing *Ayat* in Arabic over a period of twenty-three years. All the revealed verses over a period of 23 years ,ending in 632 CE, were compiled in the book known as Qur'an. The name Qur'an appears in the revealed verses. The Qur'an is not a literary work of Mohammed (pbuh); it is a direct revelation of the Lord. The

Qur'an does not contain even a word from the Prophet. The Prophet's sayings, actions, and approvals are recorded separately in collections known as Hadith.

"Al-Qur'an"(the Arabic word) literally means the recitation. The Qur'an contains God's final message to mankind as it was revealed to Prophet Muhammad (pbuh). The book was recited publicly in front of Muslim and non-Muslim communities during the life of Muhammad (pbuh). It was also completely written during the life of Muhammad (pbuh), and numerous companions of the prophet memorized the entire Qur'an word-for-word as it was revealed.

The total number of chapters in the Qur'an is 114, beginning with 'al-Fatiha' the opening chapter. Ever since Muslims have maintained the same text in its original Arabic language, stressing the importance of leaving the Qur'an unaltered.

The mission of Prophet Muhammad (pbuh) was to restore the worship of the One True God, the creator and sustainer of the universe, as taught by Prophet Ibrahim and all Prophets of God, and to demonstrate and complete the laws of moral, ethical, legal, and social conduct and all other matters of significance for the humanity at large.

Muhammad (pbuh) began to recite revelations to people in public and invite them to Islam. The Quraish, leaders of Mecca, took his preaching with hostility. The most hostile and closest to the prophet was his uncle Abu Lahab and his wife

At this time, Mecca was a prosperous city whose wealth and influence were based on the caravan trade and on the Ka'aba, a shrine and a place of pilgrimage housing the pagan deities then being worshipped by the Arabs. Muhammad (pbuh)'s message, heralding a new socio-religious order based on allegiance to one God-Allah-was unpopular among the leaders of

Mecca, and they forced Muhammad (pbuh) and his followers to emigrate north to the oasis town Yathrib (Medina). This occurred in 622, the year of the hijra, or "emigration," which marks the beginning of the Muslim calendar.

The people of Medina accepted Mohammed's faith readily because it was plain, simple and direct. With their help in 630 C.E, Prophet Muhammad (pbuh) marched to Mecca with an army consisting of 3000 Muslims of Medina and Muslims from other Arab communities that joined him on the way, totalling ten thousand Muslims. Before entering the city he sent word to citizens of Mecca that anyone who remained in his home, or in Abu Sufyan's home, or in the Ka'aba would be safe. The army entered Mecca without fighting and the Prophet went directly to the Ka'aba. He prayed to Allah for the triumphant entry in the holy city.

The people of the city expected general slaughter in view of their persecution and torture of Muslims for the past twenty years. While standing by the Ka'aba, the Prophet promised clemency for the people of Mecca.

The Prophet declared:

Allah made Mecca holy the day He created heavens and earth, and it is the holy of holies until the Resurrection Day. It is not lawful for anyone who believes in Allah and the last day to shed blood therein, nor to cut down trees therein. It was not lawful to anyone before me and it will not be lawful to anyone after me.

The people of Mecca then accepted Islam including the staunch enemies of the Prophet.

PILLARS OF ISLAM

There are five acts of worship that are so fundamental that the Prophet grouped them together as the five pillars of Islam. Every Muslim is expected to fulfill these obligations. They are:

1. Al- Shahadah (Testimony - Bearing witness to the one and only God)

Allah in Arabic implies the one and only true God, the beginning and the end of everything, neither born nor giving birth. The Qur'an states that He is beyond human description, but is referred to in the Qur'an by ninety-nine attributes, such as the merciful, the compassionate, the forgiving. Together with the command to bear witness and acknowledge the singularity, centrality, unity, and uniqueness of God, the believer is enjoined to confess that Muhammad (pbuh) is God's messenger and prophet.

2. Al-Salah (Prayer)

A Muslim must offer prayer (*salat*) 5 times a day. The Qur'an does not state the number and manner of prayers; these were established by the Prophet. Prayers are recited with the face towards the Ka'aba at Mecca. The five prayers are:

- **Fajr** (Morning Prayer) which is performed some time between the break of dawn and just before sunrise.
- **Zuhr** (Noon Prayer) offered from just after midday to afternoon.
- **'Asr** (Afternoon Prayer) offered from late afternoon until just before sunset
- **Maghrib** (Sunset Prayer) offered between sunset and darkness

■ **Isha** (Night Prayer) offered at night time, often just before sleeping.

All five prayers in Islam are congregational and are to be offered in group, but they may be offered individually if, for some reason, a person cannot be present with a congregation. When conducted in congregation, the prayers are led by an Imam, who is usually either a person schooled in Islam or simply one among the group who is more knowledgeable, older, or recognized by the others as being especially pious.

Muslims stand shoulder to shoulder and kneel a number of times, depending on whether it is the morning prayer (twice) or the late-night prayer (four times). Standing shoulder to shoulder, irrespective of status in life, symbolizes equality before God. In Islam, as the Prophet said, no man is better than another save for his piety, which only Allah can judge. At each kneeling, the Muslim places his forehead on the ground (*Sijdah*), a symbol of the equality of all men, humility, worship of the Creator, and the fact that from earth we come and to earth we return. Each part of the prayer ends after *Sijdah* with *Salam,* turning the face to the right and to the left, i.e. invoking peace and blessing of Allah on all the people . All Muslims at prayer face Mecca, where the Ka'aba is located. It is the *qibla* (the direction) which provides unity and uniformity for all Muslims. At an earlier time, it was the practice to face Jerusalem, the second holiest city in Islam. The Ka'aba holds the remnants of Abraham's temple.

Special early afternoon prayers are offered on Fridays in congregational mosques. These are preceded by a sermon from the pulpit by the Imam, also called the *Khatib.* On the two annual religious festival days called Eids, there are special prayers followed by sermons in the morning. These prayers are held in large congregational mosques and also in large open enclosures , called *Eidgahs*.

Before prayers, Muslims are required to perform ablutions, which include washing the face, arms, and feet in a ritual prescribed by the Prophet.

3. Al-Siyam (Fasting during Ramadan)

Fasting during the month of Ramadan, the ninth month in the Islamic lunar calendar, is required of those whose health permits. (The Islamic lunar calendar is 11 days shorter than the Gregorian calendar, thus the annual shift of Ramadan's occurrence in relationship to the Gregorian calendar.) It is a complete fast, requiring Muslims to abstain from food, drink and sexual activity from dawn to sunset.. During Ramadan there is an emphasis on piety and religious observances. Those who are sick, elderly, or on a journey, and women who are pregnant or nursing are permitted to break the fast and make up an equal number of days later in the year. If they are physically unable to do that, they must feed a needy person for every day missed or contribute to the Zakat.. Children begin to fast (and to observe the prayer) from puberty, although many start earlier.

4. Al-Zakat (Almsgiving - Charity)

Although required by the Qur'an, *zakat* is specified in detail only in the practice and teachings of the Prophet and in later interpretations. *Zakat* literally means purification. In practical terms, it means setting apart for Allah every year a certain portion of one's savings and wealth (generally 2.5 percent) and spending it upon religious duties and on needy members of the community. It is now common under Muslim governments for the *zakat* to be calculated at a per cent of the accumulated wealth of a man or his family at the end of each year and to be levied by the government. In non-Muslim countries, the collection and distribution of the *zakat* is undertaken by the Muslim community.. A pious person may also give as much as he or she pleases as *sadaqa*. But *zakat* is different from sadaqa. *Sadaqa* is voluntary charity, depending upon circumstances. It is both tangible and intangible. A kind word, for example, may be a form of *Sadaqa*. But *zakat* is compulsory and tangible. It is paid at the end of the Ramadan fast . Zakat is not due from infant or mad person, *mokatib,* insolvent debtor, from the necessities of life such as dwelling houses, articles of clothing, household furnitures, cattle kept for immediate use or slaves employed as actual servants or armours and weapons and from uncertain property. Jewellery not for trade or investment purpose is totally exempted from *zakat*.

5. Al Hajj (The Pilgrimage)

The pilgrimage to Mecca (Hajj) once in one's lifetime is required of all those who have the physical and financial ability to make the journey. The practice derives from the divine mandate given by the Prophet to rebuild the first temple of worship to God in Mecca. The pilgrimage requirement makes this desert city a gathering place for people from all parts of the world once a year. The rituals of the Hajj were established by the Prophet. They emphasize repentance, resulting in forgiveness by God. The practice also strengthens the bond among the faithful from all walks of life and regions of the world.

Each year in the 12th month of the Islamic calendar, Dhu al-hijja, Muslims around the world begin observing activities associated with the annual Hajj, or pilgrimage to Mecca. Hajj activities take place during six days (8th-13th) of the month . The pilgrims enter into a state of self-control called *ihram*, during which pilgrims are forbidden to disturb living creatures or even raise the voice in anger. The state of *ihram* is signified (for men) by the wearing of two pieces of un-sewn white cloth. (No specific clothing is prescribed for female pilgrims.)

In the great mosque of Mecca, they walk seven times around the Ka'aba and then walk seven times back and forth between the hills of al-Safa and al-Marwa. This is to remind the pilgrims of the distress of Hagar (one of Abraham's wives) and her son Ishmael in the desert, when God saved them by causing the spring of Zamzam to well up out of the sand of the desert. The pilgrims then drink from this well, its water believed to have miraculous powers, before continuing a few kilometres further to Mount Arafat. Here is reached the high point of pilgrimage with the pilgrims standing in meditation and prayer from noon to sunset. After sunset, they walk to nearby Mina, breaking their journey in Muzdalifa where they spend the night and collect pebbles which, on the following morning in Mina, are thrown onto three heaps of stones.. The stoning indicates the pilgrims' rejection of evil deeds This custom is a reminder of the steadfast faith of Abraham and the wondrous rescue of his son, Ishmael. To commemorate this, the believers sacrifice sheep and camels as a sign of their humility, and have their hair cut to symbolize the completion of the Hajj. The Feast of Sacrifice (Eid al-Adha) lasts for four days and is celebrated throughout the Islamic world. The meat of the sacrificial animals is given to the poor.

THE ARTICLES OF FAITH

Islam considers the following fundamental beliefs to be the foundation of the faith:

A single, indivisible God: God, the creator, is just, omnipotent and merciful. "Allah" is often used to refer to God; Allah has no partner, son, daughter, helper, or competitor. He neither begets nor is begotten. There is nothing that even remotely resembles Him. He is unique.

All of the messengers and prophets of Allah: Muslims believe in a chain of prophets starting with Adam and including Noah, Abraham, Ishmael, Isaac, Jacob, Joseph, Job, Moses, Aaron, David, Solomon, Elias, Jonah, John the Baptist, and Jesus, peace be upon them. But Muhammad (pbuh) is the last prophet (peace be upon him). Muhammad (pbuh)'s message is considered the final, universal message for all of humanity. God's final message to man, a reconfirmation of the eternal message , a summing-up of all that has gone before, and revealed to Prophet Muhammad (pbuh) through Gabriel. is Qur'an.

The original messages revealed through Allah's prophets and messengers: The purest of these is the Qur'an, for it was recorded during the lifetime of the Prophet and under his direct supervision. The revelations mentioned in the Qur'an as having been received by other prophets, such as the Suhuf of Abraham, the Torah of Moses, the Zubur (Psalms) of David, and the Injeel (Bible) of Jesus, have all been either lost or corrupted.

The existence of angels as part of the unseen world: They are spiritual beings who have no need for food, drink, or sleep.

The Day of Judgement: The Qur'an teaches that life is a test for each individual; for everyone must choose whether he will or will not follow the commands of Allah. On the Day of Judgement, a person will be resurrected and asked to account for what he did while he was alive. Those with good records will be rewarded and enter paradise, while those with bad records will be punished by being sent to hell. This belief develops within the individual an awareness of Allah's presence and a desire to obey His laws sincerely and voluntarily

The supremacy of God's will and God's complete authority over human destiny and in life after death: Muslims believe that every thing is pre-ordained by God and that nothing happens without the knowledge and permission of Allah. But at the same time they also believe that God has given human being the option to choose between right and wrong as given in the Qur'an and each individual would be accountable for his action. While we may not understand why certain things happens, it is part of the divine plan for our lives

KALIMAH - CARDINAL BELIEF

A man joins the fold of Islam by honestly believing in and professing faith in the oneness of God and the prophethood of Muhammad (pbuh). Both of these beliefs are epitomized in the *kalimah* (the article of faith):

La ilaha illa Allah, Muhammad Rasul Allah. (There is no god except Allah; Muhammad (pbuh) is His Prophet.)

The first part of the *kalimah* presents the concept of *tawhid* (the oneness of God) and its second part affirms the prophethood of Muhammad (pbuh).

HOLY SCRIPTURES
Qur'an

The Qur'an is a record of the exact words revealed by God through the Angel Gabriel to Prophet Muhammad (pbuh) . It was memorized by Muhammad (pbuh) and then dictated to his companions, and written down by scribes, who cross-checked it during his lifetime. Not one word of its 114 chapters, *Suras*, has been changed over the centuries, so that the Qur'an is in every detail the unique and miraculous text

which was revealed to Muhammad (pbuh) fourteen centuries ago.

The Qur'an, the last revealed Word of God (THE LAST TESTMENT), is the prime source of every Muslim's faith and practice. It deals with all the subjects which concern us as human beings: wisdom, doctrine, worship, and law, but its basic theme is the relationship between God and His creatures. At the same time it provides guidelines for a just society, proper human conduct and an equitable economic system

The *Sunna* of the Prophet

The *Sunnah* consists of the teachings, sayings, and actions of Prophet Muhammad (pbuh). These were recorded in writings called *Hadiths,* which help to interpret Qur'an. It is essentially an elaboration of the Qur'anic verses that shows how they are to be implemented in one's daily life.

The Quran gives legitimacy to the *Hadith*. It states: "Nor does he say aught of his own desire. It is no less than inspiration sent down to him"(53:3-4). However, the writings are not regarded as having the same status as the Holy Qur'an; the latter is considered to be God's word.

The Arabic word *sunnah* has come to denote the way Prophet Muhammad (pbuh) lived his life. The *Sunnah* is the second source of Islamic jurisprudence, the first being the Qur'an.

Both sources are indispensable; one cannot practice Islam without consulting both of them.

The Arabic word *hadith* (pl. *ahadith*) is very similar to *Sunnah,* but not identical. A *hadith* is a narration about the life of the Prophet or what he approved - as opposed to his life itself, which is the *Sunnah* .

MAIN GROUPS - SUNNIS & SHIAS

Islam spread quickly, stretching from Spain in the west to India in the east within a century after the prophet's death. Islam also succeeded in uniting an Arab world of separate tribes and castes, but disagreements concerning the succession of the prophet caused a division in Islam between two groups, *Sunnis and Shi'ites*. The Shi'ites rejected the first three successors to Muhammad (pbuh), claiming the fourth, Muhammad (pbuh)'s son-in-law Ali, as the rightful leader.

The Sunnis (from the word tradition), the largest division of Islam (today more than 80%), believe in the legitimacy of the first three successors. Among these, other sects arose (such as the conservative Wahhabi of Saudi Arabia), as well as different schools of theology

Another development within Islam, beginning in the eighth and ninth centuries, was *Sufism,* a form of mysticism. This movement was influential for many centuries and was instrumental in the spread of Islam in Asia and Africa.

Islam has expanded greatly under Muhammad (pbuh)'s successors. It is the principal religion of the Middle East, Asia, and the northern half of Africa.

Sunni Muslims, who make up more than 80% of the world's Muslims, are followers of the Hanifa, Shafi, Hanibal and Malik schools They are considered to be main stream traditionalists. Because they are comfortable pursuing their faith within secular societies, they have been able to adapt to a variety of national cultures, while following their three sources of law: the Qur'an, Hadith and consensus of Muslims

Shi'ite Muslims are followers of the Jafri school who constitute a small minority of Islam. They split from the Sunnis over a dispute over the successor to Muhammad (pbuh) . Their leaders promote a strict interpretation of the Qur'an and close adherence to its teachings. They believe in 12 heavenly Imams (perfect teachers) who led the Shi'ites in succession. Shi'ites believe that the 12th Imam, the Mahdi (guided one), never died but went into hiding waiting for the optimum time to reappear and guide humans towards justice and peace.

Sunni and shia traditions

The Sunni tradition differs from Shia tradition,. The distinction between the two traditions essentially derives from different approaches to governance. The Sunni believe, based on specific provisions of the Qur'an and the Sunna, that the Muslim people are to be governed by consensus (*ijma'*) through an elected head of state, the *khalifa*, according to democratic principles. The Shia, however, believe that the leader of Islam, whom they refer to as the *Imam* rather than the *khalifa*, must be a descendant of the Prophet. The concept is the basis for a hereditary hierarchy in the Shia tradition

The Shia movement dates from the period when a group of Muslims wanted Ali ibn Abu Talib, the cousin and son-in-law of the Prophet, to become the *khalifa* instead of Abu Bakr, who had been elected the first *khalifa* following the death of Muhammad (pbuh) in the year 632. They advanced his candidacy on the basis of heredity. However, they were out-voted. Ali ulti-

mately became the fourth *khalifa,* succeeding Uthman, who succeeded Umar, who succeeded Abu Bakr. But Ali was overthrown by the rebellion of Muawia, the governor of Syria, whose seat was in Damascus. Muawia rebelled against Ali because he attributed the assassination of his kinsman Uthman to Ali's followers. Ali was subsequently assassinated after losing the *Tahkim* (arbitration) to Muawia.

In 680 Hussain, one of Ali's sons, led a number of Muslims who were then rebelling against the ruling *khalifa* to try to establish in the area between Iran and Iraq a Imamat based on heredity from the Prophet. However, Hussain was lured into Iraq, and there at a place called Karbala he and his followers were massacred. Hussain's martyrdom spurred the Shia movement in Iraq and Iran. The anniversary of Karbala, called *Muharram* - a ten-day mourning - is commemorated every year by the Shia population. In Iran, in particular, it is conducted by means of a large popular demonstration in which people publicly weep and flagellate themselves as a sign of their remorse.

Difference in approach

The political rift between followers of the principle of election and those favoring descent from the Prophet generated some other differences between Sunni and Shia approaches to jurisprudence. For example, the Shia view the sayings of Fatima, the daughter of the Prophet, and his cousin Ali (Fatima's husband), the fourth khalifa of the Islam, as equally authoritative as the Sunna of the Prophet. The Sunni do not. There are other differences involving the structure of Islam, such as existence of an organized Shia clergy, which does not exist in the Sunni tradition. Among them the Shia allow the *imam* much wider latitude in government than the Sunni ever could in light of the principles of consensus and equality. The most important of all differences between Sunni and Shia relates to the interpretation of the Qur'an. The Sunni look more to the letter of the Qur'an; the Shia look more to its spirit. In Arabic the distinction is referred to as *al-dhaher* (the apparent) versus *al-baten* (the hidden) meaning of the Qur'an. Thus the Shia religious hierarchy plays a determining role in interpreting the Qur'an. This role reinforces their spiritual and temporal influence in Shia society.

Common features

Sunnis & Shias have many things in common. They follow the same book - Qur'an.

They follow the same prophet Muhammad (pbuh). Both offer their prayers five time a day.

Both fast in the month of Ramadan. They both go for Hajj, pilgrimage to Mecca

SUFISM

There is a third stream and a third school of thought among Muslims, namely Sufism.

Sufism is a mystic tradition in which followers seek inner knowledge directly from God through meditation and ritual and dancing. It developed late in the 10th century CE as an ascetic reaction to the formalism and laws of the

Qur'an. It reflects the need of individuals to transcend formal religious practices in order to attain higher levels of spiritual fulfillment. There are Sufis from both the Sunni and Shi'ite groups.

Sufism does not constitute a sect but is rather a spiritual or transcendental practice which persists despite criticism from orthodox theologians. Sufis believe they follow the Prophet's mysticism, particularly during the Meccan period of the revelations. Thus, in their practices there is much meditation and solitary or group recitation of prayers and incantations of their own religious formulas. They seek a life of ascetic piety, shunning worldly pleasures and seeking the inward purity of a relationship with God through love, patience, forgiveness, and other higher spiritual qualities.

Their influence on the development of Islam is more significant than is usually recognized. What marks Sufis out is their "inwardism"or belief that the Sharia only regulates external conduct, whereas inward feelings are matter strictly between each person and the Creator. Because of their emphasis on the love of God, they have developed the doctrine of Tawakul (reliance on God), which is central to the relationship between Man and God.

ISLAMIC CALENDAR

Unlike the Gregorian calendar which is based on the astronomical solar year — the length of time it takes for the earth to revolve around the sun — the Islamic calendar is based on the lunar year. It has 12 lunar months like the calendar based on the solar year. However, since each month begins and ends with the new moon — a period lasting 29 days, 12 hours, 44 minutes, and 2.8 seconds - each lunar year contains only 354 days (or 355 in leap years) as opposed to

Some important dates in the life of Prophet Muhammd (pbuh)

570 C.E.	53 B.H.	The birth of Prophet Muhammad (pbuh) in Mecca on 12th Rabi-al-Awwal
	48 B.H..	Death of Amina, mother of the Prophet
	46 B.H.	Death of Abdul Muttalib, the Prophet's grandfather
595 C.E.	28 B.H.	The Prophet Muhammad (pbuh) marries Khadijah(Radhi Allaho Anha), a noble lady of the Quraish tribe
610 C.E	14 B.H.	The Prophet Muhammad (pbuh) was visited by the Angel Gabriel (pbuh) who asked him to recite from the Holy Qur'an. (Surah 96, verses 1-5, the first revelation)Khadijah, Abu Bakr and Ali were the first to accept Islam
620 C.E.	4 B.H.	Death of Khadijah, the first wife of the Prophet
622 C.E.	1 A.H.	Prophet Muhammad (pbuh) and fellow Muslims migrate to Medina. The beginning of the Islamic calendar from Hijrah year 1.1.01 A.H., on Friday, July 16, 622 C.E.
630 C.E.	8 A.H.	Triumphant and bloodless return to Mecca
632 C.E.	1 A.H.	The Prophet Muhammad (pbuh) died in the city of Medina on Monday, the 12th Rabi-al-Awwal, at the age of 63

365 and 1/4 days for the astronomical year. As a consequence of the fewer number of days in the lunar year, the lunar calendar does not conform to the progression of the seasons. The difference in the length of the lunar year accounts for some of the difficulty in converting dates from the Islamic (Hijri or "Hijrah") system to the Gregorian and vice versa. The following equation can be used to calculate the Hijrah year in which the corresponding Gregorian year began:

$$A.D. = 622 + (32/33 \times A.H.)$$

The Islamic calendar was devised in the seventh century by caliph Umar ibn al-Khattab to mark the triumph of the Islam. It takes July 16, 622 A.D., the date of the Hijrah or the Prophet's sojourn from Mecca to Madina, as the starting point of the calendar of the Muslim era.

The Muslim months are:

Muharram	Jumada al-Awwal	Ramadan
Safar	Jumada al-Thani	Shawwal
Rabi' al-Awwal	Rajab	Dhu al-Qi'dah
Rabi' al-Thani	Sha'ban	Dhu al-Hijjah

MUSLIM HOLIDAYS

The following holidays are observed among Muslim communities throughout the world:

'Eid ul-Fitr, also known as the Little Feast. It is a day of jubilation and festivity marking the successful completion of one month of fasting in the month of Ramadan. It occurs on the first day of the month of Shawwal. It is an occasion for acts of kindness, and in particular, giving money and food to the poor.

'Eid ul-Adha, the Feast of Sacrifice, also

known as the Great Feast, falls seventy days after 'Eid ul-Fitr, on the 10th of the month of Dhu al-Hijjah, the last month of Islamic calendar. It is celebrated at the end of the religious pilgrimage, the Hajj by all Muslims except those on Hajj. Eid Ul-Adha recalls an event reported in the Qur'an and also in slightly different versions, in the Torah and the Old Testament. Ibrahim was asked by God to sacrifice his beloved son, Ishmael, to show his obedience. Just as Ibrahim was about to kill Ishmael, God provided a ram to take Ishmael's place. The festival celebrates Ibrahim's faith and God's mercy. Eid is an Arabic word meaning 'festival'. On the occasion of both the Eids, Eid ul-Fitr and Eid ul-Adha, Muslims get up early, bathe and put on new clothes before going to the mosque. There they pray. The prayers on these occasions are slightly different from the usual prayers. After worship at the mosque, Muslims visit their friends and family, exchange presents and cards and share meals.

Ra's al-Sannah, New Year's Festival, falls on the first of the month of Muharram.

Mawlid an-Nabi, the Prophet's Birthday, is celebrated on the 12th day of the month of Rabi' al-Awwal.

Lailat al Isra' wa al-Mi'raj, this festival commemorates the Prophet's miraculous journey, from Mecca to Jerusalem to heaven and then back to Mecca in the same night, is celebrated on the 27th day of the month of Rajab.

ISLAMIC LAW-THE SHARIA

The Qur'an is the principal source of Islamic law, the Sharia. It contains the rules by which the Muslim world is governed (or should govern itself) and forms the basis for relations between man and God, between individuals, whether Muslim or non-Muslim, as well as between man

and things which are part of creation. The Sharia contains the rules by which a Muslim society is organized and governed, and it provides the means to resolve conflicts among individuals and between the individual and the state.

Unquestionably, the Qur'an is the basis of the Sharia and that its specific provisions are to be scrupulously observed. The *Hadith* and *Sunna* are complementary sources to the Qur'an and consist of the sayings of the Prophet and accounts of his deeds. The *Sunna* helps to explain the Qur'an, but it may not be interpreted or applied in any way which is inconsistent with the Qur'an.

Though there are other sources of law-i.e., *ijma',* (consensus), *qiyas,* (analogy), *ijtihad,* (progressive reasoning by analogy)-the Qur'an is the first and foremost source, followed by the *Hadith* and *Sunna*. Other sources of law and rules of interpretation of the Qur'an and the Hadith and Sunna follow in accordance with a generally accepted jurisprudential scheme.

CHILDREN OF PROPHET MUHAMMAD (PBUH)

Prophet Muhammad (pbuh) and his first wife Khadijah were blessed with six children, two sons and four daughters. Sadly their first born, a son called Qasim, died shortly before his second birthday, and their second son Abdullah died in infancy. Abdullah was also called affectionately as 'Tayyab' and 'Tahir' because he was born after Muhammad (pbuh)'s prophethood. Their four daughters were Zaynab, Ruqayyah, Umm Kulthum, and Fatimah .

Zaynab married her cousin Al'Ass Ibn Al-Rabeah. Zaynab had only one child who died as a baby. Zaynab died in 630 A.D.

Ruqayyah was the wife of Othman Ibn affan. She had one boy who died possibly from an infection after a rooster pecked his eye. She died in 624 A.D..

Umm Kulthum was also married to Othman after Ruqayyah's death . She had no children. She died in 631 A.D.

Fatimah married Ali Ibn Aby Talib who was the cousin of the Prophet and who later became the fourth Calipha. He died in 662 A.D. They had two sons, Al-Hassan and Al-Hussein and one daughter Om Kolthoom. Fatimah died in 632 A.D.

The Prophet's first wife , Khatijah, died in 622 CE. The Prophet did not take another wife while she lived

In March 630 CE, the Prophet's wife Mariah gave birth to a son whom the Prophet named Ibrahim. He was the only child born after the six children from Prophet's first wife Khadijah. Ibrahim died when he was ten months old.

MUSLIM POPULATION

(Source: Adherents.com   Last updated 27 January 2000)

Followers of Islam, called Muslims, re esti-mated to be between 900 million and 1.3 billion, with 1 billion being a figure frequently given in comparative religion texts.

World's Most Muslim Nations

(About 99.5% or more of the native popula-tions -Listed alphabetically)

1. Bahrain	9. Qatar
2. Comoros	10. Somalia
3. Kuwait	11. Saudi Arabia
4. Maldives	12. Tunisia
5. Mauritania	13. United Arab Emirates
6. Mayotte	14. Western Sahara
7. Morocco	15. Yemen
8. Oman	

Largest National Muslim Populations
(Source: CIA's World Factbook 2002) *

Name	Muslim population	Percentage of total
Indonesia	201,025,326	88%
India	138,000,000	13.4%
	(2001 Census Report)	
Pakistan	140,278,140	97%
Bangladesh	108,953,984	83%
Nigeria	94,976,720	75%
China	76,386,677	6%
Turkey	66,360,982	99.8%
Iran	65,433,321	99%
Egypt	65,364,446	94%

World population: 6,068,708,934:
Muslim population: 1,509,819,727 (25 %)

* These estimates differ from those in www.adherents.com

THE COMMANDMENTS OR PROHIBITIONS IN ISLAM

(Based on questions-answers in "Inquiries about Islam" by Imam Mohamad Jawad Chirri, Director of the Islamic Center of America)

Islam commands its followers to avoid many things. Some of them are prohibited because they contradict some of the doctrines in which a Moslem is supposed to believe. Some of them are prohibited because they are immoral or unethical or unhealthy or because they represent disobedience to the devotional duties. These prohibitions may be regarded as Islamic com-mandments, the violation of which may consti-tute a major sin.

A Muslim is prohibited:

1. To ascribe to God a partner or associate:
2. To deny revelation of God to His prophets.
3. To deny any of the prophets who are recog-nized by the Qur'an, such as Jesus, Moses,

Abraham, and Noah. The denial of the revelation or any of the recognized prophets is a denial of Islam.

4. To feel safe in opposition to God:
5. To lose hope in mercy of God:
6. To swear in the name of God falsely:
7. To break a covenant deliberately:
8. To kill a human being premeditatively.
9. To be traitor to the right cause of one's own nation.
10. To help defeat it militarily by retreating at the battlefield when the nation is defending itself against aggression:
11. To steal.
12. To cheat in measuring or weighing in selling or purchasing:
13. To use an orphan's fund in a way that is not in his interest:
14. To insult one's own parent:
15. To commit adultery:
16. To scandalize people, especially women:
17. To spy on others for no purpose of protecting your nation or yourself.
18. To backbite others, exposing to those who do not know, some shameful doing:
19. To gamble.
20. To drink intoxicants:
21. To eat pork or any swine's products.
22. To eat or drink blood. (This does not include transfusion of blood for necessity.)
23. To eat meat of an animal that dies by itself, or the meat of an animal on which the name of other than God is invoked when it is slain:
24. To lie deliberately or testify falsely or falsify the word of God willingly:
25. To conceal a testimony when called to testify in a litigation:
26. To deliberately hinder a good cause.
27. To spread hatred by conveying to a person a bad

word about him spoken by another person:
28. To violate the terms of a dead man's will:
29. To oppress the people.
30. To aid an oppressor.
31. To be proud, looking down on the people:
32. To be envious, wishing people ill:
33. To antagonize a relative for no right cause:
34. To neglect any of the five daily prayers.
35. To break fasting in the days of Ramadan without a legitimate excuse.
36. To withhold the "Zakah" which is the share of the poor in the self-supporting person's wealth.
37. To neglect the duty of pilgrimage to Mecca which has to be done once in a life-time by every person who is physically and financially able to make it.
38. To neglect the duty of advising the people to do good and avoid evil when such an advice is needed and likely to be effective.

The last five are regarded as major sins, because the prayer, fasting, paying Zakah, making pilgrimage and enjoining good and prohibiting evil are Qur'anic duties.

NIKAAH - MUSLIM WEDDING AND OTHER RITUALS
Muslim rituals
MusliNikahg Nikah - Muslim wedding

In some Muslim families, parents choose marriage partners for their children. But either partner can refuse if he/she is not agreeable to the alliance. The formal offer of marriage and its acceptance have to be witnessed by at least two persons. Local wedding customs vary from place to place but some common ones are as follows:-

Mehndi ceremony

On the eve of the wedding or a couple of days before, Mehndi ceremony is held at the home of the bride. The female relatives of the bride-to-be or a *mehndiwali* or both apply *mehndi* (turmeric paste) on her hands and feet . The event has a festive feel with the women singing traditional songs. The bride-to-be wears sober clothes. According to custom , after *mehndi* ceremony she must not step out of the house until her marriage. The bride's cousins sometimes apply a dot of *mehndi* on the palm of the groom.

Nikaah Ceremony

On the day appointed for marriage, the groom arrives at the wedding venue with his *baraat* . He is invited to share a drink of *sherbet* with the bride's brother. The bride's sisters play pranks and slap the guests playfully with batons made of flowers.

The *Nikaah* - **wedding ceremony** - is conducted at the home of the bride or at any other convenient venue. *A Qazi* (priest) in the presence of close family members and relatives conducts the ceremony. In orthodox Muslim communities, the men and women are seated separately. The *'Walis'* (the father of the bride and of the bridegroom) play an important role in the ceremony. The *Qazi* reads selected verses from the Qur'an . After the *Ijab-e-Qubul* , that is after the boy's side proposes and the girl's side conveys her assent, the *Nikaah* -wedding ceremony - is complete. The mutual consent of the bride and groom is of great importance for the marriage to be legal. On the day of the *Nikaah* , the elder members of the two families decide the amount of *Mehar* . The *Mehar* is a compulsory amount of money agreed to be given by the groom's family

The *Nikaahnaama* is a document in which the marriage contract is registered. It contains a set of terms and conditions that must be respected by both the parties. For the contract to be legal, it must be signed by the bridegroom, the bride, the *Walis,* and the *Qazi*. After the Nikaah ceremony, the groom receives blessings from the older women and offers them his *salaam*. The guests pray for the newly-weds. The newly-weds sit together for the first time. Their heads are covered by a *dupatta* while they read prayers under the direction of the *Qazi* The Qur'an is placed between the couple and they are allowed to see each other through mirrors.

Rukhsat: The bride's father gives her hand to her husband and the bride's family bids her a tearful farewell.

Arrival of Bride in the Groom's house: (some hold that it is not in Islamic tradition.)

The groom's mother receives the bride and the bridegroom in her house. She holds the Quran above the head of her new daughter-in-law as she enters her new home for the first time after the wedding.

Chauthi: (This too is not a universal Islamic tradition.)The Chauthi is the fourth day after the wedding, when the bride visits the home of her parents. She receives a joyous welcome on this day.

Valimah: The Valimah is the lavish reception that the groom's family hosts after the Nikaah. It is a joyous occasion that brings together the two families, their relatives and other well-wishers

Birth

According to the Muslims, the first words that a child should hear are the words of God. Hence the *Azaan* is spoken into the new -born's right ear and the *iqamat* is spoken into his left ear.

There are no specific rituals following the birth of a child. If there are, then they are dependant on the local customs and habits of the region.

Incense is used to clean the labour room. On the seventh day following delivery the mother is bathed in warm water. The midwife is given clothes and money by the relatives.

Circumcision

In India, the custom of circumcision varies from region to region. The ritual takes place as follows. First the child is made to take bath and then wear clothes brought by his maternal uncle. Then he is taken to the mosque to offer *namaz*.

At the house, a barber is usually called. But nowadays a doctor or a surgeon does the circumcision. Inside the house, a cloth screen is erected on all sides and the child sits on the lap of his maternal uncle. Women are not allowed to watch the rite. The doctor with a sharp razor or surgical blade cuts off the foreskin of the penis. Then some antiseptics are applied to prevent any bleeding. The child is then given some drinks like milk, etc and is taken care of. After the ceremony there is a community feast.

Talak or Divorce

According to Muslim personal law if a man and woman find it impossible to live together for any kind of reason then there is provision for them to separate. The *talaq* (divorce) is to be given by saying, "I hereby give you talaq", and three times with a gap of one calendar month between each talaq. There is also a provision by which a woman can also seek divorce from her husband. This is called *Kullahi.*

After *talaq* (divorce), a woman has to observe *iddat* before she can remarry. *Iddat* is the probation period of three months and thirteen days during which a woman has to be confined to her house and observe purdah from all men. Her husband should pay her the *nano - nafka* or the money for her maintenance during that period. It includes the money for her clothes, food and housing

Death

When a Muslim dies, people recite a phrase in Arabic meaning "We have come from God and unto him we shall return". The Muslim law forbids loud wailing and display of grief on the death of a person.

First the corpse is purified through a ritual bath called *ghusl*. Only close relatives of the sex of the deceased bathe the body. Then the body is wrapped in a white cloth called *Kafan,* from head to toe. Incense sticks are lighted in the house. Then the corpse is taken to the burial ground on the shoulders of mourners. People may take turns in carrying the corpse. The procession is called *Janasa.* A prayer called *dua* is recited enroute There is a congregational prayer before the corpse is buried. The grave is sprinkled with perfumed water. After lowering the body into the grave, the head of the deceased is tilted to face towards the Ka'aba. The grave is then neatly sealed with wooden boards, stones or bamboo sticks. The mourners then toss handfuls of sand over the covering. The grave is finally covered and all present recite the *Fatiha* for the deceased and depart.

KA'ABA - BAIT-UL ALLAH
House Of Allah On Earth

The Ka'aba: It's Size and History!

The Ka'aba is the building towards which Muslims face five times a day, everyday, in prayer. This has been the case since the time of Prophet Muhammad (pbuh) over 1400 years ago.

The Ka'aba is an oblong stone building located approximately in the centre of the quadrangle of the Grand Mosque in the Holy City of Mecca. The front and back walls are 40 feet in length; the side walls are 35 feet long; the height of the walls is 50 feet .

Set in a silver surround in the east corner of the Ka'aba, some four feet above ground level, is the Black Stone. This sacred Stone, the focal point of the Hajj, is the only remnant of the shrine which Abraham built when it was given to Abraham by the angel Gabriel.

The Stone (which may be of meteoric origin) is believed to go back still further, to the time of the first man, Adam.

This small building has been constructed and reconstructed by Prophets Adam, Ibrahim, Ismail and Muhammad (peace be upon them). No other building has had this honour.

The other names of the Ka'aba

Literally, Ka'aba in Arabic means a high place with respect and prestige.

Some of these other names include:

"Bait ul Ateeq-which, according to one mean-ing, means the earliest and ancient. According to the second meaning, it means independent and liberating.

"Bayt ul Haram-the honourable house

Scholars and historians say that the Ka'aba has been reconstructed between five to twelve times.

The very first construction of the Ka'aba was done by Prophet Adam. Allah says in the Qur'an that this was the first house that was built for humanity to worship Allah.

Reconstruction of the Ka'aba In 1996

A major reconstruction of the Ka'aba took place between May 1996 and October 1996.

This was after a period of about 400 years (since Sultan Murad Khan's time).

What is inside the Ka'aba?

The President of the Islamic Society of North America (ISNA) is stated to have had the opportunity to go inside the Ka'aba in 1998. He described the following features:

"there are two pillars inside (others report 3 pillars)

"there is a table on the side to put items like perfume

"there are two lantern-type lamps hanging from the ceiling

"the space can accommodate about 50 people

"there are no electric lights inside

"the walls and floors are of marble

"there are no windows inside

"there is only one door

"the upper inside walls of the Ka'aba were covered with some kind of curtain with the Kalima written on it

In the Name of Allah, the Most Compassionate, the Most Merciful

PROPHET MUHAMMAD (PBUH) 'S LAST SERMON

[This sermon was delivered on the Ninth Day of Dhul-Hijjah 10 A.H. in the 'Uranah valley of Mount Arafat' in Mecca.]

After praising and thanking Allah, the Prophet (PBUH) said:

"O People, lend me an attentive ear, for I know not whether after this year I shall ever be amongst you again. Therefore listen to what I am saying very carefully and take these words to those who could not be present here today.

O People, just as you regard this month, this day, this city as Sacred, so regard the life and property of every Muslim as a sacred trust. Return the goods entrusted to you to their rightful owners. Hurt no one so that no one may hurt you. Remember that you will indeed meet your Lord, and that he will indeed reckon your deeds.

Allah has forbidden you to take *usury* (interest), therefore all interest obligations shall henceforth be waived. Your capital is yours to keep. You will neither inflict nor suffer any inequity. Allah has judged that there shall be no interest and that all the interest due to Abbas ibn 'Abd'al Muttalib [the Prophet's uncle] be waived.

Every right arising out of homicide in pre-islamic days is henceforth waived and the first such right that i waive is that arising from the murder of Rabiah ibn al Harithibn.

O People, the unbelievers indulge in tampering with the calendar in order to make permissible that which Allah forbade, and to forbid that which Allah has made permissible. With Allah the months are twelve in number. Four of them are holy, three of these are successive and one occurs singly between the months of Jumada and Shaban.

Beware of Satan, for the safety of your religion. He has lost all hope of that he will be able to lead you astray in big things, so beware of following him in small things.

O People, it is true that you have certain rights with regard to your women but they also have rights over you. Remember that you have taken them as your wives only under Allah's trust and with His permission. If they abide by your right, then to them belongs the right to be fed and clothed in kindness. Do treat your women well and be kind to them for they are your partners and committed helpers. And it is your right that they do not make friends with anyone of whom you do not approve, as well as never to be unchaste. O People, listen to me in earnest, worship Allah, say your five daily prayers, fast during the month of Ramadhan, and give your wealth in Zakat. Perform Hajj if you can afford to.

All mankind is from Adam and Eve, an Arab has no superiority over a non-Arab nor a non-Arab has any superiority over an Arab; also a white has no superiority over a black nor a black has any superiority over a white - except by piety and good action. Learn that every Muslim is a brother to every Muslim and that the Muslims constitute one brotherhood. Nothing shall be legitimate to a Muslim which belongs to a fellow Muslim unless it was given freely and willingly. Do not therefore do injustice to yourselves. Remember one day you will meet Allah and answer your deeds. So beware: do not stray from the path of righteousness after I am gone.

O People, no prophet or apostle will come after me, and no new faith will be born. Reason well, therefore, O People, and understand my words which I convey to you. I leave behind me two things, the Qur'an and my Sunnah and if you follow these you will never go astray.

All those who listen to me shall pass on my words to others and those to others again; and may the last ones understand my words better than those who listen to me directly. Be my witness, O Allah, that I have conveyed Your message to Your people."

MESSENGERS OF ALLAH

Below are the names of the 25 Rasuls (Messengers of Allah)

1. Adam(PBUH); (Peace be upon him)
2. Idris(PBUH).
3. Nuh (Noah)(PBUH).
4. Hud(PBUH).
5. Saleh(PBUH).
6. Lut (Lot)(PBUH).
7. Ibrahim (Abraham) (PBUH).
8. Ismail (Ishmael) (PBUH).
9. Ishaq (Isaac) (PBUH).
10. Ya'qub (Jacob) (PBUH).
11. Yousuf (Joseph)(PBUH).
12. Shuaib (PBUH).
13. Harun (Aaron) (PBUH).
14. Musa (Moses) (PBUH).
15. Dawood (David) (PBUH).
16. Sulaiman (Solomon) (PBUH).
17. Ayub (Job) (PBUH).
18. Zulkifl (Ezekiel) (PBUH).
19. Yunus (Jonah) (PBUH).
20. Elyas (Elijah) (PBUH).
21. Al-Yasa' (Elisah) (PBUH).
22. Zakariyah (Zechariah) (PBUH).
23. Yahya (John) (PBUH).
24. `Isa (Jesus) (PBUH).
25. Muhammad (pbuh) (PBUH)

REMEMBERING ALLAH (SWT) AT ALL TIMES

When starting to do something	Bism-illah
When intending to do something in future	Insha-Allah
When in pain and distress	Ya-Allah
When expressing appreciation	Masha-Allah
When thanking someone	Jazak-Allah Khayran
When awakening from sleep	La-ilaha-illallah
When thanking Allah or When sneezing	Alhamdu-lillah
When someone else sneezes	Ya-Rehmak Allah
When repenting of a sin	Astagh-Firullah
When taking oath	Wallah/Billah
When someone supplicates	Ameen
When death message is received	Inna-Lillahi-wa- inna-ilaihe Raji-aun

ISLAMIC LAWS REGARDING FOOD

Islam has provided detailed rules and regulations regarding food and drinks. The Qu'ran states in this regard:

"Forbidden to you (as food) are dead animals, blood, the flesh of swine and the animals on which has been invoked any name other than that of Allah and which has been killed by strangling, or by a violent blow or killed by a fall or that which has been gored to death, that which has been (partly) eaten by wild animal unless you are able to slaughter it in due form, that which is sacrificed on shrines"(5 : 4).

The Prophet has also prohibited meat of ass, carnivorous animals like tiger, foxes, dogs, leopard which kill their prey by using their paws. He has also prohibited eating of birds which eat flesh by using their nails and by tearing their food (for example vulture).

The meat of lawful animals (grazing quadruped mammals resembling camel, cow, goat, and sheep *"an'am"*) will be lawful only if the animals are slaughtered in accordance with Islamic law.

Islamic law has given separate rule for fish and other animals of water. The Qu'ran states:

"Lawful for you is the game of sea and its use as food"(5 : 96).

The dead fish of water is also lawful.

Alcoholic Drinks: As regards drinks, wine, alcoholic drinks and other intoxicants have been prohibited by Allah and His Prophet (p.b.u.h.).

ISLAMIC DRESS CODE

Islam emphasizes modesty. No person should be perceived as a sex object. There are certain

guidelines both for men and women. Their dresses should neither be too thin nor too tight to reveal body forms. For men, they must at least cover the area from the knee to navel. For women, their dress should cover all areas to be properly veiled. For women, acting and dressing modestly is called *hijab*. It includes covering the head, arms and legs, but the interpretation varies.

Some Muslim women in western countries wear western clothes, but often choose styles that cover their legs and upper arms.

Many Muslim women wear head scarves and plain, loose fitting long sleeved clothes to cover their bodies.

Some women wear a veil to cover the lower part of the face. Some wear *burkha* which covers everything but eyes. Some *burkhas* have mesh screen. Covering clothes are often black.

ALLAH'S NAMES AND ATTRIBUTES
Bismillah al-Rahman al-Rahim

Following is a list of Allah's Beautiful Names and Attributes.

1. **ALLAH**
Ism al-Dhat al-Qudsiyya = The Name of the Divine Essence
Ism al-Jalala = The Sublime Name
al-Ism al-A'zam = The Most Magnificent Name

2. **Al-Rahman**
The All-Beneficent

3. **Al-Rahim**
The Most Merciful

4. **Al-Malik**
The King, The Sovereign

5. **Al-Quddus**
The Most Holy

6. **Al-Salam**

Peace and Blessing

7. Al-Mu'min
The Guarantor

8. Al-Muhaymin
The Guardian, the Preserver

9. Al-'Aziz
The Almighty, the Self-Sufficient

10. Al-Jabbar
The Powerful, the Irresistible

11. Al-Mutakabbir
The Tremendous

12. Al-Khaliq
The Creator

13. Al-Bari'
The Maker

14. Al-Musawwir
The Fashioner of Forms

15. Al-Ghaffar
The Ever-Forgiving

16. Al-Qahhar
The All-Compelling Subduer

17. Al-Wahhab
The Bestower

18. Al-Razzaq
The Ever-Providing

19. Al-Fattah
The Opener, the Victory-Giver

20. Al-Alim
The All-Knowing, the Omniscient

21. Al-Qabid
The Restrainer, the Straitener

22. Al-Basit
The Expander, the Munificent

23. Al-Khafid
The Abaser

24. Al-Rafi'
The Exalter

25. Al-Mu'izz
The Giver of Honor

26. Al-Mudhill
The Giver of Dishonor

27. Al-Sami'
The All-Hearing

28. Al-Basir
The All-Seeing

29. Al-Hakam
The Judge, the Arbitrator

30. Al-'Adl
The Utterly Just

31. Al-Latif
The Subtly Kind

32. Al-Khabir
The All-Aware

33. Al-Halim
The Forbearing, the Indulgent

34. Al-'Azim
The Magnificent, the Infinite

35. Al-Ghafur
The All-Forgiving

36. Al-Shakur
The Grateful

37. Al-'Ali
The Sublimely Exalted

38. Al-Kabir
The Great

39. Al-Hafiz
The Preserver

40. Al-Muqit
The Nourisher

41. Al-Hasib
The Reckoner

42. Al-Jalil
The Majestic

43. Al-Karim
The Bountiful, the Generous

44. Al-Raqib
The Watchful

45. Al-Mujib

The Responsive, the Answerer

46. Al-Wasi'
The Vast, the All-Encompassing

47. Al-Hakim
The Wise

48. Al-Wadud
The Loving, the Kind One

49. Al-Majid
The All-Glorious

50. Al-Ba'ith
The Raiser of the Dead

51. Al-Shahid
The Witness

52. Al-Haqq
The Truth, the Real

53. Al-Wakil
The Trustee, the Dependable

54. Al-Qawiyy
The Strong

55. Al-Matin
The Firm, the Steadfast

56. Al-Wali
The Protecting Friend, Patron, and Helper

57. Al-Hamid
The All-Praiseworthy

58. Al-Muhsi
The Accounter, the Numberer of All

59. Al-Mubdi'
The Producer, Originator, and Initiator of all

60. Al-Mu'id
The Reinstater Who Brings Back All

61. Al-Muhyi
The Giver of Life

62. Al-Mumit
The Bringer of Death, the Destroyer

63. Al-Hayy
The Ever-Living

64. Al-Qayyum
The Self-Subsisting Sustainer of All

65. Al-Wajid
The Perceiver, the Finder, the Unfailing

66. Al-Majid
The Illustrious, the Magnificent

67. Al-Wahid
The One, the All-Inclusive, the Indivisible

68. Al-Samad
The Self-Sufficient, the Impregnable, the Eternally Besought of All, the Everlasting

69. Al-Qadir
The All-Able

70. Al-Muqtadir
The All-Determiner, the Dominant

71. Al-Muqaddim
The Expediter, He who brings forward

72. Al-Mu'akhkhir
The Delayer, He who puts far away

73. Al-Awwal
The First

74. Al-Akhir
The Last

75. Al-Zahir
The Manifest; the All-Victorious

76. Al-Batin
The Hidden; the All-Encompassing

77. Al-Wali
The Patron

78. Al-Muta'al
The Self-Exalted

79. Al-Barr
The Most Kind and Righteous

80. Al-Tawwab
The Ever-Returning, Ever-Relenting

81. Al-'Afuww
The Pardoner, the Effacer of Sins

82. Al-Muntaqim
The Avenger

83. Al-Ra'uf
The Compassionate, the All-Pitying

84. **Malik al-Mulk**
The Owner of All Sovereignty

85. **Dhu al-Jalal wa al-Ikram**
The Lord of Majesty and Generosity

86. **Al-Muqsit**
The Equitable, the Requiter

87. **Al-Jami'**
The Gatherer, the Unifier

88. **Al-Ghani**
The All-Rich, the Independent

89. **Al-Mughni**
The Enricher, the Emancipator

90. **Al-Mu'ti** - The Giver

91. **Al-Mani'**
The Withholder, the Shielder, the Defender

92. **Al-Nafi'**
The Propitious, the Benefactor

93. **Al-Darr**
The Distresser, the Harmer

94. **Al-Nur** - The Light

95. **Al-Hadi** - The Guide

96. **Al-Badi'**
The Incomparable, the Originator

97. **Al-Baqi**
The Ever-Enduring and Immutable

98. **Al-Warith**
The Heir, the Inheritor of All

99. **Al-Rashid**
The Guide, Infallible Teacher, and Knower

100. **Al-Sabur**
The Patient, the Timeless

ISLAMIC SAYINGS

From Prophet Muhammad (pbuh)

Remember Him in prosperity, and He will remember you in adversity

The Almighty says, "If the believer comes to Me walking, I go to him running."

The best of alms is that which the right hand giveth, and the left hand knoweth not of. Backbiting vitiates ablution and fasting.

Charity is a duty unto every Muslim. He who hath not the means thereto, let him do a good act or abstain from an evil one. That is his charity.

When you see a person, who has been given more than you in money and beauty; then look to those who have been given less.

Whoever suppresseth his anger, when he hath in his power to show it, God will give him great reward No man hath given his child anything better than good manners The greatest crimes are to associate another with God, to vex your father and mother, to murder your own species, to commit suicide, and to swear to lie.

Heaven lieth at the feet of mothers.

Those who earn an honest living are the beloved of God.

God's pleasure is in a father's pleasure; and God's displeasure is in a father's displeasure.

He who wisheth to enter Paradise at the best door must please his father and mother.

God enjoins you to treat women well, for they are your mothers, daughters, aunts.

From Qur'an: Whatever good happens to you is from God; and whatever evil happens to you is from yourself

GLOSSARY OF ISLAMIC TERMS

ADHAAN: - the call to prayer

Allah: Almighty God.

Baitul Maqdis: Also known as Masjidul Aqsa. Situated in Jerusalem. The third most sacred place in Islam. Popularly referred to as Baitul Muqaddas.

Burqah: A head covering worn by women.

Deen: Religion. Religion of Islam.

Dua: Invocation to Allah, supplication, prayer, request

Eid: Feast, festival

Eid ul-Ad'haa:. "The festival of sacrifice". On this day animals are sacrificed in the name of Allah and for His pleasure alone.

Eid ul-Fitr: The first day of Shawwaal. "Feast of breaking the Ramadaan fast". On this day the month-long Ramadaan fast comes to an end.

Eid-gah: Place where the Eid prayer is performed.

Fard: Acts and things which are compulsory on a Muslim.

Fatwa: A formal legal opinion or verdict in Islamic law.

Hadith: Sayings and actions of Prophet Muhammad (pbuh)

Hajj: Annual pilgrimage to Mecca. Hajj is the fifth pillar of Islam.

Halaal: That which is lawful or permissible in Islam.

Haraam: That which is unlawful or prohibited in Islam.

Hijaab: Seclusion of women from strangers. There are different stages of purdah, the highest of which is that the woman should not come out of her home except for some valid Islamic reason.

Hoor: Large-eyed women of paradise promised to the believers.

Ibaadat: "worship". Acts with which one renders worship to Allah Ta'ala.

Iblis: The cursed devil.

Iddah: In Islamic law it refers to the period of waiting during which a woman may not remarry after being widowed or divorced.

Iftaar: The time of breaking fast. This time commences immediately after sunset.

Ihraam: Two pieces of unstitched cloth which are donned by the person performing Hajj or Umrah.

Ilhaam: Things or ideas which Allah puts into the minds of His pious servants.

Imaan: Belief in Allah Ta'ala as the one and only God and belief that Prophet Muhammad (pbuh) is His messenger.

Jahannam: Hell.

Jannat: Heaven or paradise.

Ka'aba: The most sacred place in Islam situated in Mecca .

Kafir: Literally means "a disbeliever". In Islam it refers to one who rejects Allah and who does not believe in Prophet Muhammad (pbuh) as the final messenger of Allah.

Kalaam-e-majeed: The Holy Quran.

Kalimah: Basic tenet of Islam, i.e. bearing witness that there is none worthy of worship except Allah and that Prophet Muhammad (pbuh) is the messenger of Allah.

Khalifah: Islamic head of state. Commonly spelt "caliph".

Kufr: The state of disbelief.

Meelad: "birth, birthday".The birthday celebrations held to express respect for Prophet Muhammad (pbuh)

Mehr: Dowry which is given to the wife at the time of marriage.

Mi'raj: Ascension of Prophet Muhammad (pbuh) to the heavens wherein he communicated with Allah

Muharram: The first month of the Islamic calendar.

Musalli: One who is offering prayer

Purdah: Seclusion of women from strangers. There are different stages of purdah, the highest of which is that the woman should not come out of her home except for some valid Islamic reason.

Qiblah: The direction in which one faces when offering prayer

Qiyaamat: The day of resurrection.

Qurbaani: "sacrifice". The sacrificing of animals solely for the pleasure of Allah on the day of Eid ul-ad'haa and the two days following it.

Ramadaan: The ninth month of the Islamic calendar.

Ruku: The bowing position during prayer

Sadaqah: "charity". Also known as 'zakaat'.

Sajdah: The act of prostrating.

Salaam: Literally means "peace". In prayer it refers to the saying of "as salaamu alaykum wa rahmatullah"which denotes the end of the prayer. Also a way of greeting among Muslims.

Salaat: Prayer to Allah. One of the five pillars of Islam.

Shariah: The Islamic Law.

Sunnat: Action which Prophet Muhammad (pbuh) did or sanctioned.

Sehri: The meal partaken before dawn by the person who intends fasting.

Sub'haanallah: Glory to Allah.

Sufis: Mystics or saints.

Tasbeeh: A rosary that is used to glorify Allah Ta'ala .

◆ ◆ ◆

Christianity

THE RELIGION OF THE FATHERHOOD OF GOD AND THE BROTHERHOOD OF MAN

Table of Contents

ORIGIN

Christianity is a religion founded roughly 2,000 years ago and is practiced by nearly 2000 million people worldwide. Christianity started out as a breakaway sect of Judaism. It originated in Judea (present-day Israel) in the first century A.D. and is based on the life and teachings of Jesus of Nazareth who became known as Jesus Christ (the anointed one), thus the root of the name Christian.

Since Christianity and Judaism share the same history up to the time of Jesus Christ, they are very similar in many of their core beliefs. There are two primary differences. One is that Christians believe in original sin and that Jesus died in our place to save us from that sin. The other is that Jesus was fully human and fully God and as the Son of God is part of the Holy Trinity: God the Father, His Son, and the Holy Spirit. All Christians believe in heaven and that those who sincerely repent their sins before God will be saved and join Him in heaven.

During this period, Judea was a cross-cultural mecca of bustling cities and farms. The emperor of Rome was the ruler. The Jews at that time hated Roman rule. It was but another reminder of the historical oppression they faced as a people. The polytheistic cultural beliefs of Rome were also pagan and intrusive to Jewish life. Some Jews saw that their only hope was to conform to this change. Others became religious zealots who formed pockets of guerilla resistance against Rome. Still others withdrew themselves into the Judean wilderness to study the Jewish law and wait for the eventual coming of their promised Messiah (saviour).

JESUS CHRIST
BIRTH TO CRUCIFICATION

Nearly all that is known about the life of Jesus Christ, the founder of Christianity, is contained in the four Gospels of the New

Testament, particularly those of Matthew, Mark, Luke and John Evangelist, of which John and Matthew were Apostles .These accounts were written 60 to 100 or more years after the birth of Christ by men of different temperaments. They differ in some details but agree in all essentials. Jesus himself left no writings. Aside from mere mention by two Roman historians, in works written within a century after his death, the secular historians of his time said nothing about this man who has had such a profound influence on the life and thought of the world.

Jesus, also called Jesus of Galilee or Jesus of Nazareth, was a Palestinian Jew born between 4 and 7 B.C. in Bethlehem of Judea, about 10 kilometers from Jerusalem. Modern civilization marks his birth by dividing time B.C. (before Christ) and A.D. (Anno Domini - or the year of our Lord). Although in most countries today time is reckoned from the birth of the founder of Christianity, a mistake is believed to have occurred in fixing the date of this event. There is no record of the exact date of Jesus' birth. But it is now commonly held that the date adopted several centuries later as the beginning of the Christian Era was at least four years too late.

Joseph was the legal father of Jesus, but according to Biblical accounts, an angel appeared to Mary, a virgin, and told her that she would bear a child who would be the Son of God. Before the birth Mary and her husband Joseph, a poor carpenter from Nazareth in the northern province of Galilee, were required to go to Bethlehem to be taxed by the Roman governor. Because there was no room for them in any inn they had to lodge in a cave hollowed in a hillside and used as a stable. But Jesus was supposed to have descended from David (because Joseph descended from David clan), the great king of Israel, whose life is recounted in the Old Testament; and the New Testament holds that his birth was heralded by signs and wonders. Guided by the words of an angel, shepherds came to the cave and knelt in adoration before the holy child lying in swaddling clothes in a manger

Soon afterward wise men, or Magi, as they were called, came from the East, saying, "Where is he that is born King of the Jews? for we have seen his star in the East, and are come to worship him." The chief priests of Herod, king of Jerusalem, said the child would be found in Bethlehem. The Magi continued their journey, with the bright star--now traditionally called the Star of Bethlehem- moving ahead of them till it stopped above the place where the child lay.

Herod feared his throne would be endangered by the child if he was allowed to grow to manhood. To remove the threat, Herod ordered all children 2 years old or younger to be slain. But Joseph, having been warned by an angel in a dream, fled with Mary and the child to Egypt, where they lived for some time until Herod's death. Then they returned to Nazareth. Here Jesus passed his boyhood. Of these years, the Bible tells only one incident. When he was 12 years old, Jesus went with his parents to Jerusalem to celebrate the Passover, a Jewish festival. His parents had already travelled a long distance when they suddenly noticed that young Jesus was not with them. Anxiously returning to the Temple, they found him in the midst of the teachers of law who were astonished by his unusual interest and knowledge in religious matters. Since Jesus' parents were common people, it is assumed he attended the local synagogue school and was trained as a carpenter. The next eighteen years are often called the silent years. Since Joseph drops out of the records at this point, it is assumed that he died during this period and that Jesus took over the management of the carpenter business along with the help of his brothers and lived a traditional Jewish life, working as a carpenter.

Jesus Baptizes Jesus

John the Baptist, Jesus Christ's cousin, who was older to Jesus by a few months, had begun his ministry at the age of 27 preaching a message of repentance to the people of Jerusalem. People went out to him from Jerusalem and all Judea, and the whole region of The Jordan. Confessing their sins, they were baptized by him in the Jordan River. From the fact that he baptized his followers in the Jordan River, he is known as John the Baptist. A prophet appeared to him announcing the near approach of the long-awaited Messiah or Christ. Jesus came for baptism, and John recognized in him the Messiah whose coming he had been foretold. The word "Christ" had previously been a religious title meaning "Messiah," but it soon came to be used as a proper name for Jesus himself. As to the need for Jesus , who did no sin, to seek John's "baptism of penance for the remission of sins" , it is believed that this was the occasion preordained by the Father when Jesus should be manifested to the world as the Son of God. After Jesus was baptized in the River Jordan, and when he came out of the water, a voice from heaven said: This is my beloved Son, in whom I am well pleased" (Matt., iii, 15-17).

Jesus Starts His Ministry

Following his baptism, Jesus spent forty days in the Judean wilderness pondering over the nature of his ministry. Jesus was a Jew. He observed the Jewish faith and was well acquainted with the Jewish Law. When Jesus was about thirty he began to preach in the synagogue in Nazareth and work miracles. His ministry was a balanced portrayal of the nature of God and service to man. Many were benefited by his miracles of healing. Peter described his life succinctly: "He went about doing good."

The Message

As he preached to the townspeople at the synagogue in his home town of Nazareth, Jesus quoted the prophet Isaiah, saying:

The Spirit of the Lord is upon Me,

Because He has appointed Me to preach the gospel to the poor,
He has sent Me to proclaim release to the captives,
And recovery of sight to the blind,
To set free those who are oppressed,
To proclaim the favorable year of the Lord.

Then he outraged his neighbors with the claim: *Today this Scripture has been fulfilled in your hearing.*

His challenging words were not always appreciated by his neighbours. He travelled from village to village, teaching in the synagogues and healing those who were suffering. Jesus' teaching was revolutionary. He challenged the established religious authorities to repent from their self-righteousness and hypocrisy and realize that the Kingdom of God is rooted in service and love. Jesus' teachings stirred the hearts of people and created instability, something the Jewish religious authorities feared. He got on with the task with the help of his twelve disciples, a nucleus of a new people of God to replace the old 12 tribes of Israel. His disciples were ordinary people, fishermen, tax collectors, and merchants. Jesus taught his disciples about the will of God and about the "new covenant" God will bring to humanity through him. Jesus helped them to see that mankind is bound to the pain and futility of life as a result of sin. Due to sin, mankind lost its relationship with God. The purpose of this "new covenant" is to restore those who accept it into a renewed fellowship of forgiveness and love with God. Together they travelled the country, preaching a message of deliverance - not from Roman rule, as many believed, but of a whole new beginning for mankind . His disciples, later known as apostles, were: Peter, Andrew, James the son of Zebedee, John, Philip, Bartholomew, Matthew, Thomas, James the son of Alpheus, Thaddeus, Simon, and Judas Iscariot.

Judas Iscariot was the disciple in charge of the finances of the disciples. He covenanted with the high priest to betray Jesus for thirty pieces of silver. Repenting afterwards he threw the money on the Temple floor and hanged himself. After Pentecost, Iscariot was replaced by Matthias.

People followed him everywhere, not only to hear him speak, but also for his healings. People crippled from birth were healed and made to walk, the insane were made sane, and even the dead were raised back to life.

PROPHECY

Though most of the historical record for the start of the Christian faith is recorded in the New Testament accounts, the history of Christianity actually began with prophesying the Old Testament. There are over 300 prophecies that span over a period of 1000 years that are recorded in the Old Testament concerning the coming of a Jewish Messiah. A study of Jesus' life, death and background shows that he was undoubtedly the fulfillment of these messianic prophecies. Thus, even long before Jesus walked the earth, his mission was made known to mankind through the Word of God.

During the three years of his ministry, despite his efforts to keep a low profile, Jesus' reputation spread nationwide. The Roman governors and rulers of Israel's provinces and the leaders of the Jewish people (the religious counsel) took note of him. Jesus' key messages included:

- God loves you and is with you
- Love one another
- Immense value of each person
- Good news: kingdom of God has come to earth
  - Reality of judgment to heaven or hell
  - God forgives those who ask

JERUSALEM AD 30

Jesus entered Jerusalem on the back of a donkey for his final Passover festival. Crowds of people spread palm branches along the roadway, fulfilling the prophecy of Zechariah. The next day, furious with the way in which they had polluted the House of God, Jesus drove the money-changers from the temple.

The Last Supper (Maundy Thursday)

Knowing that the time had come, Jesus shared a solemn meal with his disciples. He rose from his meal, and laid his garment aside. Taking a towel, he filled a basin with water and proceeded to wash the feet of his disciples. When Peter objected, Christ answered him, saying, "What I do you do not realize now, but you will understand hereafter."

Turning again to the table, and to his disciples sitting there, he foretold that one of them would betray him, and told them of his coming death. Then he used the bread and the wine to symbolize that which would follow. Just as they shared the bread and the wine together, so they would share in his death. Jesus was to take the sin of the world upon himself, bringing it down into death, once and for all.

Then they went into the garden of Gethsemane, where Jesus was arrested, betrayed by Judas Iscariot, one of his twelve disciples.

Jesus' way of life and religious message had aroused the suspicion and hostility of the traditional Scribes and Pharisees. The religious leaders asked the Roman government to execute him. In each of several official trials, the Romans found that he was not guilty of breaking any Roman law. Even the Jewish leaders recognized that other than Jesus' claim to be God, Jesus followed the Jewish law perfectly. Still the religious leaders, using the argu-

The Last Supper

FINAL WORDS SPOKEN BY AND ABOUT JESUS

Words/Event Significance (Traditional Spiritual Interpretation)

Words: "Father, forgive them for they know not what they do." — Jesus prays for the executioners who do not understand or believe that Jesus is God.

Words: "My God, my God, why hast thou forsaken me?" — Jesus (quoting a line from the Jewish scriptures) cries out at a moment in time when he is not just physically punished, but spiritually separated from God, his Father. God separates Himself from Jesus because all of the evils of mankind are placed on Jesus. This spiritual separation is the heaviest sacrifice which Jesus pays of behalf of mankind, so that mankind does not need to suffer spiritual separation from God.

Words: "It is finished." — Once Jesus felt he had borne the penalty for the evils of mankind, he declared his mission as accomplished. This relates to Jesus' earlier mission statement to sacrifice himself for others: "The Son of Man did not come to be served but to serve, and to give His life as a ransom for many." (Jesus quoted by Matthew 20:28)

Words: "I promise you that today you will be with me in paradise." — These words, spoken to a thief also being executed with Jesus, indicates Jesus' belief that Jesus would continue to live in paradise (heaven) and that Jesus can choose who will be there with him.

Words: "Father, into your hands I commit my spirit." — Jesus believes his spirit, not body, now goes to heaven with God.

Event: Spear thrust into Jesus' side (recorded in John 19:34) — Roman soldier confirms Jesus is dead.
Statement by witnessing Roman soldier: "Certainly he was a good man!" (recorded in Luke 23:47)
Jesus' innocence is recognized.
Statement by witnessing Roman soldier: "Certainly this man was the Son of God." (recorded in Matthew 27:54 and Mark 15:38)
Jesus' prominence is recognized.
Based on website put up by Jesus Institute

ment of political disfavour, persuaded Pontius Pilate, Roman Governor of the Southern province of Israel, to authorize an execution.

Jesus crucified

Jesus was brutally tortured. He was made to carry his cross (wooden beam) to Golgotha, the place of crucifixion, after having been whipped by Roman soldiers and then hung by his hands, which were nailed to the cross. And Jesus, crying out with a loud voice, said, "Father, into Your hands I commit My spirit. He died in that position within three hours, with convicted thieves crucified on either side of him. As Jesus died in agony, there was an eclipse throughout the country (which is why April 3 of the year 33 has been calculated as the probable date of his death).

By late afternoon, Jesus' body had been laid in a tomb dug into the rock of a hillside. The Romans set up a guard to avoid any trouble.

RESURRECTION AND AFTER

On the first day of the week, that is three days after his burial, at early dawn, some women came to the tomb, bringing spices which they had prepared. They found that the stone had been rolled away from the entrance and, when they went inside, they found that Jesus had gone.

Over the next 40 days, Jesus journeyed in both the southern and northern provinces of Israel. Then, not once, but several times, people met Jesus, risen from the dead. They talked with him, and they ate with him. At one point, He appeared to 500 followers. He was alive. To his disciples, this was conclusive proof that Jesus' claims to be God were real. He was none other than God Himself, the Messiah. Then Jesus returned to Jerusalem, the city where he was executed, and according to witnesses, he left the earth alive by rising up into the sky.

After Jesus

Jesus' disciples were witnesses to an amazing miracle. Their teacher, Jesus of Nazareth, died and three days later rose again to become their Messiah. Compelled by a great commission to share the love that the God of this universe had imparted upon them, the disciples began to proclaim this gospel of hope throughout the territory. Their gospel message was simple: "For God so loved the world, that He gave His only begotten Son, that whosoever believeth in him should not perish, but have everlasting life." (John 3:16).

Second Coming of Jesus Christ

On the basis of Bible - New Testament - Christians believe that Jesus Christ will come again. Then the Day of Judgement will take place. Both the living and the dead will be judged on their deeds and their faith. God's kingdom will be established here on Earth. Some believe that at the second coming, people will be sent either to heaven or hell after being judged.

Bible says:

"If I go and prepare a place for you, I will come again and receive you to Myself" (John 14:3; also 21:20-23).

"Therefore you also be ready, for the Son of Man is coming at an hour when you do not expect Him (Matthew 24:44; also see Matthew 25:13).

"For as the lightning comes from the east and flashes to the west, so also will the coming of the Son of Man be" (Matthew 24:27).

"He will return in the glory of His Father with His angels" (Matthew 16:27 and 25:31)

"I am coming soon! I am indeed coming soon!" (Revelation 22:12, 20)

HISTORY AFTER JESUS

Christianity as is known today is said to have originated from St. Paul (original name Saul). The followers of Jesus Christ did not call themselves Christians in his lifetime or until sometime after his departure . It is only after Jesus' ascension to heaven that the faith which he preached was called Christianity and his followers came to be called Christians.

The early Christians were persecuted by the Romans until the fourth century. Paul of Tarsus who had been converted by the vision of Christ on the road to Damascus was primarily responsible for expanding the message of Jesus outside of the Jewish community. He wrote several New Testaments Epistles. Paul's writings have influenced the Christian Church. It is believed that Paul was beheaded in Rome by the orders of Emperor Nero. The following of Jesus Christ continued to grow . Thus, from a small group of ordinary men that lived in a small province in Judea about 2000 years ago, the history of the Christian Church began, and the Christian Faith has since spread to the rest of the world.

Christianity started as a minority sect in the eastern Mediterranean. Missionaries eventually spread the faith to Rome . Christianity became institutionalized and thus begins the history of the Christian Church. In 312 AD, the Roman Emperor Constantine granted Christians in Rome the freedom to worship and declared himself a Christian. He founded the city of Constantinople on the site of old Greek city of Byzantium and made Christianity a legal religion. In 325, he summoned a council at Nicaea (now Isnil, in Turkey) to draw up a statement of Christian belief, called the Nicene Creed. It included the idea of the Trinity (God as three persons in one: Father, Son and Holy Spirit -God's continual presence in the world). Emperor Theodosius I (347 - 395) made Christianity the State religion of the Roman Empire in the fourth century and Rome became its centre.

DIVISIONS WITHIN CHRISTENDOM
Major Splits

Initially, while the Roman Empire was united, the Christian church was also united. Beginning around 300 A D, however, the empire began to divide politically and this brought out differences within the church. In the West, Rome emerged as the undisputed leading church. There were political reasons; the absence of an Empire after 476 A D allowed the Bishop of Rome an unlimited amount of freedom. In 445 A D, the Western emperor Valentinian III ordered all western bishops to submit to the Bishop of Rome's authority .Theologically, Rome traced its authority back to its first bishop Peter, of whom Jesus had said "...you are Peter and on this rock I will build my church and the powers of death shall not prevail against it" (16:18)

Christians in the East understood things differently. They assigned pre-eminence to 5 patriarchs (Rome, Constantinople, Alexandria, Jerusalem, and Antioch) and insisted on a council of the church as ultimate authority. They were prepared to acknowledge Rome as first among equals but refused to accept the Pope as sole head of the church.

Tensions between the Pope and the Patriarch of Constantinople fluctuated between cool and formal to outright hostility. It came to a climax in 1054 A D when each leader excommunicated the other, thus resulting in the formal split of Christianity into Roman Catholic and Orthodox.

With the rise of Islam from the 7th century , Orthodox Christianity diminished. It lost nearly all of its Middle Eastern churches and was forced to move through Eastern Europe and into Russia.

In contrast, the Roman Catholicism continued to flourish. In the absence of political leadership, energetic popes assumed temporal as well as spiritual power. But there was a downside to the temporal power. Ecclesiastical offices were sold to the highest bidders. Many other malpractices crept in .

Reformation

By the sixteenth century a general call for reform was sweeping through the Christian West. A German Augustinian monk, called Martin Luther, who felt that the Catholic Church was corrupt, started the reformation movement in 1517. A new, "reformed" type of Church, known as Protestant, grew out of the protests of people like Martin Luther and John Calvin (a French). The Protestants rejected the Catholic Church's indulgences, of granting God's forgiveness in return for money. Bible, which was till then read in Latin - a language not understood by ordinary people - was translated into German and other languages. Martin Luther believed and preached that the teachings of Bible and an individual's personal faith in Christ were more important than Church rituals.

Counter-Reformation

The success of the Reformation set in motion a reform movement within the Catholic Church that became famous as the Counter-Reformation. In 1543, council, Council of Trent, that lasted from 1545 to 1564 , was formed to consider how the Church could be reformed to win the people back. The Council made a number of changes, including forbidding the sale of indulgences. Many Europeans returned to the Catholic faith, but by and large Europe became divided into a Protestant north and a Catholic south. The split of Christians between Catholic and Protestant groups led to intolerance, persecution and religious wars.

Church of England

In 1529, King Henry VIII of England challenged the supreme authority of the Pope and separated from Rome in the wake of a series of quarrels originally sparked off by the Pope's refusal to grant him dispensation to divorce his wife, Catherine of Aragon, daughter of the King Fernando and the Queen Isabel of Spain, known in history as Catholic Kings. After the divorce he married Anne Boleyn in 1533. After dissolving the monasteries he founded the Anglican State Church in 1534 and declared himself head of the Church. Initially, in many respects, the Anglican Church adopted a position somewhere between the Roman Catholic and the Protestant Churches. But subsequently, under Henry's son, Edward VI, England became Protestant country and many Catholics lost their lives. Henry's eldest daughter, Mary I, returned the country to Catholicism and, during her reign, many Protestants were killed. In 1558, Queen Elizabeth, daughter of Anne Boleyn, ascended the throne. She established the Church of England: a compromise between Protestantism and Catholicism. Today, branches of the Church of England, also known as the Anglican or Episcopalian Church, are found in many countries. Branches that follow a more Catholic tradition are known as high church and those that follow a more Protestant tradition are known as low church.

MAJOR GROUPS
Roman Catholic Church:

The Roman Catholic Church, with over a bil-

lion members, is the largest Christian church in the world. It believes in the primacy and authority of the Bishop of Rome (the Pope), who is traditionally regarded as Christ's representative on earth and the successor of St Peter (one of Jesus' disciples and the first Bishop of Rome). He administers church affairs through bishops and priests. When defining matters of faith or morals what the Pope says is regarded as infallible and

binding on all Catholics. Members accept the gospel of Jesus Christ and the teachings of the Bible, as well as the church's interpretations of these. God's grace is conveyed through the seven sacraments, especially the Eucharist or communion that is celebrated at mass, the regular service or worship. The other six sacraments are baptism, confirmation, penance, holy orders, matrimony, and anointing of the sick.

Redemption through Jesus Christ is professed as the sole method of obtaining salvation, which is necessary to ensure a place in heaven after life on earth.

The Human Soul is immortal. God is objective and exists in trinity: The Father, The Son, and the Holy Ghost. The Virgin Mary, mother of Jesus, is the mother and saviour of all humankind who is above sin.

The Vatican Council of 1869 declared the dogma of papal infallibility when the pope speaks ex cathedra. The Second Vatican Council called by John XXIII in 1958 and at meetings between 1962 and 1965 effected the most sweeping changes ever made in the Roman Catholic Church. It recognized Non-Catholics as true Christians; allowed the vernacular in the mass and more congregational participation in worship; declared Jews were not responsible for the death of Jesus; and took steps toward reconciliation with Orthodox and Protestant groups.

Eastern Orthodox Church:

Eastern Orthodox Church began its split from the Roman Catholic Church in the fifth century; the break was finalized in 1054. The split with the western church came about because of conflict over the Pope's claim to supreme authority, the excommunication by the Roman Church of the Patriarch Of Constantinople, Michael Cerularios.and a clause added to the church's creed which said that the Holy Spirit came from the Son of God as well as God. Orthodox religion holds biblical Scripture and tradition, guided by the Holy Spirit as expressed in the consciousness of the entire Orthodox community, to be the source of Christian truth. It rejects doctrine developed by the Western churches. Its Doctrine was established by seven ecumenical councils held between 325 and 787 and amended by other councils in the late Byzantine period.

Orthodox churches are largely national, each associated with a particular country The Orthodox Church includes the Church of Greece, the Church of Cyprus, and the Russian Orthodox Church. Each national Church has its own Patriarch (head of Church.). There are four ancient patriarchies ,which have special posi-

tions of honour and authority: Alexandria, Antioch, Jerusalem and Constantinople.

The Orthodox Church has two sources of Authority: Holy Scriptures and Holy Traditions. Holy Scriptures comprise the writings of both the New and the Old Testaments Holy Tradition, of which Holy Scripture is a part, includes the writings, teachings, acts of the apostles, saints, martyrs, and fathers of the Church, and her liturgical and sacramental traditions throughout the ages, the oral tradition of the early Church and the decisions of the Ecumenical Councils.

The Orthodox Church adheres to the Creed which consists of the twelve articles of the Nicene-Constantinopolitan Creed, or the "Pistevo," which is recited at each Divine Liturgy.

It believes in seven Sacraments and holds them as the visible means by which the invisible Grace of the Holy Spirit is imparted to the followers. These are Baptism ,Chrismation (anointment with holy oil) , Confession, Holy Communion, Matrimony , Holy Orders (Ordination) and Unction (anointment of the sick).

Veneration of icons is an important part of public and private worship. The Church venerates at least one saint or sacred event in the life of the Church every day of the year.

The central worship service of the Church is the Divine Liturgy which is celebrated each Sunday morning and on all holy days. The Liturgy is also the means by which followers achieve union with Jesus Christ and unity with each other through the Sacrament of Holy Communion.

Orthodox priests may marry before they are ordained. The Orthodox church operates much more independently between parishes than the Catholic church does, and there is not as much emphasis on the hierarchy of clergy.

There are over 214 million Orthodox Christians today.

Protestant Church

The name was first given to those who followed Martin Luther and who protested against certain practices and doctrines of the Catholic Church. These practices include the prominence of the Virgin Mary and the Saints in the Church, the image of Jesus on the crucifix, handy standardized prayers, confession, and indulgences of granting God's forgiveness in return for money. Later it referred to all the churches which severed connections with Rome. They believe in the acceptance of individual responsibility of Christians directly to God and not to the Church.

Protestantism holds that man is saved only "by grace, through faith (sola fide), and not by good works, and that the sole authority for doctrine is the Bible alone (sola scriptura), not any pope or council of bishops or tradition, however ancient or hallowed. The Bible for Protestants is made up of some 66 books, Old and New Testaments. It does not include seven books called the Apocrypha. It interprets the Bible in such a way that the priesthood is no longer necessary.

When Protestants display the cross, it is usually without the body of Christ.

Protestantism rejects the notion that divine authority is channeled through one particular human institution or person such as the Roman Catholic pope. Protestants look elsewhere for the authority of their faith. Most of them stress the Bible - the Hebrew Scriptures and the New Testament - as the source and the norm of their teaching.

Most Protestants share faith in the divine Trinity - God the Father, Son, and Holy Spirit. Most of them keep alive the ancient creedal wit-

ness to the fact that Jesus Christ was and is both divine and human. Most of them observe two Sacraments: Baptism and the Lord's Supper. Most Protestants do not believe that Jesus is really present in the bread and wine of the Lord's Supper (Eucharist); they consider this sacrament an act of remembrance and obedience.

Protestants allow for many styles of church government, from the Episcopal , where bishops rule, to the congregational, which acknowledges no earthly authority beyond the local. Accenting "the priesthood of all believers," they have assigned an important role to the laity. Protestants do not have monks or nuns or saints. Their pastors are allowed to marry. Increasingly during the past century and especially in recent decades, Protestant churches have ordained women to the ministry and have encouraged them to take lay leadership roles.

Aside from the main split from the Catholic Church, with the passage of time, Protestants themselves divided into many denominations which arose in response to disputes over doctrine, theology, or religious practices.

There are nearly 500 million members of Protestant Church ..

Non-conformists Groups

Some Protestants refused to conform to the established churches of northern Europe and, in the seventeenth century, began to set up Nonconformist churches. They believed that worship should be simple and churches should be plain. The Nonconformists stand split in numerous groups, each different from the other in one way or the other. A few of the groups, it is said, do not regard themselves as Christians and a few are not considered to be Christians by other groups.

Some of the more well-known Non-Conformist groups are as follows:-

Methodists: Methodism was founded in the 18th century by two English brothers, John and Charles Wesley. Methodism got its name from the methodical habits of its members whose goal was to lead ordered disciplined life. They believe in social reforms and more help to the poor.

Baptists: This is a group of Christians who broke away from the Church of England in early seventeenth century because they believed that head of the Church was Jesus and not a King or Queen. Baptists lay emphasis on the teachings of Bible as well as personal faith in Jesus. They do not baptize babies and children who, they say, are too young to understand the significance of the ceremony. They are one of the largest Protestant groups, with 40 million members worldwide.

Christian Scientists: Christian Science movement was started in 1866 in America by Mary Baker Eddy. The movement holds that the spiritual world is the true reality, compared to which the material world is an illusion. Christian Scientists believe that sin and illness can be overcome by spiritual powers. For this reason they tend to avoid medicines and medical procedures in favor of divine healing.

Church of Christ: Members of the Church of Christ follow the teachings of the New Testament strictly and reject all other traditions and creeds. They are spread in over 170 countries with the largest number of congregations in the USA, Africa and India.

Congregationalists: This group holds that each church is independent and governs itself and, as such, the beliefs of its members can vary from one church to another. Beliefs can also vary among individuals as each person is free to shape his/her own faith and develop his/her own direct relationship with God. This movement started in the sixteenth century and is found in the USA, Eastern Europe and Britain.

Holiness Movement: There are different types of churches in the Holiness Movement but all are dedicated to striving for holy living according to the teachings of Jesus Christ. The Movement rejects the materialism of modern society and stresses the importance of the spiritual life.

Jehovah's Witnesses: Jehovah's Witnesses

accept the Bible as factually true in every detail and anticipate the coming of God's kingdom after the battle of Armageddon, which is considered imminent and which is expected to be followed by a thousand-year reign of Christ on earth.. They consider it their Christian duty to preach this news from house to house. They do not believe in the Trinity.

Lutherans: The Lutheran Church is based on the ideas of Martin Luther. Lutherans are dedicated to the search for unity among Christians and hold the protection of human rights as an important Christian duty. It is the State church in Germany and most Scandinavian countries. The world's 59 million Lutherans belong to 250 different autonomous Lutheran churches around the world.

Mennonites: This movement , named after Menno Simons of the Netherlands, originated in the sixteenth century Reformation. They are similar to Baptists, follow Jesus and emphasize nonviolence. Extraordinary piety and a commitment to live as simply as possible mark the practices of active Mennonites, who refuse, on religious grounds, to hold public office or serve in any military capacity. Modern day Mennonites number almost 1 million worldwide.

Mormons: Mormons are members of the Church of Jesus Christ of Latter-day Saints, which was founded in America in 1830 by John Smith on the basis of Revelations in the "Book of Mormons: Another Testament of Jesus Christ". This is believed to be a religious account of ancient American civilizations and suggests that America would be one of the two places (the other being Jerusalem) from which Jesus Christ

would rule when he comes again. There are twelve persons who have been chosen to be present day apostles. The President of the Church is regarded as a prophet, who continues to reveal truths from God.

Pentecostalists: The Pentecostal movement began in America at the beginning of twentieth century. Its members attach great importance to the Day of Pentecost (50 days after the resurrection) and the work of Holy Spirit. Pentecostal worship is emotional and spontaneous depending on how the Holy Spirit moves each individual. They believe in faith healing: the healing of illness through the power of people's faith in the Holy Spirit.

Presbyterians: Presbyterianism is based on the ideas of John Calvin. It is a Protestant family of Churches and is found especially in the Netherlands, Scotland, the USA and Korea. The Church of Scotland is Presbyterian.

Quakers (or Friends): The proper name for Quakers is the Religious Society of Friends. The Society was founded in the seventeenth century in England by George Fox. The short name, Quakers, was derived from a speech made by George Fox in which he said: "You should quake at the word of the Lord." The Quakers reject the necessity of ordained ministers and external sacraments, viewing all aspects of life itself as sacred. This pacifist tradition holds that every believer is gifted with "inner light". Worship , which is held in Meeting Houses, is mainly silent until someone feels moved by the Holy Spirit to speak.

Salvation Army: The Salvation Army was

founded in 1865 by William Booth, who believed that he was called to fight poverty and social injustice by meeting the people's physical and spiritual needs. The Salvation Army works for providing shelters for the homeless, care homes for the elderly, schools and hospitals and helps the people with drug and alcohol addictions.

Seventh-day Adventists: Seventh-Day Adventists celebrate the Sabbath on Saturday (rather than Sunday) and anticipate the imminent Second Coming of Christ. They worship on the Sabbath: from sunset on Friday to sunset on Saturday. They live by the teachings of the Bible and are also guided by the writings of Ellen White, one of the founders of the movement.

Unitarians: The Unitarian Universalist Association, which includes both Christian non Christian members, is among the most open and tolerant of Protestant religious traditions. Unitarian Universalists reject the doctrine of the Trinity, seeing Christ as a great teacher, not a divine incarnation. They tend to avoid dogma as restrictive and even presumptuous, choosing to emphasize understanding between faiths rather than a specific religious creed.

Christian Denominations - An over-view
Most divisions within Christendom arose from the following events:
- 1054 A.D: After centuries of tension over the increasing political power of the Pope, the Roman Catholic church in Western Europe splits with the Orthodox Church in the eastern Mediterranean and Russia.
- 1521 A.D: Protesting abuses within the Catholic Church (which the Church itself later condemned), Martin Luther starts a move-

ment intended to reform the church, but ends up splitting it. Numerous Protestant churches are formed (Lutherans, Presbyterians, Baptists, Methodists, etc.).
- In the 1500s, the Church of England (Episcopal Church) takes a "middle way" between Catholicism and Protestantism, forming a church that is locally governed.

One source estimates that there are nearly 34,000 separate Christian groups in the world. These have been categorized as follows:-

Three meta-groups, (Eastern Orthodoxy, Roman Catholicism and Protestantism)

Three wings, (conservative, mainline and liberal)

Fifteen Religious families, (Adventist, Baptist, Lutheran, Reform....)

Dozens of denominations, (from the Amish to The Way), and

Many systems of belief (Arminianism, British Israelism, Calvinism...)

MAIN SIMILARITIES AND DISSIMILARITIES

Roman Catholics and Protestants agree on some major theological matters, like Angels, the Crucifixion, Jesus' incarnation, bodily resurrection, and the imminent return of Jesus to earth in the second coming, Heaven, Hell, the Trinity, and the virgin birth of Jesus. They partly agree about baptism and the makeup of the Bible. But there exists a gulf between the two groups on other matters of belief and church practice

On the surface, Eastern Orthodoxy bears marked similarities to Roman Catholicism. Both churches have priests who appear to serve as mediators between God and humanity. Both have churches which are full of religious paintings and relics. Eastern Orthodox and Roman Catholic differences over sacraments and creeds are probably greater than the differences between Roman Catholicism and Protestantism

Authority : All Christians affirm the Bible as authoritative. Additionally, Anglicans, Orthodox, and Roman Catholics cite tradition as an authoritative source, i.e., the on-going teaching, practices and worship of the church. The Orthodox look with particular reverence upon the creeds of the first seven ecumenical councils (327-787 CE). Roman Catholics accept the teachings of the councils throughout the history of the church and understand the Pope as being invested with particular grace which enables him on special occasions to be free from all error on matters regarding faith and morals.

Bible: The Bible for Protestants is made up of some 66 books, Old and New Testaments. Roman Catholics affirm those 66 books as well as some 13 other books (the apocrypha) as fully authoritative. Orthodox accept but do not count the apocrypha as authoritative as the other 66. Protestants believe in private interpretation of the Bible. Catholics believe the Church is appointed by God as custodian of the Bible to interpret the scripture.

Priesthood: Protestants believe in a universal priesthood of all believers, while Catholics have a specially ordained priesthood.

God: All Christians believe in one God. Trinity: All Christians affirm that God consists of three divine persons: God the Father, God the Son, and the Holy Spirit.

Incarnation: Though earlier there was strong disagreement among various sections, it is now generally accepted that Jesus is fully human as well as fully God.

Sin and Salvation: All Christians affirm that doing something displeasing to God is a sin. They affirm that this estrangement from God is overcome by God's initiative. Through the work of Christ, God does for us what we cannot do for ourselves.

Roman Catholic and Orthodox Churches affirm that a believer must actively receive this gift of God. There are things a person must believe, do, and have done to him/her with the aid of the church in order to be saved. Protestants believe that salvation is by grace alone; there is nothing one can do to contribute to salvation; simply believe in God's grace.

Sacraments: Roman Catholic and Orthodox believe in seven Sacraments , namely, Baptism ,Confirmation; Matrimony, Holy Orders; Extreme Unction, Confession and the Eucharist. Protestants, on the other hand, observe only three Sacraments: Baptism ,Lord's Supper(communion) and Matrimony.

Heaven, Hell, and Purgatory: Most Christians affirm the concepts of Heaven and Hell, though their perceptions of Heaven and Hell may not be same. It is believed that Heaven is where the soul resides if one lived a good life while eternal punishment awaits in Hell for those who lead a bad life. As regards Purgatory , Roman Catholics understand Purgatory as an intermediate stage in which those who have died in a state of grace are given an opportunity to purge themselves of the guilt of their sins before entering Heaven. Orthodox teaching is not entirely clear on this matter. Some accept it, others do not. Protestants reject it as having no scriptural basis.

SACRAMENTS

(Religious ceremonies and acts regarded as outward and visible signs of inward and spiritual grace)

Catholic and Orthodox Churches recognize seven (7) sacraments: baptism, confirmation, eucharist (Communion) Mass or Liturgy, confession, ordination, matrimony and extreme unction (also called the anointing of the sick). Protestantism has only two: baptism and the Eucharist (Last Supper)..

The most important sacrament is 'baptism', symbolically carried out by moistening with water. Baptism is regarded as 're-birth in Christ'. Some branches of Christianity perform it only on freely consenting adults. But most hold that baptism of children is necessary for the salvation of souls in case a child dies without having been baptized. The parents choose close friends or relations to be godparents to the child. At an infant baptism, the baby is also officially given a first name , known as christian name). For this reason, baptism is sometimes referred to as a christening.

'Confirmation' means 'confirming faith' and is meant to strengthen young people's belief. They take on the promises that were made on their behalf at baptism. For the Catholic and the Orthodox Churches it is a sacrament but it is not so for Protestants.

The Eucharist (or Mass) is for Catholics, as important a sacrament as baptism, due to the actual presence of Christ in the bread and wine, while Protestant Churches tend to see the Lord's Supper symbolically. It means "thanksgiving". It is a re-enactment of the Last Supper in which Christians eat a small piece of bread or a wafer,

and sip a drop of wine. The bread or wafer represents the body of Jesus Christ. The wine represents his blood. Together they remind Christians that Jesus gave his life so that the people could enter a new, closer relationship with God. Different branches of the Church call it by different names. In Catholic churches it is called Mass; Some Anglican churches refer to it as Holy Communion; In Orthodox churches, it is called the Divine Liturgy. Protestants often call it the Breaking of Bread or the Lord's Supper.

The sacrament of 'confession' links Christ's power to forgive sins with the granting of this power to the apostles and the position of the church as the legal successor to the apostles. The church , or rather its priests, can by proxy grant forgiveness of sins (absolution) and require penance. The abuse of the system of absolution was one of the main factors leading to the Reformation, which deprived priests of this right.

'Ordination' is a ceremony at which a person becomes a priest or equivalent or is promoted to a high level in the hierarchy of priests.

'Holy unction , or extreme unction , normally carried out only on the death bed, has now been extended in Catholicism to include ministry to the sick, which has long been the case in the Orthodox Church. It is the smearing of holy oil onto a sick or dying person by a priest, accompanied by prayers and words of comfort.

Catholicism recognizes matrimony as a sacrament. In the ceremony held in a church, a priest, acting as God's representative, joins together the couple as husband and wife. It is intended to be a lifelong commitment.

APOSTLES

Peter, Andrew's brother. Apostele Andrew was the oldest brother of Peter and both were fishermen.

Outstanding figures in the original Christian community were the apostles Peter and Paul. Peter was the spokesman for the disciples, even during Jesus' lifetime. He was one of the first persons to witness Jesus' resurrection and was called the "rock" on which Jesus said he would build the Church. Peter was called by the apostle Paul a "pillar" of the church and it was believed by the crowds, that the mere casting of his shadow upon the sick, was capable of bringing about miraculous healing. He was the sole leader of the original Christian community in Jerusalem, supported Paul's efforts to convert the Gentiles, did missionary work himself among the Jews, and finally went to Rome, where, after monstrous tortures, he was crucified in 67 A D under Roman Emperor Nero. The claim of the Pope, as Bishop of Rome and thus Peter's successor, to be the primate of the Church is based on this "rock" tradition.

Bartholomew

The apostle Bartholomew was led to Christ in the region of Galilee, possibly by the apostle Philip . It is said that he prayed a hundred times a day and a hundred times a night.. In the company of the apostle Philip, the apostle Bartholomew went to Asia Minor and laboured in Hierapolis, near Laodicea and Colosse, in what is modern day Turkey. While in Hierapolis, it is said that the wife of the Roman pro-consul was healed by the apostles Philip and Bartholomew, that she became a Christian and that her husband ordered Philip and Bartholomew to be put to death by crucifixion. Sadly, Philip was crucified, but Bartholomew escaped martyrdom, when for some special reason, the magistrates caused him to be taken down from the cross and dismissed. From there,

Bartholomew went eastward to India and then to greater Armenia. The apostle Bartholomew is said to have been martyred in the year 68 AD.

Thomas

The apostle Thomas was a fisherman by trade and a native of Galilee. After the resurrection of Jesus Christ, Thomas went to Babylon and it is believed that he established the first Christian church there. He is, also, known to have gone to Persia , and from there, he went to India and preached the Gospel making many converts. It is, also, believed that the apostle Thomas evangelized as far as China and while in India he suffered martyrdom by being killed with a lance (he was buried in Mylapore , India, which is now a

suburb of Madras.) The apostle Thomas is said to have been a fearless evangelist and a great builder of churches.

Matthew

The apostle Matthew, also called Levi, was the son of Alphaeus and the brother of the apostle James the Less, or, James, son of Alphaeus. By profession, Matthew was a tax collector before being called by Jesus to follow him. Matthew probably remained in the Holy Land, as tradition says, for 15 years and after this, encouraged by the reports of the success of other Christian leaders among the Jews (the Diaspora) and, also, among the Gentiles he went forth on several missionary journeys. It is certain

that he went to Persia and the mysterious area in Persia known as "Ethiopia." It is, also, possible that he traveled to the Ethiopia in Africa as the Roman Catholic tradition indicates and there is, also, a belief that Matthew was martyred in Egypt upon his return from Ethiopia in Africa, but, this, is not certain. There is a tradition which says that Matthew was martyred in Parthia. Matthew was a gifted writer, an devout disciple and was perhaps the best educated of the twelve Apostles. He was the writer of The Gospel of Matthew.

James

(died A.D.44) - usually called the Greater, son of Zebedee, brother of Johen, the Evangelist. He was a fisherman of Galilee and was martyred by Herod Agrippa in Jerusalem. He was the first martyr.

James

(died A.D. 62) - usually called the Less, son of Alphaens and perhaps a relative of Jesus. He was the writer of the Epistle of St. James which was into the canon of the New Testament.

John

The Evangelist, brother of James, The Greater, the loved disciple. He was the writer of the fourth gospel, of three Epistles and of the Apocalypse Book.

Paul

The apostle Paul was at first a great enemy of the Christians. Originally named Saul, a Jewish scholar, while Paul was on his way to Damascus, the glory of the Lord shone suddenly upon him, he was struck to the earth and remained blind for three days. After his recovery, he was converted and became an apostle and, lastly, suffered as a martyr for the religion which he had formerly persecuted . Paul's great abilities and earnest enthusiasm in spreading the gospel of Christ have made his name revered wherever the Christian religion is known. ... At one point , the apostle Paul was a prisoner in Rome and after being released, as part of his further missionary journeys, it is believed that he visited Gaul and Spain. It is also believed that when he returned to Rome, he was taken prisoner and was imprisoned for nine months with the apostle Peter. It was in Rome that the apostle Paul suffered martyrdom. By order of the Emperor Nero, Paul was beheaded with a sword. He is often called "the second founder of Christianity." Paul was the first to state systematically the beliefs of Christianity and is largely responsible for transforming a sect of Judaism into the early Christian Church where gentiles were welcome. He is traditionally considered to be the author of fourteen books of the New Testament His epistles to the various Christian communities, specially in the Hellenic world, which are appended to the gospels in the New Testament canon, show him to be the one of the most significant organizers and missionaries of the early church. His writings also contain the first references to the church as the (visible) "body of Christ".

John the Baptist (was not apostle!)

He was the Precursor. He was killed before Jesus Christ's death.

Son of Zachary, a priest of the order of Abia whose job in the temple was to burn incense; and of Elizabeth, a descendent of Aaron. As Zachary was ministering in the Temple, an angel brought him news that Elizabeth would bear a child filled with the Holy Spirit from the moment of his birth. Zachary doubted and was struck dumb until John's birth.

Jesus Christ and John the Baptist were related. Their mothers, Mary and Elizabeth, were cousins.. John the Baptist was born 6 months before Jesus Christ . He died about 6 months before Jesus Christ. The angel Gabriel separately announced the coming births of Jesus Christ and John the Baptist. John was a prophet whose own coming was prophesied by an earlier prophet over 700 years before (Isaiah 40:3-5)

John began his ministry around age 27, wearing a leather belt and a tunic of camel hair. People went out to him from Jerusalem and the whole region of The Jordan. Confessing their sins, they were baptized by him in the Jordan River. He converted many, and prepared the way for the coming of Jesus. He baptized Jesus, after which he stepped away and told his disciples to follow Jesus.He was considered very highly by Jesus Christ, who said about him, "Among those born of women there has not risen anyone greater than John the Baptist." (Matthew 11:11)

John's ministry, and life, came to an end when he admonished Herod for his sinful behaviour . He was imprisoned at Machaerus, a fortress about 15 kilometers east of the Dead Sea. There, he was beheaded.

Jesus responded to the news of John's death by saying, "John was a lamp that burned and gave light, and you chose for a time to enjoy his light." (John 5:35)

THE BIBLE

The "Bible" is the most sacred book, the "Word of God", for the Christians . Its theme is salvation through His Son, Jesus Christ.. It contains two main parts: The Old and the New Testament.

"What's a Testament"? Testament ,in the sense it is used in Bible, means "last will and testament", or as or as commonly called just a "will" of God. Both the Testaments are left by God for mankind .They enable mankind to enter into a covenant relationship with Him. One of the central blessings of this covenant relationship is salvation.

The Old Testament chronicles the lives of Jews and others who lived before Jesus, who had been promised a saviour by God, and were waiting for him. The Old Testament prophets hundreds of years before, foretold

the coming of a second covenant . It is made up of 66 books, written by 40 authors, covering a period of more than 1,500 years. This contains many stories about people demonstrating faith in God and also provides historical information about the era. The Old Testament was written mostly in Hebrew, with a few short passages in

Aramaic. The entire Old Testament was translated into Greek about a 100 years before the death of Christ.

The New Testament is Christ's last will and testament. It is a covenant, a divine agreement extended by God, a promise from God that He will save mankind if it obeys His Testament. The New Testament contains 27 books: Four Gospels, twenty-one Epistles, and two other books called Acts and Revelation... The New Testament was written in Greek. which was the language of educated men at the beginning of the Christian era, except Matthew Gospel that was written in Aramaic. It was translated into Latin and after Reformation, it was translated into German and other languages.

The Gospels: Gospel means "good news". Gospels were written between 70 and 100 A D by four evangelists: Matthew, Mark, Luke and John. Each gospel tells of the life, teachings, death and resurrection of Jesus from its author's viewpoint.

Acts: Acts or the Acts of the Apostles, particularly of the Apostle Paul, describe the story after the resurrection of Jesus, and relate the early development of Christianity. They were written by Luke

The epistles: An epistle is a letter. Most of the epistles in the New Testament were written about 30 years after the death of Jesus by a converted Jew named Paul. He journeyed throughout Roman Empire, telling non-Jews about Jesus and setting up churches. The Epistles also give out the ideas underlying the Christian faith of the early Christians. . The epistles are twenty-one , fourteen by Paul, three by John, two by Peter, one by James and one by   Judas

Revelations: Revelation (=Apocalypse) is the final book of the New Testament. It gives a description of the series of visions, viz., the lamb of God and the heavenly city. The author is John, the favourite Apostle of Jesus .

The Distinction between Old and New Testaments: It is believed that the Old Testament was a covenant given strictly for the Jews, or Israelites. The New Testament made no distinction. One of the great things about the New Testament is that God's message and special covenant relationship is extended to all races and peoples. The Old Testament , however, continues to have an important place in Christianity as it serves as a great source of examples that are necessary for our spiritual growth and health . Both Testaments were ushered in by "the shedding   of blood" - blood of animal sacrifices for the Old, and the blood of Christ for the New. Even the Old Testament prophets, hundreds of years before, foretold the   coming of a second covenant . New Testament is the history for the Christian   church - just as the Old Testament is the history for the Jewish religion

TEACHINGS OF JESUS
Sermon on the Mount
(New King James Version of the Bible)

The essence of Jesus' teachings is in his most famous sermon, called the "Sermon on the Mount". It emphasizes the following doctrines:-

- **Love your enemies.**
- **Do not judge others.**
- **Trust God.**
- **Don't be anxious about tomorrow.**
- **Do unto others as you would have them do unto you**

The Sermon is divided into 5 sections:

Beatitudes - Teachings that begin with "blessed." These were meant to comfort suffering believers. **New laws** - Contrasts the old law of Moses with the new law of Christ. A brief summary of Christian doctrine.

Lord's prayer - Instructions on prayer. Jesus also teaches the proper motives for fasting and offering gifts.

Money - Christian attitudes concerning the use of money. Reasons to avoid worry. Warnings - Dangers of false teachers and hypocrisy

Text of the Sermon on the Mount
The Beatitudes

1 And seeing the multitudes, He went up on a mountain, and when He was seated His disciples came to Him.

2 Then He opened His mouth and taught them, saying:

3 Blessed are the poor in spirit, For theirs is the kingdom of heaven.

4 Blessed are those who mourn, For they shall be comforted.

5 Blessed are the meek, For they shall inherit the earth.

6 Blessed are those who hunger and thirst for righteousness, For they shall be filled.

7 Blessed are the merciful, For they shall obtain mercy.

8 Blessed are the pure in heart, For they shall see God.

9 Blessed are the peacemakers, For they shall be called sons of God.

10 Blessed are those who are persecuted for righteousness' sake, For theirs is the kingdom of heaven.

11 "Blessed are you when they revile and persecute you, and say all kinds of evil against you falsely for My sake.

12 Rejoice and be exceedingly glad, for great is your reward in heaven, for so they persecuted the prophets who were before you.

Believers Are Salt and Light

13 "You are the salt of the earth; but if the salt loses its flavor, how shall it be seasoned? It is then good for nothing but to be thrown out and trampled underfoot by men.

14 "You are the light of the world. A city that is set on a hill cannot be hidden.

15 Nor do they light a lamp and put it under a basket, but on a lamp stand, and it gives light to all who are in the house.

16 Let your light so shine before men, that they may see your good works and glorify your Father in heaven.

Christ Fulfills the Law

17 "Do not think that I came to destroy the Law or the Prophets. I did not come to destroy but to fulfill.

18 For assuredly, I say to you, till heaven and earth pass away, one jot or one tittle will by no means pass from the law till all is fulfilled.

19 Whoever therefore breaks one of the least of these commandments, and teaches men so, shall be called least in the kingdom of heaven; but whoever does and teaches them, he shall be called great in the kingdom of heaven.

20 For I say to you, that unless your righteousness exceeds the righteousness of the scribes and Pharisees, you will by no means enter the kingdom of heaven.

Murder Begins in the Heart

21 "You have heard that it was said to those of old, "You shall not murder, and whoever murders will be in danger of the judgment.'

22 But I say to you that whoever is angry with his brother without a cause shall be in danger of the judgment. And whoever says to his brother, "Raca!' shall be in danger of the council. But

whoever says, "You fool!' shall be in danger of hell fire.

23Therefore if you bring your gift to the altar, and there remember that your brother has something against you,

24leave your gift there before the altar, and go your way. First be reconciled to your brother, and then come and offer your gift.

25Agree with your adversary quickly, while you are on the way with him, lest your adversary deliver you to the judge, the judge hand you over to the officer, and you be thrown into prison.

26Assuredly, I say to you, you will by no means get out of there till you have paid the last penny.

Adultery in the Heart

27 "You have heard that it was said to those of old, "You shall not commit adultery.'

28But I say to you that whoever looks at a woman to lust for her has already committed adultery with her in his heart.

29If your right eye causes you to sin, pluck it out and cast it from you; for it is more profitable for you that one of your members perish, than for your whole body to be cast into hell.

30And if your right hand causes you to sin, cut it off and cast it from you; for it is more profitable for you that one of your members perish, than for your whole body to be cast into hell.

Marriage Is Sacred and Binding

31 "Furthermore it has been said, "Whoever divorces his wife, let him give her a certificate of divorce.'

32But I say to you that whoever divorces his wife for any reason except sexual immorality causes her to commit adultery; and whoever marries a woman who is divorced commits adultery.

Jesus Forbids Oaths

33 "Again you have heard that it was said to those of old, "You shall not swear falsely, but shall perform your oaths to the Lord.'

34But I say to you, do not swear at all: neither by heaven, for it is God's throne;

35nor by the earth, for it is His footstool; nor by Jerusalem, for it is the city of the great King.

36Nor shall you swear by your head, because you cannot make one hair white or black.

37But let your "Yes' be "Yes,' and your "No,' "No.' For whatever is more than these is from the evil one.

Go the Second Mile

38 "You have heard that it was said, "An eye for an eye and a tooth for a tooth.'

39But I tell you not to resist an evil person. But whoever slaps you on your right cheek, turn the other to him also.

40If anyone wants to sue you and take away your tunic, let him have your cloak also.

41And whoever compels you to go one mile, go with him two.

42Give to him who asks you, and from him who wants to borrow from you do not turn away.

Love Your Enemies

43 "You have heard that it was said, "You shall love your neighbor and hate your enemy.'

44But I say to you, love your enemies, bless those who curse you, do good to those who hate you, and pray for those who spitefully use you and persecute you,

45that you may be sons of your Father in heaven; for He makes His sun rise on the evil and on the good, and sends rain on the just and on the unjust.

46For if you love those who love you, what

reward have you? Do not even the tax collectors do the same?

47 And if you greet your brethren only, what do you do more than others? Do not even the tax collectors do so?

48 Therefore you shall be perfect, just as your Father in heaven is perfect.

Matthew 6
Do Good to Please God

1 "Take heed that you do not do your charitable deeds before men, to be seen by them. Otherwise you have no reward from your Father in heaven.

2 Therefore, when you do a charitable deed, do not sound a trumpet before you as the hypocrites do in the synagogues and in the streets, that they may have glory from men. Assuredly, I say to you, they have their reward.

3 But when you do a charitable deed, do not let your left hand know what your right hand is doing,

4 that your charitable deed may be in secret; and your Father who sees in secret will Himself reward you openly.

Fasting to Be Seen Only by God

5 "Moreover, when you fast, do not be like the hypocrites, with a sad countenance. For they disfigure their faces that they may appear to men to be fasting. Assuredly, I say to you, they have their reward.

7 But you, when you fast, anoint your head and wash your face,

8 so that you do not appear to men to be fasting, but to your Father who is in the secret place; and your Father who sees in secret will reward you openly.

Lay Up Treasures in Heaven

9 "Do not lay up for yourselves treasures on earth, where moth and rust destroy and where thieves break in and steal;

10 but lay up for yourselves treasures in heaven, where neither moth nor rust destroys and where thieves do not break in and steal.

11 For where your treasure is, there your heart will be also.

The Lamp of the Body

12 "The lamp of the body is the eye. If therefore your eye is good, your whole body will be full of light.

13 But if your eye is bad, your whole body will be full of darkness. If therefore the light that is in you is darkness, how great is that darkness!

You Cannot Serve God and Riches

14 "No one can serve two masters; for either he will hate the one and love the other, or else he will be loyal to the one and despise the other. You cannot serve God and mammon.

Do Not Worry

15 "Therefore I say to you, do not worry about your life, what you will eat or what you will drink; nor about your body, what you will put on. Is not life more than food and the body more than clothing?

16 Look at the birds of the air, for they neither sow nor reap nor gather into barns; yet your heavenly Father feeds them. Are you not of more value than they?

17 Which of you by worrying can add one cubit to his stature?

18 So why do you worry about clothing? Consider the lilies of the field, how they grow: they neither toil nor spin;

19 and yet I say to you that even Solomon in

all his glory was not arrayed like one of these.

20 Now if God so clothes the grass of the field, which today is, and tomorrow is thrown into the oven, will He not much more clothe you, O you of little faith?

21 Therefore do not worry, saying, "What shall we eat?' or "What shall we drink?' or "What shall we wear?'

22 For after all these things the Gentiles seek. For your heavenly Father knows that you need all these things.

23 But seek first the kingdom of God and His righteousness, and all these things shall be added to you.

24 Therefore do not worry about tomorrow, for tomorrow will worry about its own things. Sufficient for the day is its own trouble.

Matthew 7
Do Not Judge

1 "Judge not, that you be not judged.

2 For with what judgment you judge, you will be judged; and with the measure you use, it will be measured back to you.

3 And why do you look at the speck in your brother's eye, but do not consider the plank in your own eye?

4 Or how can you say to your brother, "Let me remove the speck from your eye'; and look, a plank is in your own eye?

5 Hypocrite! First remove the plank from your own eye, and then you will see clearly to remove the speck from your brother's eye.

6 Do not give what is holy to the dogs; nor cast your pearls before swine, lest they trample them under their feet, and turn and tear you in pieces.

Keep Asking, Seeking, Knocking

7 "Ask, and it will be given to you; seek, and

you will find; knock, and it will be opened to you.

8 For everyone who asks receives, and he who seeks finds, and to him who knocks it will be opened.

9 Or what man is there among you who, if his son asks for bread, will give him a stone?

10 Or if he asks for a fish, will he give him a serpent?

11 If you then, being evil, know how to give good gifts to your children, how much more will your Father who is in heaven give good things to those who ask Him!

12 Therefore, whatever you want men to do to you, do also to them, for this is the Law and the Prophets.

The Narrow Way

13 "Enter by the narrow gate; for wide is the gate and broad is the way that leads to destruction, and there are many who go in by it.

14 Because arrow is the gate and difficult is the way which leads to life, and there are few who find it.

You Will Know Them by Their Fruits

15 "Beware of false prophets, who come to you in sheep's clothing, but inwardly they are ravenous wolves.

16 You will know them by their fruits. Do men gather grapes from thornbushes or figs from thistles?

17 Even so, every good tree bears good fruit, but a bad tree bears bad fruit.

18 A good tree cannot bear bad fruit, nor can a bad tree bear good fruit.

19 Every tree that does not bear good fruit is cut down and thrown into the fire.

20 Therefore by their fruits you will know them.

I Never Knew You

21 "Not everyone who says to Me, "Lord, Lord,' shall enter the kingdom of heaven, but he who does the will of My Father in heaven.

22 Many will say to Me in that day, "Lord, Lord, have we not prophesied in Your name, cast out demons in Your name, and done many wonders in Your name?'

23 And then I will declare to them, "I never knew you; depart from Me, you who practice lawlessness!'

Build on the Rock

24 "Therefore whoever hears these sayings of Mine, and does them, I will liken him to a wise man who built his house on the rock:

25 and the rain descended, the floods came, and the winds blew and beat on that house; and it did not fall, for it was founded on the rock.

26 But everyone who hears these sayings of Mine, and does not do them, will be like a foolish man who built his house on the sand:

27 and the rain descended, the floods came, and the winds blew and beat on that house; and it fell. And great was its fall."

28 And so it was, when Jesus had ended these sayings, that the people were astonished at His teaching,

29 for He taught them as one having authority, and not as the scribes.

THE LORD'S PRAYER

5 "And when you pray, you shall not be like the hypocrites. For they love to pray standing in the synagogues and on the corners of the streets, that they may be seen by men. Assuredly, I say to you, they have their reward.

6 But you, when you pray, go into your room, and when you have shut your door, pray to your Father who is in the secret place; and your Father who sees in secret will reward you openly.

7 And when you pray, do not use vain repetitions as the heathen do. For they think that they will be heard for their many words.

8 Therefore do not be like them. For your Father knows the things you have need of before you ask Him.

9 In this manner, therefore, pray:

Our Father,
who art in heaven,
hallowed be thy name.
Thy kingdom come.
Thy will be done on earth
as it is in heaven.
Give us this day
our daily bread
Forgive us our trespasses
as we forgive those who
trespass against us.

Lead us not into temptation but deliver us from evil.

For Yours is the kingdom and the power and the glory forever Amen.

"For if you forgive men their trespasses, your heavenly Father will also forgive you.

But if you do not forgive men their trespasses, neither will your Father forgive your trespasses

CHRISTIAN BELIEFS

The beliefs of Christianity can be seen in the words of the Apostles' Creed, a document which was written to distinguish Christianity from other religions and show basic Christian doctrine in a concise manner.

The Apostle's Creed

I believe in God the Father Almighty, Maker of heaven and earth.

And in Jesus Christ,
His only Son, our Lord;
Who was conceived by the Holy Spirit,
Born of the Virgin Mary, Suffered under Pontius Pilate,
Was crucified, died and was buried.
He descended into hell;
The third day He rose again from the dead;
He ascended into heaven
and is seated at the right hand of God the Father Almighty;
From there He shall come to judge the living and the dead.
I believe in the Holy Spirit,
The holy Christian Church,
The Communion of Saints,
the Forgiveness of sins,
The Resurrection of the body,
And the Life everlasting.
Amen.

TEN COMMANDMENTS

The Ten Commandments (a.k.a. Decalogue) are accepted by Judaism and Christianity as a summary of the important rules of behavior that God expects of humanity. It is believed that God gave Ten Commandments through Moses as the Law of the Old Testament. They were confirmed in the New Testament by Jesus Christ in his life and teachings.

There are three versions of the Ten Commandments . They are at Exodus 20:2-17, Exodus 34:12-26, and Deuteronomy 5:6-21.

The most commonly known
Ten Commandments are:
1. I am the Lord your God. You shall have no other gods before me.

2. You shall not take the name of the Lord your God in vain.
3. Remember to keep holy the Lord's Day.
4. Honour your father and your mother.
5. You shall not kill.
6. You shall not commit adultery.
7. You shall not steal.
8. You shall not bear false witness against your neighbour.
9. You shall not covet your neighbour's wife.
10. You shall not covet your neighbour's goods

Jesus Christ sums up ten into two

The Commandments are all about relationships When Jesus was asked what the greatest commandment was, he answered by stating that all the laws are rooted in two:

1) **Love the Lord with all your heart, and**
2) **Love your neighbor as yourself**
(Matthew 22:36-40).

CHRISTIAN MORALITY

Christian morality is quite similar to morality in other religions and cultures, and to pre-existing Jewish morality.

"Think not that I have come to abolish the law and the prophets; I have come not to abolish them but to fulfill them." - Jesus, Matthew 5:17

Christianity emphasizes two things that is often neglected in the modern world:

- **Intentions matter just as much as effects.**

"You have heard that it was said... 'Thou shalt not kill; and whoever kills shall be liable to judgment.' But I say to you that everyone who hates his brother shall be liable to judgment." - Jesus, Matthew 5:21

- **It distinguishes sin from temptation.**
Human nature is corrupted by sin, and you cannot be good by simply following your nat-

ural instincts in their present, damaged form.

"Temptations to sin are sure to come." - Jesus, Luke 17:1

"No temptation has overtaken you that is not common to mankind. God is faithful, and he will not let you be tempted beyond what you can bear." - St. Paul, I Corinthians 6:13

Christian sexual morality is based on the idea that sexual pleasure is holy and good, that God created it, that its purpose is to unite husband and wife (and, where applicable, to pro-create children), and that it has spiritual as well as physical significance. It is not a mere physical thrill, nor is it something to be ashamed of.

Jesus taught that a person's mental sex life is as important as what he or she carries out physically. This is the basis of the Christian objection to pornography and other exploitative uses of sexual desire.

Christians do not approve of sexual intercourse outside of marriage nor homosexual contact

There is no reason to expect these teachings to "change with the times. God's law is not ours to change. If it were, it wouldn't do us much good.

CHRISTIAN RITUALS
Birth

(There is a view that there is no real ritual for the birth in Christianity.)

When a woman is about to deliver a baby, the priest of the congregation is called for and he prays for a safe delivery. There are no special rituals concerned with the birth of a child. Then after 40 days of cleansing the mother takes her newborn to the church for thanksgiving. There she gives offering to the Lord.

Usually the first birthday of the child is celebrated elaborately with the parents arranging a special feast for the guests. All of them give gifts to the kid. And the child cuts a special birthday cake to be shared between the guests.

Baptism

Baptism is an important ritual in the life of a Christian. A child is admitted to the church congregation as a member only through Baptism.

According to Christian belief, a child is born tainted with the sin that passed on to him from the great sin of Adam and Eve. At Baptism, the child is relieved of this sin and he becomes a child of God and a member of the church

Baptism is done usually before the first birthday. The child is given white clothes, shoes and cap by his parents and relatives give him gifts. A feast is given to them and the priest, by the parents.

Matrimony (Today, there is no imposed ritual. There are different social customs in this regard from region to region!)

Engagement This is usually held at the brides' residence. It is more or less a family affair and only the close relatives attend the function.

The priest starts the function with a prayer. Then the girl and the boy exchange garlands, the Bible and a ring as a mark of their engagement. The priest delivers a small sermon and a feast is given for the invitees.

The girl and the boy are given time to talk and understand each other. On this day the date of marriage and other details are discussed between the groom's and the bride's side.

Marriage Marriages usually take place in the nearby churches. The marriage celebrations are influenced by local customs and practices and may vary according to the region.

On the day of marriage, the groom's party arrives at the bride's residence and the bride's father welcomes them. He welcomes the groom

meal. The guests give gifts for the newly married couple. At night a reception would be arranged at the boy's place.

Death

When a person dies, the body is laid in a cot with a cross nearby. Incense sticks and candles are lit around the cot. Perfumes are sprayed over the body. When all the relatives have gathered, the head priest holds prayers in the room.

Then the body is bathed and clothed and placed in a special coffin. The coffin is placed at an open place for people to pay their last respects. Then the arms of the body are folded across the chest. Flower garlands are laid along with lots of flowers sprinkled inside the coffin.

The Bible is read and the priest gives a small lecture on the life and deeds of the deceased. The relatives kiss the dead as a sign of farewell and the departure song is sung.

The funeral service then begins with the guidance of the priest. Usually the sons carry the coffin on their shoulders but nowadays special vehicles like a hearse- van are used for the purpose. First the coffin is taken to the church, where the bells toll in a 1.1-2 sequence. From there after a brief prayer it is taken to the cemetery

At the cemetery a special pit is dug for the purpose beforehand. The coffin is lowered into the pit and the people put handfuls of sand over the coffin and finally the pit is closed. On the 3rd or 5th day, the relatives visit the cemetry and offer garlands and milk at the spot and disperse after a prayer.

CHRISTIAN FESTIVALS
Advent

Advent begins with the fourth Sunday before Christmas and it marks the start of   the Christian Church's year. Advent means "com-

with a garland and a golden chain. Then the groom's party is given breakfast. The groom's side then goes to the nearby church accompanied by music bands. The bride's party follows suit. At the church the head priest leads the boy and the girl to the altar. Small girls with flower baskets accompany the couple ,to sprinkle flowers over the couple.

At the Altar, the priest prays for a happy life for the couple and then he blesses them. Texts from the holy Bible are read and he makes a short sermon. The father of the bride gives her hand to the groom. Then the groom ties a golden chain in the neck of the bride or slips a ring on the girl's hand.

A choir usually accompanies the service with melodious songs blessing the couple. Then they get to the bride's residence for a sumptuous

ing" or " drawing near". Christians use this period to prepare themselves for Christmas, the celebration of the birth of Jesus Christ.

Christmas

Christmas is the celebration of the birth of Jesus Christ. Although the exact date of his birth is not known, the celebration is held in the West on the 25 December. The date was chosen by Emperor Constantine to coincide with a Roman Sun festival. In the Orthodox Church, Christmas is on 6th January.

Shrove Tuesday (Carnival) and Lent

Shrove Tuesday is forty days before Easter. It is celebrated by making pancakes and traditionally having pancake races etc. Pancake race is believed to be a British celebration, not a Christian. The idea is to use up all of the rich food - eggs and flour ready for the month long fast to prepare oneself for the Easter celebration.

On Ash Wednesday (the day after Shrove Tuesday and the start of Lent) Christians remember Jesus - they go to church and have the sign of the cross marked on their foreheads in ash. Lent is the period before Easter when Christians remember their sins. Lent commemorates the 40 days and nights that Jesus spent fasting and praying in the wilderness.

Holy Week:
Palm Sunday - Maundy Thursday

On Palm Sunday - the first day of Holy week - Christians remember when Jesus rode into Jerusalem riding on a donkey - people threw palm leaves down on the road like a red carpet might be laid in front of a king. Palm crosses are given to the congregation to help them think about the week ahead. During the following week, Christians remember the events from the arrival of Jesus in Jerusalem to the day of his resurrection, Easter Day.

Maundy Thursday is a reminder of the Last Supper - when Jesus celebrated the fist communion with his apostles.

Good Friday

The day that Jesus died on the cross. There are services in all Christian churches at the time Christ was crucified. These are very solemn occasions quite unlike what will occur three days later.

Easter Sunday

The most important festival for Christians. It is a very joyous occasion marked in churches by wonderful music and flowers. Out of church by the exchange of cards and Easter eggs - a symbol of spring and new life as Jesus' death brought new life to Christians

Whitsun

On the day of Pentecost when the Jews celebrated their harvest festival. Jesus, his apostles and many people who followed him were together in Jerusalem. Suddenly it seemed like a wind rushed through the crowd, everyone suddenly could understand many languages new to them. It was a visit from the Holy Spirit and he gave everyone there new power in their bodies so that they could go and spread the word of God.

Saints' Days

There are many days of remembrance for many officially recognized saints., usually on the date of their death. On these days there may be processions and special church services .

CHRISTIANITY IN INDIA

By tradition, Christianity is said to have arrived in India with Saint Thomas, one of the apostles of Jesus Christ, who spent some years in South India and possibly died there. However, others believe that the first missionary to arrive in the country was Saint Bartholomew. Historically, Christian missionary activity started with the advent of Saint Francis Xavier in 1544. He was followed by Portuguese missionaries at first and eventually by missionaries from other countries like Denmark, Holland, Germany and Great Britain. Throughout the 18th and 19th centuries Catholic as well as Protestant missionaries preached Christian doctrines in India and also made important contributions to social improvement and education in India.

Acording to 2001 census, the Christians in India number about 24 million and consist of people from almost every denomination of Christianity.

CHRISTIAN POPULATION

Christianity: David B. Barrett's World Christian Encyclopedia (1994 update) gives an oft-cited figure of 1.9 billion Christians (or about 33% of the world population), and has projected that by the year 2000 there will be 2.1 billion Christians in the world. Regardless of the degree of accuracy of this figure, Christianity, if taken as a whole, is unarguably the largest world religion.

In India Christian population is 24 million according to 2001 Census, i.e. 2.33 % of Indian population.

The following list shows the countries with the largest numbers of Christians. Christianity,

as defined for the purpose of census and surveys, includes all those who claim to be Christian. This includes adherents of different divisions within Christianity, Catholics, Eastern Orthodox, Protestants, Pentecostals, Jehovah's Witnesses, Latter-day Saints, African Indigenous Churches and others.

Top 10 Largest National Christian Population

Rank	Nation	Number
1	USA	224,457,000
2	Brazil	139,000,000
3	Mexico	86,120,000
4	Russia	80,000,000
5	China	70,000,000
6	Germany	67,000,000
7	Philippines	63,470,000
8	United Kingdom	51,060,000
9	Italy	47,690,000
10	France	44,150,000
11	Nigeria	38,180,000

Source for these Christian statistics: Ash, Russell. The Top 10 of Everything, DK Publishing, Inc.: New York (1997), pg. 160-161; December Advance Newsletter, 1996, Kainos Press; Adherents.com.

GLOSSARY OF CHRISTIAN TERMS

Apostle- Follower/disciple

Archbishop (Archdiocese) - Chief bishop of province

Baptism- Ritual of sprinkling water on a person and accepting him/her into the Church

Bible The sacred text which records the lives of major figures in Christianity, including Jesus. Contains Old and New Testaments.

Bishop- A clergyman who is consecrated as governor of diocese

Cardinal- A leading dignitary of the Roman Catholic Church

Cathedral- Church or principal church of diocese

Chapel- Place of worship of Christians, normally a small church

Church- Place of worship of Christians

Communion- Small piece of bread also called host used to represent the body of Jesus Christ

Convent- A place where nuns or monks usually operate

Confession- Act of confessing sins (wrong-doings) to priest or God

Covenant- A pact, a decision; usually a pact with God

Cross Roman method of execution which took the life of Jesus. Now a symbol of Jesus' suffering and resurrection

Diocese- Under pastoral care of bishop

Easter The celebration of Jesus' triumphant return to life after dying on the crossEucharist-Christian sacrament

Gabriel- Angel of God; also God's messenger

Gentile- Person who wasn't a Jew

Gospel- Word of the Lord

Holy Trinity- The combination of God the Father, God the Son and God the Holy -Spirit

Lent The remembrance of the period of time leading up to and including Christ's death on the cross.

Mass- Service/Ritual carried out in catholic church where people come in groups to pray together

Messiah- Promised deliverer of Jews

Minister- Like a priest

Nun- Woman who takes vows of chastity, poverty and obedience towards the Christian church. Orthodox Church- Eastern or Greek church separated during 9th century; recognizing Patriarch of Constantinople as head.

Passover- Festival celebrating the liberation of the Israelites from the Egyptians

Pastor- Minister in charge of protestant church

Pentecost- It is a Jewish festival celebrated fitfty days after Passover. In Christianity it is a festival, fifty days after Easter, to commemorate the giving of the Holy Spirit to the Apostles.   Pope-Religious head of Roman Catholic church

Priest- Someone who is appointed by the Christian Church to conduct mass, confession, baptism and other Christian duties.

Prophet- One who is selected by God and carries out God's will. Interpreter of Gods messages.

Protestant- A sect of Christians who do not accept the Pope as the head of the Church; have a few different beliefs than Catholics. Originally started by people who protested against the wrongdoing of the Catholic Church

Purgatory- After a person has died, and they still have to account for certain sins of theirs, they go to this place temporarily to repent for their sins before they go to heaven.

Reformation A movement which resulted in the formation of the Protestant branch of Christianity. A reforming of Christianity which eliminated certain doctrines and practices of Catholicism which were deemed incorrect.Roman Catholic- Followers of the original Christian church, accept the Pope as the religious head of the church

Sabbath- The holy day of the week for resting and worshipping God . Saturday for Jews; Sunday for Christians

Sacrament- An outward sign, inward grace and the institution by Jesus Christ

Sister- Nun

Sin- Tuning away from God's love. Doing something wrong..

Synagogue- Jewish place of worship   Ten Commandments- Laws of conduct written on stone and given to Moses by God at Mt. Sinai

CHRISTIAN SAYINGS

No slave can serve two masters. For a slave will either hate one and love the other, or be devoted to one and despise the other. You cannot serve God and wealth

— Jesus Christ

This is my commandment, that you love one another as I have loved you. No one has greater love than this, to lay down one's life for one's friends.

—Jesus Christ

Love your enemies, do good to those who hate you, bless those who curse you, pray for those who abuse you. From anyone who takes away your coat do not withhold even your shirt. Give to everyone who begs from you; and if anyone takes away your goods, do not ask for them again.

— Jesus Christ

Do unto others as you would have others do unto you.

—Jesus Christ

Do all the good you can,
By all the means you can,
In all the ways you can,
At all the times you can,
To all the people you can,
As long as ever you can.

—John Wesley

If anyone says "I love God" and
hates his brother, he is a liar;
for he who does not love his brother
whom he has seen, cannot love God
whom he has not seen.

— John's First Letter

For what shall it profit a man, if he shall gain the whole world and lose his own soul?- Mark's Gospel

Sikhism

THE RELIGION OF DIVINE GRACE, HARMONY & SACRIFICE

Table of Contents

ORIGIN

Sikhism, the youngest of the major religions of the world, was founded by Guru Nanak Dev in the second half of the 15th century . Based on the divine philosophy of Guru Nanak , Sikhism evolved through a succession of nine Gurus, reaching its glory and acquiring a distinct identity under the tenth Guru, Guru Gobind Singh in the year 1699. After Guru Gobind Singh's death in 1708, personal Guruship ended and Granth Sahib, the holy scripture containing the hymns composed by Sikh Gurus was installed as, and has since been, the Guru of the Sikhs. Sikhism, which has a following of over 23 million people world-wide, preaches a message of devotion and remembrance of God, truthful living, equality of mankind and denounces superstitions and blind rituals. It stands for love, harmony, tolerance , service , sacrifice and charity .

INDIA BEFORE GURU NANAK

Before the advent of Guru Nanak, the founder of Sikh religion, in the second half of 15th century, Islam was the ruling religion in North India and the rulers had become utterly intolerant and tyrannical and had denied the very right of existence to those who did not believe in their religion. As many as 60 foreign invasions of India had taken place between the 11th century and the birth of Guru Nanak. More than conquering the country to rule over, the Muslim invaders concentrated on loot and plunder. They were ruthless , massacring non-Muslims without mercy, demolishing temples and converting Hindus to Islam at the point of sword.

Hindus were living under inhuman conditions and were facing repression of the worst order. They were persecuted systematically and those who resisted were butchered. The honour of their women was not safe. They were treated as second class citizens in their own country . They had to pay *jizia,* a tax for being Hindus. They could not build temples, nor repair the old ones. They were not permitted to mourn their dead too loudly, lest they should disturb the peace of the Muslim elite. When asked to describe the status of a Hindu, the qazi in the court of Allauddin Khilji said:

"They are payers of tribute and when the revenue officer demands silver from them, they should without question and with all humility and respect tender gold. If the tax collector chooses to spit in the mouth of the Hindu, the latter must open his mouth without hesitation."
—Guru Nank and His Times by A C Bannerjee.

Such was the havoc the successive invaders

had wrought on Hindu psyche.

The once highly spiritual character of Hinduism, to which religion most of the Indians belonged, had been obsessed with ostentatious paraphernalia and rituals. The centuries of foreign invasions, foreign misrule and persecution had produced deep depression, demoralisation and downright degradation. Hypocricy, weakness of mind, abject servility towards the ruling class had entered the Hindu character. The rigid caste distinctions, with superstitions associated with it, divided the Hindu community into innumerable water-tight compartments. A great body of fellow Hindus was treated as untouchable.

Condition of women was pitiable . Muslims had confined their women within the four walls of the house and did not allow them to move about except under a thick covering of 'Burqa'. The condition of Hindu women was worse. Since Muslim invaders and Muslim rulers used to pick up young Hindu girls for forcible marriages, the Hindus took recourse to female infanticide, and those who were lucky to escape infanticide, used to be given away in marriage early. Widows were not allowed to re-marry and quite often they immolated themselves along with their dead husbands on their funeral pyre. A number of them converted to Islam or took to prostitution.

In society in general, corruption, treachery and debauchery reigned supreme.

Hindu and Muslim religious classes had both forgotten their holy books and they indulged in evil, repression and cruel treatment towards fellow human beings. The religion in both communities consisted of only externalities. Guru Nanak, having seen this state of society , declared: There is no Hindu, no Musalman.

GURU NANAK DEV (1469-1539)

It was in such times that Guru Nanak appeared on the scene. He set out to awaken a depressed, demoralised, superstitious and priest-ridden race of Hindus. He urged both the Mohammedans and the Hindus to observe the noblest of all principles which inculcate devotion to God and peace and love towards mankind in general. He combatted the furious bigotry of the one and the deep rooted superstitions of the other. He set upon restoring the faith of the people in God. His missionary activities took him to all directions in India, east, south, north and west. He visited Sri Lanka, Tibet , Iraq ,Mecca and Medina.

Guru Nanak believed in one formless God and in total surrender to the will of God and in complete equality of mankind."God will not ask man", said Guru Nanak,"to what race and religion he belongs. He will but ask him 'What have you done?'"."Deeds, not creeds", is what the Guru asked of his disciples. He preached a philosophy which was to illuminate lives, a philosophy of love, service and sacrifice. The main principles of life enunciated by Guru Nanak were (1) earning a living by honest labour (*Kirt Karna*); (2) meditating on the Name of Lord (*Naam Japna); (3)* sharing one's earnings with the needy (*Vand Chhakna*). He exhorted his followers to the path of truth in thought, word and deed and to the company of holy and good persons (*Saadh Sangat*). He asked his followers to shed ritualism . For him, service of the people was worship of the Lord. He believed that "Truth is higher than everything; but higher still is truthful-living". He was respected by both Hindus and Muslims.

Guru Nanak gave women equal status with men and one of his '*shabads*' brought it out beautifully:"*So kyon manda aakhiye, jit jamme rajaan*"(How can you call women inferior ? They give birth to kings.) He demolished divisions between Hindus and Muslims. Guru chose two companions for his missionary tours; of them one was a Muslim and the other a Hindu. Charity moved with Guru Nanak wherever he went. He used to give away whatever he had and could to fulfil the needs of others as he believed that 'To serve God is to serve His creation'. He used to stay with the poor and the honest and spurn the tempting offers of the high-born and the rich. Towards the end of his life, Guru settled down as a farmer and did farming with his own hands and kept an open kitchen for all, thus emphasizing the dignity of labour and the importance of sharing one's income. *Sangat* (congregation of good persons for spiritual pursuits) and *Pangat* (sitting in a row for food) were two of the most valuable legacies left behind by Guru Nanak.

GURU ANGAD DEV (1504-1552)

Bhai Lehna, the most devoted disciple of Guru Nanak , who had earned the Guru's love and confidence through service and dedication , was nominated the next Guru and was named"Angad"(meaning 'my own limb') by Guru Nanak, Guru Angad Dev , the second Sikh Guru's pontificate was an extension of Guru Nanak's work. He spent most of his time in the service of the people and in meditation. He was compassion incarnate. He tended the sick and came to be known as the healer of incurable diseases.

Guru Angad was was humble and self-effacing. He believed in complete surrender to his Master, Guru Nanak Dev. He was totally obedient and carried out his Guru's instructions devotedly. But, he was absolutely fearless of the rulers. When Mughal Emperor Humayun, on being over-powered by Sher Shah, came to Guru Angad for his blessings, he had to wait for some time as the Guru was in the *sangat* of his disciples singing hymns. Humayun lost his temper and threatened to attack the Guru and his followers. Seeing the Emperor in anger, the Guru chided him and said:"When you should have used the sword, you did not; rather you ran away from the battlefield like a coward. Here with a *dervish,* you show off , threatening to attack unarmed devotees engaged in prayer".Emperor Humayun realised his mistake and sought to be pardoned.

Guru Angad loved children and took great interest in their education and physical development. He insisted that children should be taught in their mother tongue and to that end he is said to have simplified and codified Gurmukhi script which till today is the script of Sikh scriptures.

Finding most of his disciples illiterate, he taught them Panjabi in Gurmakhi script. The place of worship was used as classroom. The Guru started games and sports to promote physical culture. Literacy, physical culture and congregational prayers became essential features of daily routine.

It was Guru Angad's practice to distribute robes of honour to his devotees every six months. Amar Das, his successor, had earned six such robes. Guru Angad maintained an extensive home in which food was prepared under the supervision of his wife and provided to persons of all denominations and creeds. This open kitchen developed into a community kitchen, called "*langar*", which came to be supported by the combined contribution of the community. The"langar" came to serve as a strong bond of union among the new brotherhood and proved a powerful instrument to break the caste barriers.

GURU AMAR DAS (1479-1574)

Guru Amar Das, the third Sikh Guru, developed" *langar*" into a regular institution and made it an integral part of Sikh religion . Through this institution, Guru worked systematically towards banishing social and caste prejudices and untouchability and instilling the concept of equality among all mankind. None , not even Emperor Akbar, could meet the Guru before he or she sat on the ground with others and ate food in the '*langar*'. Guru Amar Das carrie9*d out a vigorous campaign against the most deplorable practices of '*Sati*' (widow-burning) and female infanticide which were prevalent among Hindus at that time, thus bringing in emancipation of women from social oppressions and religious bigotry. He encouraged widow-remarriage.

With a view to consolidating Sikhism and spreading Guru Nanak's message far and wide, Guru Amar Das trained a band of 146 apostles, of whom 52 were women, and sent them to various parts of the country to attend to spiritual needs of the Guru's followers.

He formalised an organisation of Sikhs and established 22 centres of Sikhism, called manjis, in which devoted Sikhs were appointed as heads to carry on missionary work .

Many of these appointees were women , who were thus given equal status with men in public life.

Guru Amar Das' teachings were as simple as his way of life. He said : Pilgrimages, penance or the rituals were all right for the three eras of *Satyug*, *Tretayug* and *Dwarpayug* they would, however, not do for the Kaliyug. It is the 'Divine Name' alone that can earn salvation in this age. He believed: God rewards patience. If anyone ill-treats you, bear it once, twice, thrice. God will Himself intervene on your behalf fourth time. The Guru said: There is no place particularly pure or impure. Where God is remembered, the place becomes sanctified. He exhorted his follower to serve God and accept His will; it is the devotion to God and service of the people in humility that brings salvation. Guru Amar Das was against women wearing veil as they were not inferior to men. He was against conceit, slander and self-glorification. He advised his followers to avoid evil company and not to look at another's wife with covetous eyes. He laid emphasis on everybody doing his duty and giving a part of his earnings in charity.

Guru Amar Das introduced simple ceremonies for the occasions of birth, marriage and death, asking the Sikhs not to cry in the hour of loss and not to forget the divine in their hour of earthly bliss. Guru prepared two volumes of the compositions of Guru Nanak, Guru Angad and of himself. What was most unprecedented was that , in these volumes, he also included the compositions of Kabir and Namdev, who did not belong to Sikh religion . This was a path-breaking act which was followed by successor-Gurus and which manifested the catholicity of Sikh Gurus' approach towards other religions.

Guru constructed in Goindwal an open well-cum-reservoir called"Baoli Sahib", with 84 steps to reach the water which became sacred for the Sikhs and, in a sense, the first pilgrimage centre for the Sikhs.

GURU RAM DAS (1534-1581)

Guru Ram Das, the fourth Sikh Guru, was a self-made man who had come to Guru Amar Das as a helpless orphan and who, for his devotion, discipline, selfless service and humility, was elevated to the position of 'Guru'. He laid the foundation of a sacred tank for a holy dip -'*Amritsar*' - the nectar of immortality. This divine pool , it is believed, removes the sins of all those who have a dip in its sacred water. Around the pool developed the town of Ramdaspur , now known as Amritsar. In the framework of Mughal empire, Ramdaspur was an autonomous town where no"*jizya*"- a tax that the Mughals used to impose on followers of other religions - was levied, nor any fine.

Guru Ram Das carried forward his predecessors' mission to rid Hindu society of meaningless rituals , superstitions and the stranglehold of priestly class. He exhorted his followers to be ready to do service to others , particularly the wayfarers and strangers. He introduced social reforms. He advised his followers not to resort to retaliation but to have faith in God and leave matters to Him.

He made wedding ceremony a simple affair .The hymn of "*Laanvaan*"composed by Guru Ram Das has since been an integral part of Sikh wedding ceremony. Another hymn ,"*Ghoriaan*", composed by Guru is sung on days preceding the wedding. He composed a large number of hymns which are a part of Guru Granth Sahib. As a missionary and nation-builder, he put Sikhism on path of development.

GURU ARJAN DEV (1563-1606)

Guru Ram Das was succeeded by his son, Guru Arjan Dev, the fifth Sikh Guru, who completed the construction of the sacred tank - Amritsar- and in the midst of the tank, he constructed a temple dedicated to God,"*Harmandir*", for singing God's praises and reciting the compositions of Gurus, called"*baani*". The foundation of '*Harmandir*' was laid by a Muslim saint, Mian Mir, a friend and admirer of the Guru.

Guru Arjan Dev followed in the traditions of his predecessors. He was the culmination of all that Guru Nanak and the three Gurus succeeding him stood for, namely, universal truth, devotion to God, meditation, service of fellow-beings and mutual understanding. Guru Arjan Dev honoured a number of saints and holy men of other religions.He gave his followers their fixed rule of religious and moral conduct. He wrote more compositions than any of his predecessor or successor. To the two volumes compiled by Guru Amar Das were added the compositions of Guru Ram Das and Guru Arjan himself. In keeping with the noble tradition set by Guru Amar Das, Guru Arjan Dev included the compositions of a much larger number of saints and sufis belonging to other religions. A comprehensive volume of all compositions was compiled and systemically arranged and named the"Granth"which later came to be known as"Adi Granth".

Guru Arjan's humility was unparalleled. There was no trace of self. He believed that more important than the Guru were the Guru's Sikhs. What they decide in a congregation must hold good. Guru respected their wishes even when his life was at stake.

Guru Arjan was against renunciation of the world. For him. it was like a soldier running away from the battlefield. He sought to abolish the distinction between the rich and the poor. He believed that one should earn by the sweat of one's own brow and share one's earnings with others. Guru Arjan said that evil must be resisted even if one may have to give one's life for it.

Guru Arjan was held in high esteem by Mughal Emperor Akbar. But his successor, Emperor Jehangir was different. At the instigation of one of his courtiers, Emperor Jehangir asked the Guru to revise the Holy Granth by deleting all references to Islam and Hinduism in it. The Guru refused. He maintained that hymns in the Holy Granth were in praise of God and no one dare alter them. Under the orders of Mughal ruler, Guru Arjan was arrested on fictitious charges and ordered to be tortured to death . He was made to sit on a red hot iron sheet. Red hot sand was poured on his body. He was dipped in boiling water. The tortures did not shake the Guru's resolve and he died a martyr's death with God's name on his lips:-

Sweet is Your Will, O God

The gift of Your Name alone I seek..

Gur Arjan Dev was the first Sikh martyr. Accepting the Will of the God, he gave his life suffering inhuman atrocities to uphold the sanctity and sovereignty of the Sikh scripture .

GURU HARGOBIND (1595-1644)

After the martyrdom of Guru Arjan Dev, Sikhism entered a new phase under the stewardship of his son, Guru Hargobind, the 6th Guru. Guru Hargobind reacted to his father's death by torture in proportion to the enormity of the injustice. He set upon the mission of making Sikh community brave and self-reliant and preparing his followers against tyranny and oppression.. He girded two swords, one symbolising the spiritual authority (*piri*) and the other his temporal power (*miri*). In addition to prayers and meditation, he encouraged his followers in martial arts, hunting and horsemanship.. He emerged as a military leader as well as a spiritual teacher. He raised an army of his followers to fight against tyranny. He organised a stable of 800 horses, 300 mounted followers and a personal guard of 60 matchlockmen. Under the Guru's stewardship, no more did the Sikhs believe in self-denial alone. They were awakened to the need to be assertive also. While they would not frighten anyone, they were not to be afraid of anyone either.

Guru Hargobind constructed a high platform opposite"Harmandir"which came to be known as"*Akal Takht*"- the immortal throne - where Guru used to hold court to conduct temporal business.

Under Guru Hargobind, the forces of good were organised and strengthened and put in action against the forces of evil and tyranny. He believed in justice even to the poorest. Though given a martial orientation , Sikhs were no less saintly than before. Guru instilled in women a spirit of duty and regard for truth and called woman"the conscience of man". Guru Hargobind was a man of God. He was equally a man of action who fought against injustice and never compromised with evil.

Guru Hargobind gave a new turn to Sikh way of life. He turned saints into soldiers. He believed that in the new times religion could not be separated from state-craft. He believed that non-violence was cowardice if it was resorted to out of helplessness or fear. When all other means fail, there is always justification to take up arms. He fought battles to defend himself and his followers but never committed an aggression.

In spite of his involvement in martial activities, Guru Hargobind laid great emphasis on social reforms and spiritual development of his followers. He insisted on reading of scriptures with understanding.

After a brief spell of good relations with Guru Hargobind , Emperor Jehangir started feeling apprehensive of Guru's increasing power and popularity and ordered Guru's detention in Gwalior fort. But the Emperor soon realised the truth and released the Guru who, thereafter, was left free to pursue his spiritual and temporal activities and to organise his followers on disciplined lines. He did not abandon his martial exercises.

GURU HAR RAI (1630-1661)

On his death in 1645, Guru Hargobind was succeeded by Guru Har Rai , the Seventh Guru, when Aurangzeb was the ruler of the Mughal empire. Emperor Aurangzeb was aggressive and intolerant towards Hindus and Sikhs .His attitude towards Sikh Guru Har Rai also changed. On a suspicion that Guru Har Rai had lent support to Aurangzeb's rebel brother Dara Shikoh, Guru was summoned by the Emperor to his court. By way of protesting against the tyrannies of Aurangzeb, Guru vowed never to see his face and refused to comply with the Emperor's summons. In stead, Guru sent his elder son, Ram Rai, with instructions not to show any miracles and not to allow the sanctity of the Sikh scriptures to be compromised. What was feared happened. In the Emperor's court, Ram Rai not only worked miracles but, while explaining a Guru Nanak's hymn

"Mitti Musalman ki pede pai kumhar" (The ashes of the Muslim get into a potter's clod) , also found fault with the hymn and said that the correct hymn was *"Mitti beiman ki pede pai kumhar"* (The ashes of the faithless get into a potter's clod). When it came to Guru Har Rai's knowledge, the Guru was distressed and he disowned his son, Ram Rai.

Guru Har Rai was the most magnanimous of men and yet a soldier, a strong, self-respecting man. . According to him, the quality of mercy is most genuine when it is practised by a man who is conscious of his strength and yet suppresses himself and is tender. Life becomes most fruitful when one meets with those who practise humility and gentleness, even when they are strong. He was a simple man of God who lived a simple life and valued simple living and devotion among his followers.

GURU HAR KRISHAN (1656-1664)

Before his death in 1661, Guru Har Rai appointed his younger son, Har Krishan, as the 8th Guru when he was five years old. Before his death, Guru Har Rai had told his son, Guru Har Krishan, never to meet Emperor Aurangzeb. Even at that early age, Guru Har Krishan remembered great many hymns of his predecessors and recited them with amazing appropriateness. The divine light of Guru Nanak kindled in him. His actions had the stamp of maturity

On being approached for intervention in the issue of succession to Guruship, Emperor Aurangzeb decided to summon Guru Har Krishan and deputed Raja Jai Singh to plead with the Guru to visit Delhi for a discussion on the subject. The Guru accepted the Raja's invitation but told him that he would not meet the Emperor. Raja arranged Guru Har Krishan's stay in his own bungalow where at present Bangla Sahib Gurdwara is located..

At that time small-pox had broken out in Delhi. The Guru and his disciples engaged themselves in the care and cure of the sick. In the course of that missionary work , Guru Har Krishna himself fell a prey to small-pox and died in 1664. Before his death,

Guru nominated his grandfather's brother, Tegh Bahadur, as his successor.

GURU TEGH BAHADUR (1621-1675)

Guru Tegh Bahadur, the 9th Guru, toured the whole of North and East India to establish contact with Sikhs settled there and to re-assure them of his concern for them. He visited Delhi, Agra, Allahabad, Varanasi, Sahasran, Patna, Monghir, Dacca and some towns in Assam. During his travels, Guru encouraged the people to stand up for their rights and protest against injustice. The Sikh congregations rallied behind the Guru and strengthened his hands with valuable gifts in cash and kind. On the other side, Emperor Aurangzeb intensified his policy of persecution of Hindus and use of force for their conversion to Islam. When Aurangzeb came to know that Sikhs were building temples in various towns in his empire, he ordered the deputies of the Guru to be driven out of the temples and to demolish the temples. In some places, after demolishing temples, mosques were built in their place..

Guru Tegh Bahadur prepared his followers to face life with courage and to shed fear of death. His compositions reveal him as a prophet of reassurance in trying situations. His increasing popularity and support among people in various parts of the country upset Emperor Aurangzeb. In 1675, Brahmins of Kashmir met the Guru with a woeful tale of religious persecution at the hands of Mughal Governor of Kashmir. On seeing his father in deep thought, when Govind Rai, the nine-year old son, asked his father Guru Tegh Bahadur about the problem bothering him, the Guru related the plight

Name	Birth year / place	Guruship/place	Death/place
The following Table shows the years of birth, assumption of guruship and death of all the ten (10) Gurus:-			
1. Guru Nanak	1469; Talwandi Nankana Sahib ,	1490? Sultanpur?	1539; Kartarpur
2. Guru Angad	1504; Nange Di Saran	1539; Kartarpur	1552;Khadur
3. Guru Amar Das	1479; Basar Ke	1552; Khadur	1574; Goindwal
4. Guru Ram Das	1534; Lahore	1574; Goindwal	1581; Goindwal
5. Guru Arjan Dev	1563; Goindwal	1581; Goindwal	1606; Lahore
6. Guru Har Gobind	1595; Wadali	1606; Amritsar	1644; Kiratpur
7. Guru Har Rai	1630; Kiratpur	1644; Kiratpur	1661; Kiratpur
8. Guru Har Krishan	1656; Kiratpur	1661; Kiratpur	1664; Delhi
9. Guru Tegh Bahadur	1621; Amritsar	1664; Baba Bakala	1675; Delhi
10. Guru Gobind Singh	1666; Patna	1675; Anandpur	1708; Nanded

of Kashmiri Brahmins and said:"They can be saved only if a great soul can offer himself for martyrdom."Promptly remarked the son , the future saint-soldier of the Sikhs:"Then who is greater than yourself"? Guru Tegh Bahadur resolved to stand up to uphold the right of Kashmiri Brahmins to live according to their faith. He advised the Kashmiris to go back and inform the Mughal rulers that they would be willing to accept Islam if Guru Tegh Bahadur could first be persuaded to embrace Islam.

Guru was arrested by Mughal administration and brought to Delhi . He was asked to embrace Islam which he refused. Three of Guru's companions were put to death in his presence to impress upon him the consequences of refusal. On Guru's persistent refusal, he was beheaded with sword in Chandni Chowk, the main market square opposite Red Fort (Delhi) on 11 November 1675 in the full view of a large multitude of people. The Guru made supreme sacrifice not only in the cause of his own faith but also in the defence of freedom of conscience in general and of Kashmiri Brahmins in particular.

Guru Tegh Bahadur had a verstile personality. He was a warrior, a family-man, a preacher of great understanding and vision. His hymns embodied a message of freedom, courage and compassion -"Fear not , frighten not". His martyrdom signified the triumph of good over evil and inspired his people to rebel against intolerance and tyranny of the Mughals.

GURU GOBIND SINGH (1666-1708)

Before his arrest by Mughal administration, Guru Tegh Bahadur had appointed his 9-year old son, Govind Rai (later Gobind Singh) as the 10th Guru. in anticipation of the coming events. Growing into man-hood, Guru Gobind Singh received literary and religious education and became a scholar in Persian and Sanskrit. He also received training in arms and inspired his followers to take up interest in martial activity. He patronised poets and urged them to compose poems of heroes and warriors. Guru himself wrote several compositions including the famous 'Chandi-di-var' in Panjabi to inspire soldiers for the coming struggle against tyranny. He laid down the principles of 'Dharm Yudh' - war for justice and righteousness.

Guru Gobind Singh had a specific mission on his mind but he found people suffering from inferiority complex vis-à-vis Mughals and not up to the task. He decided to raise a force of committed followers who would join him and stand by him in the war against tyranny. At a special assembly of his followers at Anandpur on the Baisakhi day of 1699, he unfolded his plan and invited those who were ready to lay down their lives for their Guru. Five devoted Sikhs stood up. The Guru baptised them with"Amrit". The Guru then asked the"Panj Piaras"-the Five beloved ones of the Lord - as they came to be known later, to baptise him and they in turn baptised their Guru. The Guru baptising his followers and the followers baptising the Guru was a new form of spiritual socialism in the realm of religion. Thus started a new order of Sikhs called the"Khalsa"- the pure, who were equipped with sword and certain other distinctive features which became the emblems of power and self-respect. Guru made religious fervour the backbone of his warlike doctrines. But this religious fervour was imparted to uphold"Dharma", the spiritual order, against bigoted Mughals and was not allowed to degenerate into hatred towards Muslims or their mosques.No Muslim mosque was demolished and no forcible conversion was effected in Guru's time or even afterwards. On the contrary, in battles against Mughals, under Guru's directions, wounded Muslim soldiers were tended with as much care as Sikh soldiers. There was to be no discrimination.

The Guru was aware that the need of the hour was to raise an army of saint-soldiers who could fight against the forces of evil, exploitation and repression. The Khalsa fulfilled the need fully.

In a battle against Mughal troops at Chamkaur in 1704, Guru's two eldest sons, Ajit Singh (18 yrs) and Jujhar Singh (14 yrs), and all his personal guards were killed. Later, his mother and two youngest sons, Zorawar Singh (9 yrs) and Fateh Singh (7 yrs), were captured by Mughal Governor of Sirhind. The choice before the two children was death or conversion to Islam. They refused to be converted to Islam. Both the sons were buried alive in a wall. Despite having lost his entire family, Guru stood unshaken in his resolve.

Guru Gobind Singh was approached by Mughal Emperor Aurangzeb for reconciliation and invited for a meeting in the Deccan where the Emperor then was. But before Guru could reach there, Aurangzeb died (Feb 1707). Guru Gobind Singh met the new Emperor Bahadur Shah in Agra and remained close to the imperial camp during its movements in the Deccan for nearly a year, hoping that the contentious issues could be resolved any time. But before it could materialise, Guru was treacherously stabbed and badly wounded by an Afghan under a plot hatched by Mughal chieftain Wazir Khan, who had earlier killed the Guru's two younger sons. On 7 October 1708, Guru breathed his last.

When the end came, Guru Gobind Singh addressed his Sikhs thus:-

As ordained by God, the Lord Eternal,
A new way of life is evolved..
All the sikhs are asked to accept the Holy Granth as the Guru.
Guru Granth should be accepted
As the living God.
Those who wish to meet God
Will find Him in the Word.

Guru Gobind Singh brought about a revolutionary transformation among his followers. He made them fearless, brave and strong. He instilled in them confidence that one Sikh could fight against many. They were no longer suffering from inferiority complex. He brought about equality between the lowest and the highest and all the four castes among Hindus started eating and drinking out of the same vessel.

Of the"Panj Piaras"with whom Guru started his new order, the Khalsa, , one was Khatri, one Jat and the other three were from so-called lower castes. It was a revolutionary development. Sikh women also started joining the Khalsa fraternity thus occupying an equal status with men. Guru fought against female infanticide and, at one time observed:"- with slayers of daughters whosoever has intercourse, him do I curse." Again he observed:"Whosoever takes food from the slayers of daughters shall die unabsolved."

DIVINE ATTRIBUTES

The divine light was transmitted from Guru Nanak to all succeeding Gurus and each carried forward the divine message of Guru Nanak. All of them were one. Though it is an impossible task to describe the divine attribute of each one of the ten Gurus in one word or phrase, a scholar has tried to describe it as follows :-

Guru Nanak Dev - *Ek Omkar Sat Naam*
(God is one; the eternal Truth)
Guru Angad Dev Obedience

Guru Amar Das	*Nithaaniyanw di thanw;*
	Ni-aasryanw da aasra
	(Home of the homeless;
	Strength of the weak)
Guru Ram Das	Service
Guru Arjan Dev	Supreme sacrifice
Guru Hargobind	*Miri-Piri de maalik*
	(Spiritual and temporal authority)
Guru Har Rai	Mercy
Guru Harkrishan	Dispeller of suffering
Guru Tegh Bahadur	*Hind Di Chaader*
	(Saviour of the honour of India)
Guru Gobind Singh	*Sant sipahi* (Saint-soldier)

GURU GRANTH SAHIB

Guru Granth Sahib is the Holy Book of Sikhs upon which 'Guruship' was bestowed by the Tenth Guru, Guru Gobind Singh , before his death in 1708. Adi Granth , by which name Granth Sahib was known before 'Guruship' was bestowed upon it, was compiled by the Fifth Sikh Guru, Guru Arjan Dev, with the assistance

of Bhai Gurdass and installed in the Harmandir Sahib, Amritsar, on 1 September 1604. Baba Buddha was appointed as its First Granthi. In course of time the Adi Granth passed into the custody of Bhai Dhirmal, grandson of Guru Hargobind, who refused to give it back. This Granth, which is called Kartarpuri Bir , is now in the possession of Sodhi family of Kartarpur (Punjab) who are the descendants of Bhai Dhirmal . Adi Granth contained the compositions of the first five Gurus - Guru Nanak Dev, Guru Angad, Guru Amar Das, Guru Ram Das and Guru Arjan Dev .

When the original Granth could not be taken back from the descendants of Bhai Dhirmal, Guru Gobind Singh dictated the whole Granth once again to his devoted follower Bhai Mani Singh at Damdama in the year 1706. He also included in it the hymns composed by the Ninth Guru, Guru Tegh Bahadur. Before his death in 1708, Guru Gobind Singh proclaimed, in the following words, that the Granth, as finalised by him, shall be the final and eternal Guru of the Sikhs after him :-

aagya bhai Akal ki Tabhi chalayo Panth,
Sab Sikhan ko hukum hai Guru Manyo Granth.
Guru Granth ji manyo pargat Guran ki deh.
jo prabh ko milna chahe khoj shabad men le.

As ordained by God, the Lord Eternal,
A new way of life is evolved.
All the sikhs are asked to accept the Holy
Granth as the Guru.
Guru Granth should be accepted
As the living God.
Those who wish to meet God
Will find Him in the Word.
Besides the compositions of six Gurus, Guru Granth Sahib contains the compositions of fif-

teen *Bhagats* (saints and holy man) who not only belonged to other religions but were also from all castes (low as well as high) and from various parts of India, such as, Bengal, Maharashtra, Rajasthan, U P , Sindh, Madhya Pradesh, West Punjab and Oudh. The *Bhagats* were:-

Jaidev (Brahman-Bengal)
Dhanna (Jat- Rajputana)
Sheikh Farid (Mohammedan Pir-Panjab)
Pipa (Jogi- Gangaraungarh)
Namdev (Chhima-Maharashtra)
Sain (Barber- Rewa-U.P.)
Trilochan (Brahman-Maharashtra)
Kabir (Reformer-Banaras)
Parmanand (Maharashtra)
Ravidas (Leather dresser-U P.)
Sadhna (Butcher-Sind)
Sur Das (A blind man-Oudh)
Beri (Beni?) - (origin not known)
Ramanand (Reformer-U .P.)
Bhikan (U.P.)

The Granth Sahib also contains panegyrics composed by eleven *Bhatts* (Mathra, Jalap, Harbans, Talya, Salya, Bhal, Kulh Sahar, Nal, Kirat, Gayand, Sadrang).

Guru Gobind Singh chose not to include his own compositions in the Granth Sahib. These were included in a separate volume, called Dasam Granth.

Guru Granth Sahib contains 1430 pages . It invokes the names of *Hari*-8344 times, *Ram* -2533 times, *Prabhu*-1371 times, *Gopal*-491 times, *Gobind* 475 times, *Parmeshwar*-139 times, *Narain*-85 times, *Murari*-97 times, *Allah*-46 times, *Bhagwan* 30 times, *Maadho*-27 times and *Banwari*-15 times.

Guru Granth Sahib is perhaps the only scripture which has been composed and edited by the founders of the religion themselves. It is also the only scripture which contains the compositions of holy men of other religions.

AKHAND PATH

Sikhs hold their holy book, Guru Granth Sahib, in highest esteem. On special occasions like birthdays , weddings, anniversaries, memorial service, or on other occasions marking the start, conclusion or success of an assignment or venture, *Akhand Path* (non-stop, continuous and uninterrupted reading of the whole of the Granth Sahib) , is performed in a Gurdwara or at home, depending on the convenience or wishes of the individuals organising it. *Akhand Paths* marking important dates in the Sikh calendar are held in the Gurdwara. Normally, with a group of devotees reading the holy book in relays, it takes 48 hours to complete an Akhand Path . When"uninterrupted" reading of Granth Sahib is not feasible or is not intended for some reasons, one may hold a *Saptahik Path* , which takes 7 days of intermittent reading.; or a *Sahj* or *Sadharan Path,* for which there is no time limit .

GOLDEN TEMPLE (HARMANDIR SAHIB)

Harmandir Sahib, a temple dedicated to God, was constructed in the midst of the sacred tank"Amritsar"by Guru Arjan Dev, the fifth Guru. The Guru invited a Muslim saint, Mian Mir, to lay the foundation of Harmandir in 1589 . It was completed in 1601. The"Adi Granth was installed in Harmandir Sahib in 1st September 1604.

Harmandir Sahib, also called Darbar Sahib, is a two-storeyed marble structure built on a 67 feet square platform in the centre of the sacred tank Amritsar. The Temple itself is 40.5 feet

square. It has a door each on the east, west, north and south. The four doors are symbolic of the Sikh philosophy that their Temple is open to all; that people can come here irrespective of cast, creed or sex.

Harmandir Sahib has a chequered history and it has changed hands a number of times. It was destroyed and desecrated again and again by Mughal rulers but was re-occupied and re-constructed by Sikhs through great sacrifices. Maharaja Ranjit Singh (1780-1839) beautified the Temple with gold work, gilding the upper half with gilded sheets and the lower half with marble, mosaics and semi-precious stones. (Hence the name 'Golden Temple'). During the British regime it passed under the control of a manager ("*Sarbah*") who was the nominee of the Deputy Commissioner of Amritsar. After a long , hard and non-violent struggle of the Sikh Gurdwara Reform Movement, the Sikhs succeeded in ending British regime's control on Sikh shrines. On receiving the news of handing over of keys of Harmandir Sahib to Sikh leaders , Mahatma Gandhi , in his telegraphic message, hailed it as the"first decisive battle for India's freedom won". A new law, Sikh Gurdwara Act

1925, was passed and under the Act, the control of Harmandir Sahib and other Sikh shrines in Punjab vested in Shiromani Gurdwara Parbandhak Committee, a representative body of Sikhs elected by adult franchise.

"MOOL MANTRA" OF GURBANI

The essence of Granth Sahib is in *Japji Sahib*, the first chapter of the Granth, composed by Guru Nanak. It opens with the *Mool Mantra*, the basic postulate, and reads as follows :-

Ek Omkar, sat naam, karta purakh, nirbhau , nirvair, akaal murat,ajooni , seh-bhang,Guru prasad

It means: God is one; the Eternal Truth; He is the Supreme Creator; He knows no fear and has no enmity with anyone; He is immortal; He is beyond incarnation; He is self-existent.He is realised through the grace of the True Guru.

JAPJI - THE SIKH MORNING PRAYER

Japji , the opening chapter of Guru Granth Sahib, is the morning prayer of Sikhs designed for meditation. Composed by Guru Nanak, it epitomizes his philosophy and his vision of the path to salvation. It consists of *Mool Mantra* (basic postulate), 38 stanzas, and the concluding sloka. In this composition, the Guru first poses questions as to how to know the truth and how to demolish the wall of falsehood; and then he answers the questions. Mere reading and talking or intense debate about God are of no avail in the realisation of the Divine. It is only the righteous deeds that lead man to God.. While actions determine how men are born , it is His grace alone which brings in salvation. One must submit to the will of the God. One must recite His Name, listen to His Word to attain salvation.

Japji describes the spiritual journey of the seeker through various stages . First is the stage of just and truthful living and correct behaviour, followed by realm of knowledge of the divine, realm of His grace where His blessings help and finally the realm of God, the Truth which is gained only by His grace. It is possible to achieve all this while living a family life.

Purity of mind and conduct is an absolute pre-requisite for reaching the realm of the Truth where the seeker becomes one with God.

In the Guru's vision of the Almighty, to love God is to love His creation; to serve Him is to serve the mankind.

Japji is a poetic narration of Guru's observation, understanding and analysis of the cosmos and the Divine Truth in the course of his communion with God

ESSENCE OF SIKHISM

Sikhism is a social and fraternal religion which preaches common Fatherhood of God and univer-sal Brotherhood of Man, recognises equal status to all human beings and between man and woman, and emphasizes that normal family life, lived with virtuous conduct and sincere faith in God, leads to the path of salvation. It is a faith which aims at cre-ation of a just order and believes in social equality and peaceful co- existence. Sikhism exhorts its fol-lowers to lead a social life based on the principles of *Nam Japna* (devotion to Divine Name), *Kirt Karna* (earn a living by honest labour) and vand *chhakna* (share earnings with the needy). Sikhism is a positive, joyous, spiritually-oriented, life-affirming philosophy as manifested through Divine hymns of Guru Granth Sahib. It is based on humanistic and universal values of love, equality, freedom, dignity, tolerance, harmony, brother-hood, self-realisation, self-confidence, service, char-

ity and sacrifice.

In Sikhism, it is not irreligious to acquire wealth provided it is acquired through honest and fair means and provided it is used not only to derive personal comfort for oneself or one's family but also to give comfort to society . Sikhism gives one a healthy outlook on life. It is a faith concerned with Here and Now, the realization of God within us Here and Now, not after death. It is a world-affirm-ing, not world-denying, philosophy. Sikhism rec-ommends an active life - the life of a householder-in society, not in isolation. Worldly duties are to be performed side by side with search for the Truth. It lays emphasis on social obligations and it believes that the man, being a part of society, has to work for its uplift.

Sikhs are a warm, affectionate and progressive community with a global outlook .

They have achieved remarkable success in all walks of life , have made signal contribution towards the progress of the communities they live in, and have acquired a position of influ-ence far in excess of their numerical strength, not only in India but everywhere in the world.

ARDAAS (PRAYER)

Ardaas is an integral part of Sikh religion. It is a prayer offered by Sikhs before or after any function or activity or occasion, happy or sad. Broadly, the Ardaas falls in four parts. One, it invokes the blessings of the God and the ten Gurus. Two, it recounts the achievements of the tenth Guru and the events of Sikh history, partic-ularly the sacrifices made by Sikhs in the defence of their faith and Gurdwaras. Three, the reciter mentions the purpose and the occasion for offer-ing the prayer. He then invokes the Lord's bless-ings for success of the function , the project undertaken or to be undertaken ; peace, progress, health and welfare of an individual/ family. Ardaas,offered after completion of a task , is an expression of grateful thanks to the Lord for the success granted in the execution of the task. Last, but not the least , in the Ardaas, a humble appeal is made: O Lord, save us from lust, wrath, greed, conceit and undue attachment. Let there be peace all around. O Father, grant success to everyone in his/her efforts. Bestow the bliss of the Holy Name on us all and keep us in the company of persons devoted to thyself. May your Holy Name be ever in ascendance and may peace and progress come to the entire mankind . O God, give us humility in behaviour and nobility in thought. Forgive us for our short- comings and acts of omission and commission .

While offering Ardaas, Sikhs seek God's blessings not only for the one who organises the function, not only for their own community , but also for the entire mankind, for the good of each and every creature in this world. It is not merely for material gains but also for spiritual uplift and excellence of conduct in worldly affairs.

BIRTH OF KHALSA

Baisakhi was an annual seasonal festival in Punjab. But the one in 1699 had a special significance. For this festival in 1699, Guru Gobind Singh had issued a special invitation to his Sikhs all over to visit Anandpur.

Thousands turned up. On the morning of the Baisakhi day of 1699, after the hymn singing had concluded, the Guru appeared on the dais with an unsheathed sword and asked the audience,"My sword is thirsty. It needs the blood of a Sikh to quench its thirst. Is there anyone in the audience who is willing to offer his head?"The Guru repeated this call three times. At the third call, a Sikh called Daya Ram, a Khatri from Lahore, 30 years of age, stood up and offered his head, with the words"It is yours in life and death". The Guru took him inside a tent set up close by. People heard a thud of the sword. A moment later, the Guru appeared with his sword dripping with blood. He announced:"I want another head". There were murmurs in the audience. Another Sikh, Dharam Chand, a Jat from Haryana, rose and placed his head at the disposal of the Guru. The Guru took him inside the tent. There was again a thud, followed by a stream of blood flowing out of the tent. The Guru came out and asked for another head, the third. A Sikh, Mohkam Chand from Dwarka, stood up to offer his head and was taken inside. The same frightful thud followed with blood streaming out. The Guru asked for the fourth head. There was panic in the assembly. But there it was ; another Sikh, named Himmat Rai from Jagannath Puri, rushed to the Guru and was treated like three of his predecessors . The Guru came out again with his dripping sword and made similar announcement. The crowd had by then started thinning. Sahib Chand of Bidar rushed to the Guru and offered his head. The fifth Sikh was treated likewise. The Sikhs in the audience were stunned. They had started wondering as to what was going on. They had assembled there to celebrate the festival of Baisakhi and here the Guru had started killing them. They did not know what to do when suddenly, from behind the tent, they saw the five faithful Sikhs emerge one after the other, radiant and glorious. They were followed by the Guru glowing with a new confidence. The audience burst into spontaneous joy and hailed the Guru with slogans,"The Guru is great","Long live the Guru","Glory to the Guru". The Guru silenced them and announced,"Great are these five faithful! Glory to them! They are the chosen ones. They have found immortality. Those who know how to die, only they win deliverance from the cycle of birth and death."(The Guru had killed only goats inside the tent)

The Guru then called for a steel vessel and poured water into it. The five faithful Sikhs were asked to recite hymns from the sacred scripture while the Guru stirred the water with a double-edged dagger. The Guru prepared *Amrit* - nectar - to baptize the five faithful Sikhs to turn them into *Khalsa* - the pure. As the *Amrit* was being prepared , the Guru's wife came in with *patashas* -sugar candy - as her offering. The Guru hailed it as a"timely gift". Taking the *patashas* from his wife, the Guru put them in the vessel and said ,"It is marrying valour to compassion. The dagger was to turn my Sikhs into heroes; the *patashas* will foster in them the milk of human kindness."The Guru baptised the five beloved faithful, *Panj Piaras,* with the nectar, the draught of immortality.

After the Sikhs had been thus baptised, the Guru stood before them with hands folded and prayed to them to baptise him in return. Thus the Guru turned himself into a disciple. The moment he had the sip of *Amrit* , from Guru Gobind Rai, he became Guru Gobind Singh. So were the five faithful Sikhs and thousands of the Guru's devotees who had gathered there. This was the birth of the *Khalsa*. Every Sikh became a Singh, a lion. The Guru enjoined upon his devotees to keep long unshorn hear, wear a steel *Karra* - a bangle, *kachha* - short pants, *a kanga* - a comb in the hear and carry a *kirpan* - a sword - as a weapon of defence .

At the end of the function, the Guru hailed his followers with a new form of greeting: *Waheguu ji ka Khalsa; Waheguru ji ki Fateh.* (Hail the Khalsa who belongs to God. Hail the God to whom belongs the victory).

Baisakhi of 1699 thus became immortal and an unforgettable part of Sikh history and it is celebrated with great fervour every year.

PANJ KAKKE (FIVE 'K'S)

Sikhs are an easily identifiable community because of the five distinguishing symbols they wear, called *panj kakke* (Five 'K's). These were introduced by Guru Gobind Singh on the occasion of birth of the Khalsa on the Baisakhi of 1699.

The *panj kakke* (Five 'K's) are: *Kesh* - uncut hair and unshaved beard which symbolise saintliness. *Kanga* - a comb with which to maintain the hair. *Karra* - a steel bangle worn on the right wrist. It symbolises strength and fearlessness. It is also to remind the Sikhs of their commitment to truth. *Kaccha* - a knee-length pair of breeches worn by soldiers of the time. It ensures briskness of movement at times of action. *Kirpan* - a sword which symbolises power and dignity, to be used only in self-defence or to uphold justice."When all other means have failed, it is righteous to draw the sword."(**Guru Gobind Singh**).

Significance of figure 'FIVE"- *Panj Piare, Panj Kakke, Panj Takhts*

The figure 'five' has a special significance for the Sikhs. On the day of Baisakhi of 1699, Guru Gobind Singh created the Khalsa by initiating the first five of his followers into the new order at Anandpur Sahib, called the *Panj Piare*. He ordained his followers to wear five distinguishing symbols, namely, *Kesh, Kanga, Karra,*

Kachha & *Kirpan* (Five Kakke). The figure five was given further importance when Guru Gobind Singh directed the Khalsa to elect five persons from amongst themselves to take decisions on matters affecting the community.

As time passed, the most momentous matters concerning the Sikh community were to be decided by heads of five seats of Sikh authority, called *Takhts*. The five *Takhts* are:

Akal Takht (Amritsar)
Takht Sri Harmandir Sahib (Patna)
Takht Sri Kesgarh Sahib (Anandpur)
Takht Sri Damdama Sahib (Talwandi Sabo)
Takht Sri Hazur Sahib (Nanded)

SIKH CEREMONIES

Following are the most widely observed Sikh ceremonies:-

Naming ceremony
Dastar Bandhi (Turban Tying ceremony)
Amrit Chhakna (Sikh baptism)
Anand Karaj (Sikh wedding ceremony)
Death ceremony

All the ceremonies are simple and have a religious tone. They are held in thepresence of Guru Granth Sahib and include *Kirtan* (the singing of appropriate hymns for the occasion), offering of *Ardaas* (formal Sikh prayer), and distribution of *Karah Parshad* (sanctified pudding)) to the congregation.

ANAND KARAJ (SIKH WEDDING)

A Sikh wedding is called *Anand Karaj* (blissful union) . A distinct system of Sikh marriage was initiated by Guru Amar Das, the third Guru. It consisted of recitation of Anand Sahib composed by Guru Amar Das (hence called Anand Karaj). Later on, Guru Ram Das composed the Laanvaan (wedding hymn) for solemnising Sikh marriages. It was

given statutory recognition by the Anand Marriage Act 1909, passed by the Indian Legislature.

Anand Karaj is performed in the presence of Guru Granth Sahib. The bride and the groom sit in front of the holy scripture, the bride sitting on the left side of the groom. The main ceremony consists of recitation of *Laanvaan* (Wedding hymn) which has four stanzas. Each stanza is first recited by the *Granthi* (preacher) and then sung by the *Raagi* . While it is sung by the *Raagi*, the couple (groom closely followed by bride) circumambulate around the Guru Granth Sahib , in all four times. In *Laanvaan*, the Guru describes four steps to achieve complete union with God. Each stanza conveys a direction to the couple to understand each other in order to unite two bodies into one soul. The hymn compares the progression of love between husband and wife with that between the soul (bride) and God (husband).After the couple goes round the holy scripture four times accompanied by the singing of the *Laavnaan,* the marriage ceremony is practically complete and marriage stands duly solemnised.

Of husband-wife, **Guru Amar Das said:** ”They are not said to be husband and wife, who merely sit together. Rather they alone are called husband and wife, who have one soul in two bodies.”(Pauri, pg. 788)

PROMINENT SIKH SAINTS & MARTYRS
Bhai Mardana (1459 to 1520)

Lifelong companion and first disciple of Guru Nanak, Bhai Mardana was born in 1459 at Nankana Sahib to Muslim parents . He belonged to a sect of musicians who sang and danced at festivals and weddings. Bhai Mardana and Guru Nanak were friends from childhood. Mardana was 10 years older than Guru Nanak. He accompanied Guru Nanak on most of his journeys. He used to play the rebeck (a string instrument) while Guru Nanak composed and sang his hymns. Three of Bhai Mardana's hymns are also included in the Guru Granth Sahib. Bhai Mardana passed away in 1520 on the banks of the river Khuram in Afghanastan when he was returning with Guru Nanak from Mecca. Guru Nanak personally performed the last rites of Bhai Mardana.

Bhai Bala

Bhai Bala , a Sandhu Jat , was a long time companion of Guru Nanak. He wrote *Janamsakhi* of Guru Nanak.

Baba Buddha (1506 to 1631)

Baba Buddha (originally named Bura Randhawa) was born in 1506 in the village of Kathu Nangal (Punjab). He was a contemporary of the first six Sikh Gurus. He was a young boy herding cattle in the fields in his village when he first met Guru Nanak .Guru Nanak was so highly impressed by the boy that he exclaimed that though young in age, he was a *Buddha* (an old man) in terms of maturity and wisdom. Baba Buddha became an exemplary disciple of the Gurus. For his devotion and understanding of Sikh philosophy, Baba Buddha was conferred the unique honour of performing the "guruship"ceremony of five Gurus after Guru Nanak , staring from Guru Angad upto Guru Hargobind. Baba Buddha was the first high priest of Harmandir Sahib . He was associated with the construction of the Akal Takht and a number of other Sikh shrines.. Baba Buddha passed away in 1631 at village Ramdas. His last rites were performed by Guru Hargobind.

Bhai Gurdas (1560 to 1629)

Bhai Gurdas ,born around 1560 at Goindwal (Punjab), was a great Sikh scholar and a contemporary of the third, fourth, fifth and sixth Guru. He was the scribe of the original copy of the Adi Granth under the guidance of Guru Arjan Dev. He was son of Datar Chand , the younger brother of Guru Amar Das. Following Guru Amar Das's death, Bhai Gurdas was sent by Guru Ram Das as a missionary to preach Sikhism at Agra. Bhai Gurdas met the Mughal Emperor Akbar and convinced him that the Guru Granth Sahib was not derogatory to Islam. Bhai Gurdas was a great writer . He composed 40 *vaars* (ballads) in Panjabi and 556 *kabits* (couplets) in Braj which were recognized as the key to the Adi Granth . While Guru Hargobind was imprisoned at

Gwalior Fort, Bhai Gurdas along with Baba Buddha managed the affairs of the Sikh community. Bhai Gurdas was also associated with the construction of the Akal Takht. He passed away in 1629 at Goindwal. His last rites were performed by Guru Hargobind.

Bhai Nand Lal (1633 to 1715)

Bhai Nand Lal, a great poet and close associate and follower of Guru Gobind Singh, was born in 1633 at Ghazni (Afghanistan) where his father was a high government official. A respected scholar of Persian and Arabic, he was one of the 52 poets whom Guru Gobind Singh had honoured in his court.. He wrote 10 books, 7 in Persian, 2 in Panjabi and 1 in Hindi. *Zindgi Nama* and *Tankhah Nama* are his famous works. *Tankha Nama* serves as a code of discipline for the Khalsa. Bhai Nand Lal had accompanied Guru Gobind Singh to Deccan where the Guru was assassinated. Bhai Nand Lal died in 1715 at Multan.

Bhai Daya Singh (1669 to 1708)

Born in a Khatri family in Lahore in 1669, Bhai Daya Singh (originally named Daya Ram), was the first amongst the *Panj Piaré* who offered their heads to Guru Gobind Singh in response to his call on the Baisakhi day of 1699. Bhai Daya Singh participated in nearly all the battles of the Khalsa. As *Jathedar of the Panj Piaré,* he was with Guru Gobind Singh when he left the fortress of Chamkaur (1704) and served him till his death. As emissary of the Guru, he was sent to deliver Guru Gobind Singh's letter, the Zafarnamah, to Emperor Aurangzeb in the Deccan. He died at Nanded in 1708, just one month before the demise of Guru Gobind Singh. A Gurdwara there jointly preserves the memory of Bhai Dharam Singh and Bhai Daya Singh.

Bhai Dharam Singh (1666 to 1708)

The second Beloved One who offered his head in response to Guru Gobind Singh's call on the Baisakhi day of 1699 at Anandpur Sahib, Bhai Dharam Singh (originally named Dharam Das) was born to Jat parents at Hastinapur near Delhi in 1666. He took part in the battles of Anandpur. He was with Guru Gobind Singh when Anandpur and thereafter Chamkaur was evacuated. He accompanied Guru Gobind Singh to Nanded and served him till the Guru's death in 1708. A Gurdwara in Nanded stands in the memory of Bhai Dharam Singh and Bhai Daya Singh.

Bhai Mohkam Singh (1666 - 1704)

The third Beloved One of Guru Gobind Singh, Bhai Mohkam Singh (originally named Mohkam) was the son of Tirath Chand, a calico-printer of Dwarka (Gujarat). He practised martial arts and took part in the battles which Guru Gobind Singh fought against the Hindu hill chiefs and Mughal imperial troops. He died fighting in the battle of Chamkaur in 1704.

Bhai Sahib Singh (1662 to 1704)

The fourth Beloved One to have offered his head to Guru Gobind Singh in response to his call on the Baisakhi day of 1699, , Bhai Sahib Singh (original name Sahib Chand) was born in a barber family of Bidar (Karnataka). He came to Anandpur at the age of 16, and attached himself permanently to Guru Gobind Singh. He won a name for himself as an extraordinary marksman and in one of the battles at Anandpur he shot dead the Gujjar chief Jamatullah. In another action the Raja of Hindur, Bhup Chand, was seriously wounded by a shot from his musket following which the entire hill army fled the field . He died fighting in the battle of Chamkaur in 1704.

Bhai Himmat Singh (1661 to 1704)

The fifth Beloved One of Guru Gobind Singh , Bhai Himmat Singh (original name Bhai Himmat) was the son of a water carrier of Jagannath (Orissa). . He came to Anandpur at the age of 17, and became a devotee of Guru Gobind Singh. Bhai Himmat Singh proved to be an extraordinary warrior and took part in the battles which the Guru fought against the hill chiefs and imperial forces. He died fighting in the battle of Chamkaur in 1704.

Bhai Mani Singh (1670 to 1737)

Bhai Mani Singh was a great Sikh scholar and martyr who was the scribe of the final version of the Adi Granth under the guidance of Guru Gobind Singh and who also compiled the Dasam Granth following the death of Guru Gobind Singh. Bhai Mani Singh was born to Jat parents at the village of Sunam in 1670. He was the younger brother of Bhai Dyala who was martyred along with Guru Tegh Bahadur in 1675. Bhai Mani Singh was raised from a young age with Guru Gobind Singh by the Guru's mother Mata Gujri. Bhai Mani Singh spent almost a year with Guru Gobind Singh at Damdama Sahib compiling the final and current version of Guru Granth Sahib in 1705. After the death of Guru Gobind Singh, Bhai Mani Singh was installed as the head granthi at the Harmandir Sahib in 1721. In 1737 Bhai Mani Singh took permission from the Muslim Governor of Lahore for the Sikhs to celebrate Diwali at the Harmandir Sahib on assurance of payment of a certain amount as tax. Not enough people attended Diwali that year because they were afraid of the Muslim authorities and as a result not enough money was collected. The Muslim authorities arrested Bhai Mani Singh and publicly executed him in Lahore

Banda Singh Bahadur (1670 to 1715)

The great Sikh soldier and martyr, Banda Bahadur (originally named Lachhman Das) was born in 1670 at Rajouri in Jammu to Rajput parents. He spent many years in Hindu shrines in central India and established an ashram at Nanded (Maharashtra) where he lived for fifteen years before he came into contact with Guru Gobind Singh. He was called Banda, meaning devoted servant of the Guru. Following his initiation into the Khalsa brotherhood, he was named Gurbax Singh but continued to be popularly known as Banda. When Guru Gobind Singh was in the Deccan, he sent Banda to Punjab to punish the enemies of the Khalsa. Banda Bahadur attacked Samana in 1709 and captured Sirhind in 1710. The killer of Guru Gobind Singhs' two sons Wazir Khan (the ruler of Sirhind) was also killed. Banda Bahadur became the leader of the Khalsa following the death of Guru Gobind Singh and struck coins in the name of Guru Gobind Singh. In 1712 Banda conquered the Lohgarh Fort. A huge army of 20,000 men amassed by the Muslim Governor of Lahore besieged Banda for eight months at a fort in Gurdaspur in 1715. Banda Singh Bahadur and 600 Sikhs were finally captured and brought to Delhi where they were all tortured to death for refusing to convert to Islam.

Baba Deep Singh (1680 to 1762)

Baba Deep Singh was a great Sikh scholar who became a soldier and martyr in the cause of

Sikhism. He visited Anandpur Sahib in 1700 and joined Khalsa brotherhood. There he learnt horse riding, archery and use of other arms training from Bhai Mani Singh. Baba Deep Singh met Guru Gobind Singh at Damdama Sahib where Guru Gobind Singh told him to start preaching the message of Sikhism. Between 1715 and 1728 Baba Deep Singh and Bhai Mani Singh produced a number of hand written copies of Guru Granth Sahib for distribution among the Sikhs. When Bhai Mani Singh became the *head granthi* at the Harmandir Sahib, Baba Deep Singh stayed on as the head at Damdama Sahib. In 1710 Baba Deep Singh joined Banda Singh Bahadur in the battle of Sirhind. In 1762 when Ahmed Shah Abdhali, the Afghan invader, raided the Harmandir Sahib and desecrated the sacred pool , Baba Deep Singh came out of scholarly retirement at Damdama Sahib and mobilised Sikhs to march with him to Amritsar to avenge the desecration. On the way to Amritsar, hundreds of Sikhs joined Baba Deep Singh. On the outskirts of Amritsar Baba Deep Singh and the heavily outnumbered Sikhs fought two fierce battles against a large Mughal force . In the second engagement Baba Deep Singh was seriously wounded in the neck but vowed to continue fighting till the end. Baba Deep Singh fought on until he was able to make his way to the sacred pool of the Harmandir Sahib where he finally fell down dead.

The *Sahibzadas*

Guru Gobind Singh had four sons who sacrificed their lives for Sikhism and are remembered every day in *Ardaas* (the common prayer).

Baba Ajit Singh (1687 to 1704) and Baba Jujhar Singh (1689 to 1704) Baba Ajit Singh , the eldest son of Guru Gobind Singh, was born on January 7, 1687 at Anandpur Sahib. Baba Jujhar Singh, the second son, was born in March 1689. Both brothers received religious education as well as training in the weapons of war. During the battle of Chamkaur in 1704 in which the Guru and 40 Sikhs fought against overwhelming odds, both the brothers went out to fight against enemy troops with the permission of their father and died fighting like heroes.

Baba Zorawar Singh (1696 to 1704) and Baba Fateh Singh (1698 to 1704) Baba Zorawar Singh, the third son of Guru Gobind Singh, was born in 1696 while Baba Fateh Singh, the fourth, was born in 1698. During the crossing of the River Sarsa following the departure of the Guru and his family from Anandpur Sahib, the Sikhs were attacked by the Mughals treacherously after they had been guaranteed safe passage. During the ensuing battle and confusion, both the sons along with Mata Gujri, Guru Gobind Singh's mother, were separated from the others and eventually fell into the hands of Nawab Wazir Khan, the Governor of Sirhind. The Nawab gave the two young brothers a choice of either converting to Islam or being put to death. On their refusing to convert to Islam, both the sons were bricked alive in a wall and had their heads cut off .

SIKH SHRINES

1. Akal Takht

Meaning ,Eternal Throne. Set up by Guru Hargobind opposite the Golden Temple, Amritsar, as seat of temporal authority where decisions of importance concerning Sikhs were and are taken.

2. Anandgarh Fort

Nearly 3 Kilometer from Anandpur Sahib. Set up by Guru Gobind Singh

3. Bandi Chhor Sahib

Gurdwara set up at Gwalior to commemorate the release of Guru Hargobind who was imprisoned there under the orders of Emperor Jehangir.

4. Bangla Sahib

New Delhi. Dedicated to Guru Harkrishan who stayed there during his visit to the capital. It was the residence of Raja Jai Singh of Jaipur.

5. Baoli Sahib Goindwal (near Amritsar).

The first centre of Sikhism established by Guru Amar Das. Eighty-four steps lead to the baoli (well). It is believed that whosoever takes a bath in the baoli and recites the Japji at each step ,will obtain release from the cycle of birth and death.

6. Chaubara Sahib Goindwal (near Amritsar).

Abode of Guru Amar Das. Birth place of Guru Arjan Dev

7. Damdama Sahib Talwandi Sabo(near Bhatinda).

The place where Guru Gobind Singh stayed for a short while and brought out a rendition of Adi Granth.

8. Dera Sahib Lahore (now in Pakistan).

The spot where Guru Arjan Dev attained martyrdom.

9. Dukh Niwaran Sahib Patiala.

During temporary stay here, Guru Tegh Bahadur blessed a woman whose children used to die of common diseases:"Whosoever will take bath in the sacred tank there on the occasion of Panchami with full faith will have his/her desire fulfilled."

10. Harmandir Sahib Amritsar.

Principal seat of Sikh Panth. Commonly known as
Darbar Sahib) Golden Temple. Constructed by Guru Arjan Dev

11. Harmandir Sahib Bihar.

Birthplace of Guru Gobind Singh (Patna)

12. Hazur Sahib Nanded (Maharahtra).

The place where Guru Gobind Singh (Sach Khand) breathed his last after he was stabbed by an Afghan The plot to kill the Guru was hatched and executed by Wazir Khan, the infamous Governor of Sirhind, who had earlier killed the Guru's two younger sons.

13. Hem-Kunt Sahib Literally, lake of snow.

The place at a level of over 17000 feet in the Himalays in U.P.(India) where Guru Gobind Singh is believed to have meditated in his previous birth. This place was traced by Sikhs and its authenticity was confirmed by Bhai Vir Singh. A Gurdwara has been built there which is visited by thousands of Sikhs every year.

14. Kesgarh Sahib Anandpur Sahib (Punjab).

Founded by Guru Tegh Bahadur Guru Gobind Singh lived here for a number of years. It is the birthplace of the Khalsa.

15. Khadur Sahib

Near Goindwal-Taran Taran. Home of Guru Angad Dev

16. Kiratpur Sahib

Near Anandpur Sahib. Founded by Guru Hargobind. The seventh & eighth Gurus were annointed here. The ninth and tenth Gurus were also connected with this place. Guru Hargobind and Guru Har Rai breathed their last here. Ashes of Guru Har Krishan were immersed in the river here.

17. Majnu Ka Tilla Sahib Delhi.

The place where Guru Nanak met a Muslim Fakir, called Majnu, and blessed him. Guru Hargobind also stayed here for a while.

18. Moti Bagh Gurdwara Delhi.

The place where Guru Gobind Singh stayed on way to Deccan to meet Emperor Aurangzeb. This is the spot from where Guru Gobind Singh is said to have shot two arrows in the direction of Red Fort to inform Prince Muazzam, who later became Emperor Bahadur Shah, of his arrival.

19. Nanak Mata Sahib Near Pilibhit (U.P.)

It was a centre of Yogic cult. Here Guru Nanak met yogis and enlightened them about the importance of meditation on the Holy Name.

20. Nanak Jhira Sahib Bidar (Karnataka).

The place where Guru Nanak met Pir Jala-ud-din, head of Muslim monastry, and spotted the source of water supply for the people there.

21. Nankana Sahib Talwandi (now in Pakistan).

About 48 miles from Lahore . The place where Guru Nanak was born.

22. Panja Sahib Hasan Abdal (now in Pakistan),

48 KMs from Rawalpindi..The place where Wali Kandhari, a Muslim Fakir rolled a boulder towards Guru Nanak in anger .The boulder was stopped by the Guru with his hand, leaving impression of fingers on the boulder (hence 'Panja Sahib'). Wali Kandhari felt repentant and became Guru's admirer.

23. Paonta Sahib

About 80 miles from Ambala (in Himachal Pradesh). Here Guru Gobind Singh stayed for nearly 3 years, practised riding, hunting, and martial arts and engaged in literary activities. The Guru held court here and engaged 52 poets to compose poems on heroic and religious themes.

25. Rakab Ganj Sahib New Delhi.

The place where the headless body of Guru Tegh Bahadur was cremated by Lakhi Shah Lubana by placing the body in his own house there and setting it alight

26. Sheesh Ganj Sahib Delhi.

The place where Guru Tegh Bahadur was beheaded under the orders of Emperor Aurangzeb for refusing to convert to Islam.

27. Taran Taran Sahib

Near Amritsar. The place where Guru Arjan Dev built a Gurdwara in the memory of Guru Ram Das.

MAJOR SIKH FESTIVALS

Sikh festivals are generally called Gurpurabs connected with the birth and death anniversaries of the Gurus or special historical events. The most important festivals are as under:-

(1) **Guru Nanak's Birthday-** It is celebrated on *Puranmasi* (Full moon) day in Kartik , 8th month of Bikrami calendar year, which falls in October/November.

(2) **Guru Gobind Singh's Birthday -** It is celebrated according to Bikrami calendar and falls in December/January.

(3) **Baisakhi** - Apart from being a harvest festival in Punjab which normally falls on 13 April,

it is an historic day of great importance for Sikhs. On this day in 1699, Guru Gobind Singh founded the Order of Khalsa in Anandpur. For Sikhs, it is not merely a festival but also the beginning of a new phase.

(4) **Diwali** - This festival falling in October/November is celebrated by Sikhs because on this day in 1621 Guru Hargobind reached Amritsar after release from Gwalior prison. Golden Temple is specially decorated for this event. Illuminations, fireworks and display of treasures, relics and weapons are also held.

(5) **Holla Mohalla** - In place of Holi, Guru Gobind Singh started the celebration of Holla Mohalla when mock battles, military exercises, contests in swordsmanship, archery, wrestling and fencing (Gatka) are held, especially at Anandpur Sahib (Punjab).

6) **Other Gurpurabs** - There are other Gurpurabs held to commemorate the martyrdom days of Guru Arjan Dev and Guru Tegh Bahadur. Guru Granth Sahib day and the foundation day of the city of Amritsar are also celebrated.

WHO IS A "SIKH"?

According to Sikh Gurdwara Act 1925, passed by Punjab Legislature,

"Sikh" means a person who professes the Sikh religion or, in the case of a deceased person, professed the Sikh religion or was known to be a Sikh during his lifetime.

If any question arises as to whether any living person is or is not a Sikh, he shall be deemed respectively to be or not to be a Sikh according as he makes or refuses to make in such manner as the (State) government may prescribe the following declaration:-

"I solemnly affirm that I am a Sikh, that I believe in Guru Granth Sahib, that I believe in the ten Gurus, and that I have no other religion."

SIKH POPULATION

Country	Number	Percent
India	19,000,000	1.84 %*
United Kingdom	500,000	1
Canada	225,000	0.6
USA	100,000	
Malaysia	50,000	
Singapore	20,000	

* 2001 census

Sikh population in some States (India & Abroad)

States	Percent	Number
Punjab, India	61.00%	11,000,000
Haryana, India	5.81	956,836
British Columbia, Canada	2.30	100,000
French Guiana	2.00	1,200
Rajasthan, India	1.48	649,174
Himachal Pradesh, India	1.01	400,000
Manitoba, Canada	0.32	3,500
Alberta, Canada	0.54	13,600
Ontario, Canada	0.50	50,100
Fiji	0.50	4,000

Uttar Pradesh, India 0.49 675,775
As on 9 March 2000
Source: www.adherents.com

In 2002, total population of Sikhs in the world was approximately 23 million (2.3 crore) (www.adherents.com) .They are spread in almost all the important countries of the world. In as many as 49 countries, they have established their own Gurdwaras.

GLOSSARY OF SIKH TERMS

Akhand Paath: Uninterrupted reading of the whole of Guru Granth Sahib by a team of readers in relay.(It takes about 48 hours.)

Amrit: Holy water. Water sanctified by the touch of the sacred. Nectar made from sugar and water.

Ardaas: The Sikh prayer.

Bani(Gurbani): Hymns composed by Gurus and

forming part of Guru Granth Sahib. Also scriptures compiled by Gurus.

Bhog: Conclusion of the reading of Granth Sahib, followed generally by singing of hymns and ardaas. Also, conclusion of a function in general.

Chaur: Yak hair whisk waved as a symbol of respect for the scriptures.

Five K's: Panj Kakke (Kesh, Kanga, Karra, Kaccha & Kirpan) . The five distinguishing symbols worn by Sikhs.

Giani: One who is well-versed in Sikh scriptures. In general, a person who is well-read and possesses knowledge.

Granthi: A professional reader of the Granth Sahib. A functionary in charge of a Gurdwara

Gurdwara: Sikh Temple.

Gurmukhi: The script in which Granth Sahib is written. Script for Panjabi language.

Gurpurab: A Sikh festival connected with Gurus.

Gursikh: A true devotee of the Gurus.

Harmandir: "The house of God"- The central shrine of the Sikhs in Amritsar, commonly known as Golden Temple .

Hukamnama: Religious commandment issued by a recognised authority of Sikhs

Kaccha: Knee-length breeches; Short underpants.

Karra : Steel bangle worn by Sikhs.

Karah Parshad: A sacramental pudding first offered to God and then distributed among all those present at a Sikh religious gathering. It is made of wheat flour, sugar and clarified butter (Ghee).

Kar Sewa: Voluntary service done by devotees in Gurdwara or in any activity connected with religious project.

Kesh: Hair. Unshorn hair.

Khalsa: The pure one; the brotherhood of baptised Sikhs. Commonly used to refer to Sikh community.

Kirpan: Sword.

Kirtan: Singing of hymns from Sikh scriptures. In general, singing of devotional songs in praise of God.

Langar: Community kitchen; community eating. The kitchen attached to Gurdwara from which food is served to all regardless of caste or creed

Miri: Temporal authority.

Nishan Sahib: Saffron-coloured triangular-shaped Sikh flag , usually reinforced in the middle with Sikh insignia in blue. It is usually mounted on a long steel pole (which is also covered with saffron-coloured cloth) headed with a Khanda

Panj Piare: The five beloved ones; the first five Sikhs who were baptised by Guru Gobind Singh in 1699.

Piri: Spiritual authority.

Raagi: Musicians and vocalists who sing devotional hymns, particularly hymns from Sikh scriptures.

Sangat (Saadh Sangat): Religious congregation. A congregation of Sikhs. Assembly of good persons on a religious occasion.

Sarovar: A sacred pool, lake.

Sat Guru: True Guru

Sat Nam: True name; God's name; truth

Sat Sri Akal: Sikh greeting, meaning truth is immortal.

Shabad: Sacred hymn from Guru Granth Sahib, sung in devotional style.

Singh: Lion; an essential part of male Sikh name.

Waheguru: God.

Waheguru Ji Ka Khalsa: Hail the Khalsa who belongs to God.

Waheguru Ji Ki Fateh: Hail the God to whom belongs the Victory

QUOTATIONS FROM GURU GRANTH SAHIB

He who eats what he has earned by his own labour and gives some to others - Nanak, he it is who knows the true path. - *—Guru Nanak Dev*

In words we are good but in deeds bad ..Within mind we are impure and black but are white from without.

The pity is that we shamelessly stand in competitiom with those who stand and serve at the Lord's door.

—Guru Nanak Dev

Of what use is the bathing in sacred waters, if the mind is defiled by sin. **—Guru Nanak Dev**
Shame to him who commits adultery .

—Guru Arjan Dev

As one lies with a venomous serpent, so it is if one sleeps with another's wife.

—Guru Arjan Dev

His mind is full of deceit.
And he calls himself a saint.
His desires are not fulfilled,
And he meets his end in shame.

—Guru Amar Das

The heart is full of spite,
Yet he talks sweetly,
He meets his end in misery

—Guru Arjan Dev

I am slave to him, Who does good actions.

—Guru Amar Das

Of what use is wealth, amassed by wrongful means? *— Guru Arjan Dev*

Son, why do you quarrel with your father,
Due to him you have grown to this age?
It is a sin to argue with him.- Guru Ram Das
Why call woman inferior who gives birth
to kings ? *—Guru Nanak*
Do not harbour ill-will for any person,
For the Lord resides in all.

—Guru Arjan Dev

He who is full of jealousy of others, shall never get peace. *—Guru Ram Das*

When His Nam resides in the mind, anger and conceit are washed away. *— Guru Amar Das*

Vanity is the root of all evil. *— Guru Amar Das*

Whoever think high of themselves and low of others, I saw them going to hell, because of their thoughts, words and deeds.

—Bhagat Kabir

Without contentment, No one can get true tranquility of mind. *—Guru Arjan Dev*
He who is proud, shall be burnt in the fire of His wrath. *—Guru Ram Das*
Pride is a disease of the mind. *—Guru Ram Das*
The corrupt man has no protection,

The backbiter has no honour, —*Guru Nanak Dev*
He, whose heart is corrupt and yet who calls himself a saint, is a hypocrite and can never realize God.

—*Guru Amar Das*

His mind is full of deceit.
And he calls himself a saint,
His desires are not fulfilled,
And he meets his end in shame.

—*Guru Amar Das*

Meet you the Lord of the universe,
For now is the time,
After several births you have attained the human body, Lose not this opportunity.

—*Guru Arjan Dev*

The society of saints removes all sins.

—*Guru Arjan Dev*

We shall all have to render, an account of our actions. —*Guru Nanak Dev*

There can be no worship, without doing good actions. —*Guru Nanak Dev*

Those who keep false books, And earn wealth by dishonest means; And those who love falsehood, Shall be burnt in the fire of hell. —*Guru Amar das*

SIKH CALENDAR

Unto 1998, the Sikhs used a Hindu lunar calendar to determine their religious holidays. Starting in 1999 a new Nanakshahi calendar was introduced. All religious holidays are now being observed according to the new Nanakshahi Calendar. The Sikh New Year begins with Chet 1 which in the Common Era (Gregorian) calendar is March 14. In 1999 it was the year 531 Nanakshahi. The years of the Nanakshahi calendar start with the birth of Guru Nanak Dev in 1469 Gregorian . The modification is that now the calendar is based on the length of the tropical solar year, instead of the lunar cycle, meaning that dates will not fluctuate from year to year as they did previously.

Features of the new calendar

- a solar calendar
- called Nanakshahi after Guru Nanak (founder of Sikhism)
- year one is the year of Guru Nanak's birth (1469 CE)
- uses most of the mechanics of the Western calendar
- year length is same as Western calendar (365 days 5 hours 48 minutes 45 seconds)
- contains 5 months of 31 days followed by 7 months of 30 days
- leap year every 4 years in which the last month (Phagun) has an extra day

Month	Start Date	Days in Month
Chet	14 March	31
Vaisakh	14 April	31
Jeth	15 May	31
Haarh	15 June	31
Saavan	16 July	31
Bhaadon	16 August	30
Assu	15 September	30
Kattak	15 October	30
Maggar	14 November	30
Poh	14 December	30
Maagh	13 January	30
Phagun	12 February	30 (31 in leap year)

Buddhism

THE RELIGION OF PEACEFUL, ETHICAL SELF-CULTURE

Table of Contents

ORIGIN

Buddhism is one of the major religions in the world .It began as an offspring of Hinduism in India around 2,500 years ago when Siddhartha Gautama discovered how to bring happiness into the world. His aim was to free man from the cycle of reincarnations as ultimately life means suffering, transitoriness and death.

Historians, religious scholars, and various Buddhist sects debate the actual year of the Buddha's birth. It may have been as early as 644 BC or as late as 540 BC. The years 566BC, 563 BC and 560BC are believed to be the most probable years of his birth.

Siddharth Gautam was born in Lumbini in the small kingdom of Kapilavastu (Nepal) His father was King Suddhodana , king of Shakya tribe, and his mother was Queen Maya. Gautam Buddha's mother died at childbirth and he was brought up by his mother's sister Prajapati

Gotami . Soon after Prince Siddhartha was born, the wise men predicted that he would become a Buddha. When the king heard this, he was deeply disturbed, for he wanted his son to become a mighty ruler. He told Queen Maya, "I will make life in the palace so pleasant that our son will never want to leave."

At the age of sixteen, Prince Siddhartha married a beautiful princess, Yasodhara. The king built them three palaces, one for each season, and lavished them with luxuries. They passed their days in enjoyment and never thought about life outside the palace. They had a son, Rahul.

THE FOUR SIGHTS

At the time of Siddhatha Gautam's birth, people were looking for new answers to certain questions, especially questions about suffering. They wanted to know why people had to suffer and how it could be avoided. Siddhartha became interested in the problem and set about finding new ways of solving it.

Siddhartha became disillusioned with the palace life and wanted to see the outside world. He made four trips outside the palace and saw four things that changed his life. On the first three trips, he saw sickness, old age and death. He asked himself, "How can I enjoy a life of pleasure when there is so much suffering in the world?"

On his fourth trip, he saw a wandering monk who had given up everything he owned to seek an end to suffering. "I shall be like him." Siddhartha thought.

Prince Siddhath left the palace and the loved ones behind in search of the truth about life and an answer to the problem of pain and human suffering. He was 29 then.

He became a wandering monk. He cut off his hair to show that he had renounced the worldly lifestyle and called himself Gautam. He wore ragged robes and wandered from place to place. In his search for truth, he studied with the wisest teachers of his day. He studied the Hindu scriptures, but became disillusioned with the teachings of Hinduism. He then devoted himself to a life of extreme asceticism in the jungle. It is believed that he eventually learned to exist on one grain of rice a day which reduced his body to a skeleton. But he came to the conclusion that asceticism did not lead to peace and self realisation ; it merely weakened the mind and body.

ENLIGHTENMENT

After six years of various experiments, Gautam eventually turned to a life of meditation. While in deep meditation under a fig tree known as the Bodhi tree (meaning, "tree of wisdom"), in the city of Bodhgaya in India, Gautama experienced enlightenment, the highest degree of God-consciousness. This meant freedom from the cycle of re-birth , and so freedom from suffering. Gautam then became known as Buddha, the "Enlightenment one."

For 45 years, Buddha spread his message of a spiritual life with 8 - fold path towards salvation . Buddha died at the age of 80 years..

Seven days after the Buddha's death at Kushinagara (modern Kasia), his body was cremated and the relics were divided equally among eight clans. Each of these built a sacred cairn over the relics, a form of memorial known as a *stupa,* which later became the focus for Buddhists' devotions. For the next two centuries, there was a steady growth of Buddhism in India.

The word 'Buddha' is a title and not a name. It means 'The Awakened one' , 'The Enlightened

one'. The Buddha was not a God and he made no claim to divinity. He did not claim to be a God and he has never been regarded as such by Buddhists. .. He was a human being who, through tremendous efforts, became Enlightened, understanding life in the deepest way possible.. Buddhists see him as an ideal and a guide who can lead one to Enlightenment . Some Hindus believe that Buddha was one of the *avatars* of Lord Vishnu himself

BUDDHA'S DISCOURSE AFTER ENLIGHTENMENT

Soon after Enlightenment, the Buddha told his followers of the three components that make up the essence of what he had learned during his meditation.

The first component is to live a moral life - to live according to the *Dharma* or universal law that governs both the physical and moral order of the universe. Good deeds result in a person gaining positive *Karma* and bad deeds lead to negative *Karma*.

Second, to become enlightened, the Buddha taught that one must practice meditation. This will give the calmness to gain understanding of the true nature of existence.

Third, using insight meditation, one gains the wisdom. This wisdom reveals that even those things that seem most intimate, one's thoughts and emotions, are transient states that come and go. Through this wisdom, a great burden is lifted. The clamouring ego with its desires and disappointments is silenced. When a person gains this wisdom, a deep and lasting sense of peace and contentment replaces selfish craving and gratification.

Buddha believed that an order existed in the universe but he did not claim that God created the order. Also, Buddha did not teach that humans had a soul. In this, Buddha set himself apart from the Hindu religious tradition which claims that each person possesses an eternal soul.

However, the Buddha did believe in reincarnation. Death, for the Buddha, is merely an incident between one life and another. A legend about the life of the Buddha reports that when he achieved enlightenment he gained the ability to recall many of his previous lives.

When the Buddha taught about what he had learned, he always cautioned his followers not to accept his teachings uncritically. He encouraged them to evaluate his teachings in the light of their own experience. According to another legend, he said something like this:

Believe nothing, O monks, merely because you have been told it . . . or because it is traditional, or because you yourselves have imagined it. Do not believe what your teacher tells you merely out of respect for the teacher. But whatever, after due examination and analysis, you find to be conducive to the good, the benefit, the welfare of all beings -- that doctrine believe and cling to, and take it as your guide.

The most simple teaching of the Buddha was to do good, to avoid evil and to purify the heart. According to Buddha, the hearts of ordinary men are not pure. They are filled with greed, ill will and delusion. Greed and hatred are impurities caused by desires, and ignorance is the cause of delusion, especially delusion of self. Ignorance, in fact, is the cause of desire and thus the primary cause of all suffering and of rebirth. The Buddha said that one may purify his heart: 1. By practicing self-control and self-restraint 2. By meditating upon one's own self . 3. By following the Eight-Fold Path that leads to the end of all suffering All of these features are the basic essence of Buddhism.

Buddha's teachings in a nutshell
Sabba papassa akaranam, kusalassa upasampada
Sacittapariyodapanam, etam Buddhana sasanam

To cease from doing all evils, to cultivate good
To purify one's mind, this is the advice of Buddha.

The essence of Buddha's teachings was:-
1. *Prajna:* Understanding as against superstition and supernaturalism
2. *Karuna:* Love
3. *Samata:* Equality
That is what man needs for good and happy life on earth

ESSENCE OF BUDDHISM

(a) The three Universal Truths

One day, the Buddha sat down in the shade of a tree and noticed how beautiful the countryside was. Flowers were blooming and trees were putting on bright new leaves, but among all this beauty, he saw much unhappiness. A farmer beat his ox in the field. A bird pecked at an earthworm, and then an eagle swooped down on the bird. Deeply troubled, he asked, "Why does the farmer beat his ox? Why must one creature eat another to live?"

During his enlightenment, the Buddha found the answer to these questions. He discovered three great truths. He explained these truths in a simple way so that everyone could understand them.

1. Nothing is lost in the universe

The first truth is that nothing is lost in the universe. Matter turns into energy, energy turns into matter. A dead leaf turns into soil. A seed sprouts and becomes a new plant. Old solar systems disintegrate and turn into cosmic rays. We are born of our parents, our children are born of us.

We are the same as plants, as trees, as other people, as the rain that falls. We consist of that which is around us, we are the same as everything. If we destroy something around us, we destroy ourselves. If we cheat another, we cheat ourselves. Understanding this truth, the Buddha and his disciples never killed any animal.

2. Everything Changes

The second universal truth of the Buddha is that everything is continuously changing. Life is like a river flowing on and on, ever-changing. It is smooth and gentle in some places, but later on snags and rocks crop up out of nowhere. As soon as we think we are safe, something unexpected happens. Once dinosaurs, mammoths, and saber-toothed tigers roamed this earth. They all died out, yet this was not the end of life. Other life forms like smaller mammals appeared, and eventually humans, too. Our ideas about life also change.

3. Law of Cause and Effect

The third universal truth explained by the Buddha is the law of cause and effect. The law of cause and effect is known as *karma*. Nothing ever happens to us unless we deserve it. We receive exactly what we earn, whether it is good or bad. We are the way we are now due to the things we have done in the past. Our thoughts and actions determine the kind of life we can have. If we do good things, in the future good things will happen to us. If we do bad things, in the future bad things will happen to us. Every moment we create new *karma* by what we say, do, and think.

(b) The Four Noble Truths

The Buddha did not try to explain whether there was an ultimate God or not, or what the proper rituals and sacrifices were to achieve oneness with God. Instead, he taught that we must strive through our own efforts to achieve liberation from anguish and suffering. The Buddha espoused an easily understood philosophy, based on the Four Noble Truths:

1. Suffering

There is suffering in the world. Everyone suffers from these thing:-

Birth- When we are born, we cry.

Sickness- When we are sick, we are miserable.

Old age- When old, we will have aches and

pains and find it hard to get around.

Death- None of us wants to die. We feel deep sorrow when someone dies.

Other things we suffer from are:

Being with those we dislike,

Being apart from those we love,

Not getting what we want.

The Buddha did not deny that there is happiness in life, but he pointed out it does not last forever. Eventually everyone meets with some kind of suffering.

2. The cause of suffering: desire

All suffering is caused by craving, greed, desire , attachment and ignorance. We are the cause of our suffering. People are ignorant of the law of *karma* and are greedy for the wrong kind of pleasures. When we long for something but are unable to get it, we feel frustrated. When we expect someone to live up to our expectations and he does not, we feel let down and disappointed. When we want others to like us and they don't, we feel hurt. Even when we are able to get what we crave for, this may not often lead to happiness either because it is not long before we feel bored with that thing, lose interest in it or, after getting it, start wanting something else. Put simply, even getting what we want does not guarantee happiness..

3. The end of suffering : stop desire

Suffering can be overcome and happiness attained. To end suffering, stop doing what causes suffering. Stop greed , ignorance, desire and attachment. The state in which all suffering ends is *Nirvana*. *Nirvana* is an everlasting state of great joy and peace. The Buddha said, "The extinction of desire is *Nirvana*." This is the ultimate goal in Buddhism

4. The path to the end of suffering:

The path to end suffering is the **Noble Eight-fold Path**. It is also known as the **Middle Way**.

These four Truths are called 'Noble' because they ennoble one who understands them.

NOBLE EIGHT-FOLD PATH

When the Buddha gave his first sermon in the Deer Park, he began the 'Turning of the Dharma Wheel'. He chose the beautiful symbol of the wheel with its eight spokes to represent the Noble Eight-fold Path. The Buddha's teaching goes round and round like a great wheel that never stops, leading to the central point of the wheel, the only point which is fixed, Nirvana. The eight spokes on the wheel represent the eight parts of the Noble Eight-fold Path. Just as every spoke is needed for the wheel to keep turning, we need to follow each step of the path.

1. Right Understanding

Right understanding is the knowledge of the Four Noble Truths. In other words, it is the understanding of oneself as one really is. It is to see the world with wisdom and compassion. Wrong view occurs when we impose our expectations onto things; expectations about how we hope things will be, or about how we are afraid things might be. Right view occurs when we see things simply, as they are

2. Right Thought.

Right thought is right volition, decision, and contemplation. It means not having thoughts of greed, hatred, and ignorance. These three poisons of greed, hatred, and ignorance are main obstacles on the road to Enlightenment. They continually occupy our minds and contaminate our pure nature. It is not easy to be rid of these three poisons. We have to exert effort constantly to maintain the right thinking needed to overcome these three poisons and enter the path of Buddhahood.

Right Thoughts are threefold. They are:
(a) The thoughts of renunciation which are opposed to sense-pleasures.
(b) Kind thoughts which are opposed to ill-will.
(c) Thoughts of harmlessness which are opposed to cruelty. These tend to purify mind

3. Right Speech.

Right speech means that we do not tell lies. We refrain from backbiting, slander and rumor-mongering as they bring about disharmony in people . We do not use harsh or malicious language, or utter frivolous speech. If we say something inappropriate, we not only hurt others but also hurt ourselves. It is very important that we choose our words carefully. Ethical conduct is based on Right Speech. By speaking kind and helpful words, we are respected and trusted by everyone. We should say what needs to be said, very simply in a genuine way.

4. Right Conduct.

Right conduct is refraining from killing, stealing, intoxicants and improper sexual behaviour. It helps one to develop a character that is self-controlled and mindful of rights of others . . Be honest . Observe discipline; it implies renunciation. No matter what we say, others know us from the way we behave. Before we criticize others, we should first see what we do ourselves. Besides abstaining from doing evil deeds, we also need to actively perform good deeds.

5. Right Livelihood.

This means choosing a work that does not hurt others. The Buddha said, "Do not earn your living by harming others. Do not seek happiness by making others unhappy." Right livelihood refers to proper way of making a living and abstaining from unethical occupations such as operating gambling houses, selling alcoholic beverages or instruments that can kill, operating slaughterhouses, trading in animals for slaughter and the like. Right livelihood enables us to have a happy family life and a stable society.

It is only natural and right that we should earn our living. Often, many of us may not be happy with our jobs. Often, we may feel that our job is not in keeping with the image we want to project. The right course is that so long as we hold a job, we should do it well. Whatever it is ,we need to perform it properly and honestly, with attention to detail.

6. Right Effort.

A worthwhile life means doing our best at all times and having good will toward others. This also means not wasting effort on things that harm ourselves or others. Right effort doesn't involve violence at all. When we see things as they are, we can work with them, gently and without any kind of aggression whatsoever. We must be persistent in preventing evil and unharmonious state of mind from coming to be. We must also be persistent in promoting good and harmonious state of mind..

Right Effort is a mental discipline. It is fourfold, namely:
(a) the endeavor to discard evil that has already arisen.
(b) the endeavor to prevent the arising of unrisen evil.

(c) the endeavour to develop that good which has already arisen.

(b) the endeavour to promote that good which has not already arisen..

The Buddha teaches that attaining happiness and enlightenment depends upon one's own efforts. Effort is the root of all achievement. One must put the teaching into practice before one can expect to obtain the desired result.

7. Right Mindfulness.

Right Mindfulness is the awareness of one's deeds, words and thoughts. It involves precision and clarity. We should be mindful of the tiniest details of our experience. We should be mindful of the way we talk, the way we perform our jobs, our posture, our attitude toward our friends and family, every detail.

- Right Mindfulness is also four-fold:
- mindfulness with regard to body
- mindfulness with regard to feeling
- mindfulness with regard to mind
- mindfulness with regard to mental objects.

We should be ever aware of what our body is doing, what we sense and feel, and what our mind is thinking about. We should attempt to be detached from these things

If we always remember impermanence, suffering, and selflessness, we will not be greedy for the trifling advantages of this world. We will then strive for the Truth diligently

8. Right Meditation:

Right Meditation means the gradual process of training the mind to concentrate and focus on a single object and to remain fixed upon the object without wavering. The constant practice of meditation helps one to develop a calm and concentrated mind and help to prepare one for the attainment of wisdom and enlightenment ultimately. What it really means is that we should concentrate our volition and thoughts through meditation . By doing this, we can be quiet and attain true peace of mind. This precept strengthens mental discipline

TRIPLE JEWELS

The Buddha knew it would be difficult for people to follow his teachings on their own. So he established the Three Refuges for them to rely on. These Refuges are the most precious things in Buddhism, namely, the Buddha, the *dharma,* and the *sangha* These are also known as the Three Jewels. .

- The Buddha is the guide.
- The *Dharma* is the path. It refers to sacred and profound teachings of the Buddha
- The *Sangha* is the community of monks, hermits, teachers and companions along the way.

There is a special ceremony for taking refuge with the Triple Jewels. With a sincere mind, one recites the following verse in front of an ordained monk or nun:-

1. I go to the Buddha for refuge
   — *Buddhm saranam gacchami*
2. I go to the Dhamma for refuge
   — *Dhammam saranam gacchami*
3. I go to the Samgha for refuge
   — *Samgham saranam gacchami*

For a Buddhist, taking refuge is the first step on the path to enlightenment. Even if enlightenment is not achieved in this life, one has a better chance to become enlightened in a future life.

The *Dhamma*

The Dhamma could simply mean the teachings of the Buddha. No doubt there were many scriptures and expositions made by him, the most concise essence of the Truth could be found in the Four Noble Truths taught by the Buddha.

The Sangha - Lifestyle of Monks

The community of monks and hermits is called *"Sangha"*. Their code prescribes a strict self-monitoring, purity laws and a warning against the life of the senses and its temptations. Monks live in monasteries . The monastic rules have three ideals: poverty, celibacy and peace-ableness. Monks live a simple life. They have no possessions apart from begging bowl, sewing needle, prayer beads, razor and drinking water filter. They are required to suppress both desire and sex as a way of relaxation . Lately, however, there are some married monks. No one should harm anyone else. Everyone should have compassion for all other living beings . Besides the Five Precepts (given below) laid down for all followers of Buddhism, the monks are required also to observe the following rules in life: (1) Avoid eating too much or eating after mid-day; (2) Avoid dancing and frivolous singing; (3) Avoid wearing adornments and perfumes; Avoid sleeping too much, or in a soft bed; and (5) Avoid handling gold and silver (money).

FIVE PRECEPTS

All religions have some basic rules that define what is good conduct and what kind of conduct should be avoided. In Buddhism, the most important rules are the Five Precepts. These have been passed down from the Buddha himself.

1. Not to deprive a living thing of life
    —Respect for life
2. Not to take what is not given to you
    —Respect for others' property
3. Not to engage in illicit sexual conduct

    —Respect for our pure nature
4. Not to lie
    —Respect for honesty
5. Not to take intoxicating drinks
    —Respect for a clear mind

Not to deprive a living thing of life.- No killing: The Buddha said, "Life is dear to all beings. They have the right to live the same as we do". We should respect all life and not kill anything. Killing ants and mosquitoes is also breaking this precept. We should have an attitude of loving-kindness towards all beings, wishing them to be happy and free from harm. Taking care of the earth, its rivers and air is included. One way that many Buddhists follow this precept is by being vegetarian.

Not to take what is not given to you - No stealing: If we steal from another, we steal from ourselves. Instead, we should learn to give and take care of things that belong to our family, to the school, or to the public.

Not to engage in illicit sexual conduct- No sexual misconduct: Proper conduct shows respect for oneself and others. Our bodies are gifts from our parents, so we should protect them from harm. Young people should especially keep their natures pure and develop their virtues. It is up to them to make the world a better place to live. In happy families, the husband and wife both respect each other.

Not to lie : This precept means and includes no lying, no gossip, no back-biting, no harsh words and no idle speech. Being honest brings peace into the world. When there is a misunderstanding, the best thing is to speak the truth and sort the matter out.

Not to take intoxicating drinks. - The fifth precept is based on keeping a clear mind and a healthy body. One day, when the Buddha was speaking the Dharma for the assembly, a young drunkard staggered into the room. He tripped over some monks who were sitting on the floor and started cursing loudly. His breath reeked of alcohol and filled the air with a sickening stench. Mumbling to himself, he reeled out the door. Everyone was astonished at his rude behavior, but the Buddha remained calm. "Great assembly!" he spoke, "Take a look at this man! He will certainly lose his wealth and good name. His body will grow weak and sickly. Day and night, he will quarrel with his family and friends until they abandon him. The worst thing is that he will lose his wisdom and become stupid."

These prohibitions along with other teachings help achieve the ultimate goal of life, that is *Nirvana,* a state of peace and freedom from the cycle of re-births, which, according to Buddhism, should be the goal of life.

WHEEL OF LIFE

Buddhists do not believe that death is the end of life. When one dies, one's consciousness leaves and enters one of the six paths of re-birth.

- Heavenly Beings
- Humans
- *Asuras* are beings who have many good things in life, but still like to fight. They appear in the heavens or on earth as people or animals.
- Hungry ghosts are beings who suffer from constant hunger.
- Hell-beings

These are the six states on the wheel of life. At the top are the heavens, where everyone is happy. At the bottom are the hells where the suffering is unbearable. Beings can rise or fall from one path to another. If one does good deeds, one will be born into the paths of gods, humans, or asuras. If one does evil deeds, one will be born into the

paths of animals, hungry ghosts, or hell-beings. From one life to the next one can suddenly change from a human to an animal or from a ghost to a hell-being, according to the acts one has done.

How to Escape the Turning Wheel

The wheel of life and death is kept turning by the three poisons of greed, hatred, and ignorance. By cutting off the three poisons, we can escape the wheel and become enlightened

Nirvana:

Nirvana' literally means "blowing out" or "extinction". According to Buddhism, this is the ultimate goal of life and can be described in various words. It is a cessation of all sorrows, which can be achieved by removing desire by following the Eight Fold Path.

BUDDHISM - THE MIDDLE PATH

Buddhism is a path of practical and spiritual development leading to ones insight into the true nature of life. Buddhist practices such as meditation are means of changing oneself in order to develop the qualities of awareness, kindness, and wisdom. Buddhism is not about teaching or learning but it is all about experiencing.

Buddhist ideology does not advocate the practice of worshipping a creator God. Hence, quite often it is not really seen as a religion in the normal sense. The basic tenets of Buddhist teaching are straight forward and practical: Nothing is fixed or permanent; actions have consequences; change is possible. It teaches practical methods (such as meditation) which enable people to realise and utilise its teachings in order to transform their experience, to be fully responsible for their lives and to develop the qualities of Wisdom and Compassion.

There are over 360 million Buddhists followers all over the world. They follow many different forms of Buddhism, but all traditions are characterised by non-violence, lack of dogma, tolerance of differences, and, usually, by the practice of meditation.

Buddha preached a Middle course to be adopted by his followers for leading a peaceful life He was against the two extremes of self-indulgence and self-mortification. To him neither way is right. He preached for a third way, a Middle Path. The path that is based on the principle of moderation. He advised his followers : Enjoy desires in moderation. Be kind to all other people. Do not harm living creatures of any kind . Help people less fortunate than yourself.

BUDDHIST SCRIPTURES

Historical research shows that the original teachings of Buddha can never be known. It seems that Gautam Buddha's teachings were memorized by his disciples. His disciples remembered his talks and recited them regularly. Only after 400 years of the death of Buddha were his teachings and doctrines written down. These were collected into books called *Sutras*. There are many *Sutras*. Thus Buddhism does not have just a single holy book, like the Christian Bible or the Qur'an of Islam.

The first *Sutras* were written on palm leaves in Pali and Sanskrit, ancient Indian languages. They have been gathered together in a collection called the *Tripitaka,* which means 'three baskets'. It is divided into three parts.

- *Sutra Pitaka* ~ Sutras and their explanations
- *Vinaya Pitaka* ~ Rules for monks and nuns
- *Abhidharma Pitaka* ~ The psychology and philosophy of the Buddha's teachings

Buddhists treat *Sutras* with great respect and place them on the highest shelves in the most respected areas.

HISTORY OF BUDDHISM
BUDDHISM IN THE EAST

Buddhism was first introduced into Sri Lanka from India in the 3rd century BC by Mahinda, the son of King Ashoka. There it achieved great popularity and is still flourishing.

In the early centuries AD, Buddhism was taken to Southeast Asia by merchants and missionaries. The great monuments like Borobudur in Indonesia and Angkor Thom in Cambodia are evidence of the splendour of Buddhism in these regions.

In the 1st century AD, Buddhism reached China where many *Sutras* were translated into classical Chinese. In the 4th century AD, Buddhism found its way to Korea and Japan.

BUDDHISM IN THE WEST

Even before the 17th century, people in the West had heard of the Buddha and his teachings from early travellers such as Marco Polo and Christian missionaries.

By the early 20th century, many Europeans had travelled to the East to study Buddhism. Some of them became monks and inspired Buddhism in the West. In the 19th century, Chinese and Japanese immigrants brought many different traditions of Buddhism to America. Today, there are numerous Buddhist centers spread across Europe and North and South America.

DIFFERENT FORMS OF BUDDHISM
TWO SCHOOLS OF BUDDHISM

In the centuries following the Buddha's lifetime,

his followers faithfully preserved his teachings and spread them to many countries in Asia. Today, there are two main schools of Buddhism: *Theravada* and *Mahayana*. They have different practices, but they have some fundamental similarities.

Theravada Buddhism: Theravada means 'the teachings of the elders'. It is practiced in Burma, Sri Lanka, Thailand, and other parts of South East Asia. It is often called Southern Buddhism because of the path it took through Southern India to Southeast Asia. This system remains true to the original teachings of Gautam Buddha (also known as Sakyamuni Gautama Buddha), that are found in the Pali scriptures. The Four Noble Truths and the Eight-Fold Path are the main focus of the school.

They believe that the Buddha was a man who liberated himself through meditation and contemplation. They look upon him as a teacher as opposed to a deity, and so images of the Buddha in these lands are revered or venerated, not worshipped. In this system, each individual must strive to liberate oneself through enlightened actions. Neither gods nor magic spells can assist the process.

Theravada monks follow the practices that have been passed down by the senior monks from the Buddha's time, such as living in the forests and meditating. The goal in *Theravada* Buddhism is to become an *Arhat,* a person who is free of suffering, who is holy and wise of the highest level , and who has destroyed worldly pleasures and passions.

Mahayana Buddhism : The *Mahayana* school is known as the Greater Vehicle .It incorporates many of the concepts found in Hinduism and in the original Tibetan religious beliefs. It is practiced in East Asia, especially in Tibet, China and Japan. It reached these lands via Central Asia.

This system introduced new metaphysical concepts such as the notion of "nothingness" or *"sunya"* through Sanskrit scriptures written by scholars such as Nagarjuna, Asanga, Vasubandhu and Asvaghosha. Hsuan-tsang of China visited India in search of these texts which were then translated into Chinese and Japanese. This system also introduced the concept of *Bodhisattva* and the goddess called Tara. The goal in *Mahayana* Buddhism is to follow the *Bodhisattva* Path. *Bodhisattva* means "Buddha-to-be" or " Developing Buddha". A *Bodhisattva* is one who enlightens oneself as well as others. People no longer had to take up difficult vows to attain *'nirvana'*; they could simply earn merits and liberate themselves by worshipping Bodhisattvas who, in their infinite compassion, worked for human welfare. In *Mahayana* Buddhism , while the Sangha is important, becoming a monk is not considered to be essential. A person can seek *nirvana* while still being involved in society

Mahayana Buddhism formed distinctive branches; three of these are:

Vajrayana Buddhism, also known as Tibetan Buddhism.

Pure Land Buddhism. It began in China and spread to Japan. The central figure is Buddha known as *"Amida Buddha"*.

Zen Buddhism. It also spread to China and Japan. *Zen* means "meditation". *Zen* Buddhists try to spend as much time as possible being "mindful", or meditating on reality.

Both *Theravada* and *Mahayana* Buddhism are found in the West.

BUDDHIST FESTIVALS

Buddhists have many festivals throughout the year. These festivals celebrate events in the lives of Buddha, Bodhisattvas and famous teachers.

During these occasions people can also take refuge and precepts, or leave the home life to become monks and nuns.

Buddha Day- *Wesak*

For the Buddhist community, the most important event of the year is the celebration of Wesak, the Birth of the Buddha, his Enlightenment and Nirvana. It falls on the full-moon day in May. On this day, Buddhists take part in the ceremonial bathing of the Buddha. They pour ladles of water scented with flowers over a statue of the baby Siddhartha. This symbolizes purifying one's thoughts and actions.

The temples are elaborately decorated with flowers and banners; the altars are laden with offerings; vegetarian meals are provided for all; and captive animals, such as birds and turtles are set free. This is a very joyous day for everyone.

Dharma Day - *Asalha Puja*

Asalha Puja, known as 'Dharma Day', is celebrated during full-moon in July. This celebration commemorates the first sermon of the Buddha to the five monks in the Deer Park at Varanasi (Benares).

Sangha Day- *Kathina Day*

Sangha Day or *Kathina* Day is usually held in October. In the *Theravada* tradition, monks and nuns go on a three-month retreat during the rainy season. After the retreat, the laity offers robes and other necessities to them. This day symbolizes the close relationship between the *Sangha* and laity.

Ullambana Day

The observance of *Ullambana* is based on the story of Maudgalyayana, a disciple of the Buddha. When Maudgalyayana's mother died, he wanted to know where she was reborn. Using his spiritual powers, he travelled into the hells and found her suffering miserably from hunger. He brought her a bowl of food, but when she tried to swallow it, the food turned into hot coals. The distressed Maudgalyayana asked the Buddha, "Why is my mother suffering in the hells?" The Buddha replied, "In her life as a human, she was stingy and greedy. This is her retribution." He advised, "Make offerings to the *Sangha*. The merit and virtue from this act will release your mother and others from the hells." As a result of Maudgalyana's offering, his mother and thousands of others were released from their unhappy state. After this, making offerings to release departed relatives and others from the hells became popular in *Mahayana* countries. Usually, it takes place in September.

Losar Festival

Losar is a major Tibetan festival that is celebrated at the full moon in February. It marks the Buddha's early life and teachings and also marks the beginning of the new year.

Obon Festival

Obon is a Japanese festival held in July. It is a festival during which people pay their respects to family ancestors.

MEDITATION

Meditation is at the heart of the Buddhist way of life. It is basically a method for understanding and working on our own mind. We first learn to identify and overcome our negative mental states known as 'delusions', and learn how to develop peaceful and positive mental states or 'virtuous minds'.

Out of meditation we try to maintain the virtuous minds we have developed and use our wisdom to solve the problems of daily life. As our mind becomes more positive, our actions become more constructive, and our experience of life becomes more satisfying and beneficial to others.

Though basic meditation has great benefits, according to Buddhism, one needs to progress beyond basic meditation for which one requires faith in the Three Jewels - Buddha, *Dharma* and *Sangha*.

Technique of meditation

Concentration on the Breath

A very simple way of meditating is concentrating on your breath. The breath is like a bridge between your body and mind. When you concentrate on your breath for a while, your body becomes relaxed and your mind becomes peaceful.

■ Sit in a comfortable position with your back straight.

■ Place your hands in your lap with the left hand on the bottom.

■ Keep your eyes half-closed or closed.

■ Concentrate on the tip of your nose. Notice your breath going in and out.

Lotus posture

Full lotus is the best sitting posture. Begin by sitting in half-lotus, then work your way up to full lotus.

■ Full-lotus- Sit on the edge of a cushion. Place your left ankle on your right thigh. Then lift your right ankle onto your left thigh.

■ Half-lotus- Lift your left ankle onto your right thigh.

Note: It is best to sit at the same time and place everyday. Increase your sitting time little by little. You may sit in a chair or stand if necessary.

Calming meditation - Insight meditation

The legend of the life of Siddhartha does not describe the instructions his teachers gave him when he learned to meditate. They may have advised him to concentrate on his breathing or to repeat a mantra silently to himself, or focus thoughts on an object a few feet away . The goal of these exercises is for the mind to become completely engrossed until the awareness of subject and object dissolves into a unified field of consciousness.

This meditation is a "calming meditation." Siddhartha found it to be only a temporary escape from human suffering. In the legend, as he sat under the tree at the age of thirty-five, he created a new form of meditation, "insight meditation." After achieving peace and calmness using calming meditation, Siddhartha began to meditate on his own state of mind

He examined his subjective experience, his physical sensations, his feelings, his mood and his thoughts. The realization came to him that he was free to choose how to react in all situations. A new sense of freedom replaced the grip of long-standing desires and compulsions. From this detached observation it gradually became clear to Siddhartha that even his conscious mind was but a process like everything else. He saw that the stream of consciousness is just another facet of the complex interactions of the body. Awareness developed that the body and the mind were nothing more than a temporary assemblage of bones, nerves, and tissues, not objects with which to become infatuated or excessively attached. This realization, this insight that Siddhartha had at the age of thirty-five, was his enlightenment.

PLACES OF PILGRIMAGE

The following are the principal Buddhist pilgrimage sites , with the most important ones located in the Ganges Valley of India.

Lumbini: The most important place of Buddhist pilgrimage is Lumbini, located near the Nepal-India border. This is where Gautam Buddha was born The great Buddhist ruler Ashoka visited the site two centuries after Buddha's birth and constructed a stupa (mound, usually of earth) and pillar in recognition. Although largely destroyed now, there remain important marks of the Buddha's birthplace.

Bodhgaya: The Buddha attained enlightenment in the city of Bodhgaya in India. After settling under a tree, the Buddha made the resolve not to move until he had achieved enlightenment. After three days and nights of profound meditation this goal was realised. The Bodhi tree under which the Buddha sat has been destroyed both intentionally and naturally, many times since this time of enlightenment. It has continued to re-sprout and is visible today.

The Mahabodhi Temple marks Bodhgaya. The origins of the Temple are unclear. Some claim the Temple could have been built as early as the third century by Ashoka; others claim the Temple was built between the fifth and seventh centuries. A thriving Monastic Order continues in the area today, with three monasteries catering for locals and foreigners alike.

At **Sarnath** in the Ganges valley of India, the Buddha proclaimed the law of faith. It was here that he taught the keys aspects of Buddhism: the four noble truths, the eight-fold path and the middle way philosophy. The Buddha encouraged followers to avoid extremes of austerity or

pleasure. The remains of monasteries dating from the third century B.C.. to the first century A.D.. indicate a thriving monastic community.

Shravasti: Another of the most commonly visited places of Buddhist pilgrimage is Shravasti. It is here that the Buddha is said to have performed great miracles.

In **Sankashaya** the Buddha descended from the Tushita Heaven. It is said that during the forty-first year of the Buddha's life, he went to the Tushita Heaven to teach Dharma to his mother. Ashoka later built a Temple on the site. This is the only important place of Buddhist pilgrimage where no temples, or monasteries exist today.

Nalanda is important both because it was blessed with the presence of the Buddha, and because of the famous monastic university developed there. This university also named Nalanda (meaning 'insatiable in giving') played a central role in the development of Buddhism in India.

Rajgir is another place in the Ganges valley where the Buddha preached and where he converted two of his future disciples, Sariputra and Maudgalyayana.

PLACES OF WORSHIP

Stupas / Pagodas

Stupas are mounds that were built to hold relics of the Buddha or his chief disciples. They were also built to mark important events of the Buddha's life or lives of his disciples. King Ashoka is said to have built 84,000 stupas all over India, from the original relics of the Buddha. In Sri Lanka stupas are called dagobas; in Burma, Thailand and China they are know as pagodas and in Tibet they are called chortens.

Temples and Monasteries

A temple is a place where monks or nuns live and Buddhist religious ceremonies are held. A large temple is called a monastery. Most temples also have a stupa and a Bodhi tree.

Among other symbols made to remember the Buddha were stone pillars or columns. King Ashoka erected many stone pillars inscribed with Buddhist texts and royal instructions. The most important pillar is at Lumbini, the Buddha's birthplace.

The stone pillar at Lumbini, marking where the Buddha was born, was erected by King Ashoka around 243 BC - it has an inscription about the king carved on it. The most famous of Ashoka's columns has a Four-Lion Capital . The lion symbolizes both Ashoka's imperial rule and the kingship of the Buddha.

BUDDHIST RITUALS
Wedding

1. A Buddhist wedding is very traditional.
2. After consulting the lama (priest), the groom's family chooses an auspicious day to visit the bride's house to ask her parents for their daughter's hand in marriage.
3. *Chessian* is the betrothal ceremony. The maternal uncle of the parent of the bride sit on a raised platform and the lama, or the priest, recites a prayer and distributes a religious drink, madyan, among those present.
4. The date of marriage is fixed in consultation with the astrologer.
5. A Buddhist *lama* (priest) presides over the wedding.
6. The wedding ceremony is conducted at the bride's home. The *lama* leads the couple through the religious rites that include the groom's family offering the mother of the bride the price of milk.
7. Then depending on the horoscope, the bride accompanies her husband on the same day, or the next.

Funeral Rites for the Dead

The early Buddhists followed the Indian custom of burning the body at death. The Buddha's body was cremated and this set the example for many Buddhists, even in the West. When someone is dying in a Buddhist home, monks come to comfort them by chanting verses to them, such as:

"Even the gorgeous royal chariots wear out; and indeed this body too wears out. But the teaching of goodness does not age; and so Goodness makes that known to the good ones."

After death, while the dead person is being prepared for the funeral fire, the monks continue to chant in order to help the dead one's good energies to be released from their fading personality. The monks come with the family to the funeral. The family and all their friends give food and candles to the monks. Goodwill is created by these gifts and it is believed that the goodwill helps the lingering spirit of the dead person.

BUDDHIST POPULATION

World estimates for Buddhism vary between 230 and 500 million, with most around 360 million.

Top 10 Largest National Buddhist Populations

Country	Number of Buddhists
China	102,000,000
Japan	89,650,000
Thailand	55,480,000
Vietnam	49,690,000
Myanmar	41,610,000
Sri Lanka	12,540,000
South Korea	10,920,000
Taiwan	9,150,000
Cambodia	9,130,000
India	7,900,000*

*(0.76% of Indian population. 2001 census)

Top 10 Countries with the Highest Proportion of Buddhists

Country	Percent
Thailand	95%
Cambodia	90
Myanmar	88
Bhutan	75
Sri Lanka	70
Tibet	65
Laos	60
Vietnam	55
Japan	50
Macau	45
Taiwan	43

As on 6 September 2002

Source: www.adherents.com

GLOSSARY OF BUDDHIST TERMS

Amitabha: The Bodhisattva whose name means "Budha of Boundless Light" and who dwells in the paradise called the Pure Land. He is also the founder of this sect of Buddhism.

Arhat: A Buddhist monk who who has destroyed worldly pleasures and passions, is free from all illusions and who has achieved personal enlightenment. This term is used primarily in Theravada Buddhism.

Bikshu: Bhikkhu: A fully ordained monk who has left his home and renounced all his possessions in order to follow the Way of the Buddha

Bodhisattva: A being in the final stages of attaining Buddhahood, who has vowed to help all sentient beings achieve Nirvana, or enlightenment, before he himself achieves it.

Bodhi/Bo Tree: The tree beneath which the meditating Gautama sat before he achieved enlightenment.

Brahman: the Ultimate Reality. Similar to a Supreme Being.

Buddha: Enlightened One Ch'an: Forms of Mahayana Buddhism in China. Japanese version is called Zen.

Dharma: The ultimate law, or doctrine, as taught by Buddha, which consists of the Four Noble Truths and the Eightfold Path.

Gautam/Gotama: Another name for Buddha.

Hinayana: Literally, "small vehicle." A term used by the Mahayanists to describe earlier orthodox sects of Buddhism (Theravada School). Their scriptures are written in Pali, an ancient Indian language.

Karma: Literally, "deed." A concept that binds its followers to an endless cycle of birth, death, and rebirth and, according to one's deeds in life, determines the condition of one's rebirth.

Lama: Literally, "superior one." A Buddhist monk of Tibet.

Mahayana: Literally, "great vehicle." One of the three major forms of Buddhism, Mahayana is considered the more liberal and practical. Its scriptures are written in Sanskrit.

Maya: Queen Maya, mother of Buddha. · Moksha: Literally, "release." An idea originally developed from Upanishadic teachers. By leading a highly spiritual life (or several lives), a soul could be reunited with Brahman, the Ultimate Reality.

Nirvana: Literally, "extinction." The ultimate goal of Buddhists, characterized as the extinction of both craving and the separate "ego." The state of peace and quietude attained by extinguishing all illusions.

Parinirvana: Death of the Buddha. · P u r e Land: A sect of Mahayana Buddhism founded by Amitabha Buddha. The Pure Land is a paradise in the "west" where people can go when they die. People must call on Amitabha to enter this paradise.

Sakyamuni : Another name of the Buddha · Samsara: The continuous cycle of birth, death, and rebirth (reincarnation)

Sangha: An organized assembly of Buddhist monks. · Stupa: A dome, or pagoda, in which sacred relics are deposited. Sutra: Literally, "thread" or "string." A scripture containing the teachings of Buddha.

Theravada: Literally, "School of the Elders." Aso known as Hinayana. One of the three major forms of Buddhism, Theravada is considered to be the original and orthodox form of Buddhism.

Tripitaka: Literally, "Three Baskets." According to Buddhist belief, the scriptures were stored in three baskets, dividing Buddha's teachings into the code of discipline for monks, his sermons and discourses, and the higher doctrine (Buddhist philosophy and psychology)

Zen: Forms of Mahayana Buddhism in Japan. Chinese version is called Ch'an.

SAYINGS OF BUDDHA

Dhammapada I have been insulted! I have been hurt! I have been beaten! I have been robbed! Anger ceases in those who do not harbour this sort of thought.

It is not the shortcomings of others, nor what others have done or not done that one should think about, but what one has done or not done oneself.

Like a solid rock is not shaken by the wind, so the wise are not moved by praise or blame.

Four principal things increase in the man who is respectful and always honours his elders - length of life, good looks, happiness and health.

All fear violence, life is dear to all. Seeing the similarity to oneself, one should not use violence or have it used.

Health is the supreme possession. Contentment is the supreme wealth. A trustworthy friend is the supreme relation. Nirvana is the supreme happiness.

There never has been, there never will be, and there is not now any man exclusively criticised or exclusively praised.

The thoughtless man who consorts with another man's wife encounters four things - accumulation of demerit, disturbed sleep, thirdly disgrace, and hell fourth.

For hate is never conquered by hate. Hate is conquered by love. This is an eternal law.

If you speak and act with pure thoughts - happiness follows you.

We are not punished for our sins, we are punished by our sins.

Suffering because life cannot satisfy selfish desire is like suffering because a banana tree will not bear mangoes.

Jainism

THE RELIGION OF ASCETICISM

Table of Contents

LORD MAHAVIR

Jainism is one of the oldest living religions of the world. It is a religious faith of India that is usually said to have originated with Mahavira, a contemporary of the Buddha (6th century BC). But Jains believe that the religion is far older, extending in fact to the remotest antiquity. Mahavira, they believe, was the twenty-fourth and last of the *Tirthankars*.

About 2600 years ago Mahavir or Vardhaman (599BC - 527 BC), the twenty fourth and the last *Tirthankara* of this era revived the Jain philosophy previously preached by his predecessor Lord Parshva (950BC - 850 BC) in India. He expanded the code of conduct and implemented daily rites for his followers. He felt that such changes are essential for proper religious practice. The present Jain scriptures reflect only his teachings.

Mahavir was born in 599 B.C., into the royal family of King Siddharth and Queen Trishala. After his conception, the wealth, prosperity and influence of the family increased. So his parents named him Vardhaman, the increaser of prosperity. Later, his followers named him Mahavir, the great hero.

Mahavir was born in the same border region of India and Nepal as the Buddha, just 50 kilometres north of modern Patna.. Thus he was about 35 years older than the Buddha.

Mahavira's parents were followers of Parshva, the penultimate Tirthankara, who lived about 250 years earlier in Varanasi. The historicity of Parshva is proved by the modern historians and scholars. So Mahavira was not the founder of Jaina religion. He was the rejuvenator, propagator and exponent of Jaina religion which had been taught by Parshva and other omniscient teachers of his ever present and imperishable Jaina tradition.

Although a born prince, Mahavir showed indifference towards worldly pleasures from his early age. At the age of thirty, he renounced the world, adopted the lifestyle in harmony with nature and remained engaged in meditation. He spent the next twelve years in deep silence and meditation to conquer his desires, feelings, and attachments. He carefully avoided harming

other living beings including animals, birds, insects, and plants. He also went without food for long periods of time. He was calm and peaceful against all unbearable hardships. During this period, his spiritual powers fully developed and, at the age of 42, he realized perfect perception, perfect knowledge, perfect power, and total bliss. This realization is known as *keval-jnana*. or the perfect enlightenment

Mahavir spent the next thirty years travelling barefoot around India preaching the eternal truth he realized. The ultimate objective of his teaching is how one can attain total freedom from the cycle of birth, life, pain, misery, and death, and achieve the permanent blissful state of one's self. This is also known as liberation, *nirvana,* absolute freedom, or *Moksha.*

Lord Mahavir organized his followers, into a four fold order, namely monk (*Sadhu*), nun (*Sadhvi*), layman (*Shravak*), and laywoman (*Shravika*). His followers are known as Jains

At the age of 72 (527 BC), Lord Mahavir attained *nirvana* (death) and his purified soul left his body and achieved complete liberation. He became a *Siddha*, a pure consciousness, a liberated soul, living forever in a state of complete bliss. On the night of his *nirvana,* people celebrated the Festival of Lights (Dipavali) in his honour.

LORD MAHAVIR'S MESSAGE

Lord Mahavir made religion simple and natural, free from elaborate ritual complexities. His teachings reflected the internal beauty and harmony of the soul. Mahavir taught the idea of supremacy of human life and stressed the importance of the positive attitude of life. His message of non-violence (*Ahimsa*), truth (*Satya*), non-stealing (*Achaurya*), celibacy (*Brahma-charya*), and non-possession (*Aparigraha*) is full of universal compassion. Mahavir said that, "A living body is not merely an integration of limbs and flesh but it is the abode of the soul which potentially has perfect perception (*Anant-darshana*), perfect knowledge (*Anant-jnana*), perfect power (*Anant-virya*), and perfect bliss (*Anant-sukha*). Mahavir's message reflects freedom and spiritual joy of the living being. Mahavir empha-

sized that all living beings, irrespective of their size, shape, and form how spiritually developed or undeveloped, are equal and we should love and respect them. This way he preached the gospel of universal love. Mahavir rejected the concept of God as a creator, a protector, and a destroyer of the universe. He also denounced the worshiping of gods and goddesses as a means of material gains and personal benefits. In the matters of spiritual advancement, as envisioned by Mahavir, both men and women are on an equal footing. His message of renunciation and liberation attracted women as well. Many women followed Mahavir's path and renounced the world in search of ultimate happiness.

Lord Mahavir was the twenty-fourth and the last *Tirthankara* of the Jain religion. According to Jain philosophy, all *Tirthankaras* were born as human beings but they attained a state of perfection or enlightenment through meditation and self realization. They are the Gods of Jains. *Tirthankaras* are also known as *Arihants* or *Jinas.*

Arihant - One who destroys his inner enemies like anger, greed, passion, ego .Jina - One who conquers his inner enemies like anger, greed, passion, ego, love and hate, pleasure and pain, attachment and aversion, and has thereby freed 'his' soul from the *karmas.*

The "Jains" are the followers of the *Jinas*.The Jains refer to the Jina as God.

Unlike Buddhism, Jainism never spread beyond India

BASIC TEACHINGS OF JAINISM

The heart of Jainism is non-violence. Positively stated, Jainism is a religion of compassion, universal love and friendliness. It aims at the welfare of all living beings, and not of men and women alone.

It is one of the tenets of Jainism that all living beings desire life and not death. No one has the right to take away the life of any other being. To kill a living being is the greatest of sins. Life is dear to everyone, and we must have respect for life. Not only "Love and Let Live" but "Live and Help Others Live" should be our principle.

Principle features of Jainism are:

- Religious tolerance
- Ethical purity
- Harmony between self and one's environment
- Spiritual contentment

Three Jewels

Along with other Indian systems, Jainism prescribes a path to liberation (*Moksha*), which consists of the three jewels (trinity or *ratna-traya*) of Jainism:

Right Perception
Right knowledge, and
Right conduct.

Right perception creates an awareness of reality or truth; right knowledge impels the person to proper action; and proper conduct leads him to the attainment of total freedom. They must coexist in a person if one is to make any progress on the path of liberation.

Right Perception (*Samyak Darsana*):

Right perception consists in seeing the true nature of every substances of the universe. Jainism advocates that one should first try to know, comprehend, and understand the nature of reality, one's own self, religious goal, and the path. One should analyze it, examine it, test it, and verify it, and then, if satisfied, be convinced of its truth and efficacy.

From the practical point of view, perception in the nature of the reality means to have a total faith in the preachings of *Tirthankars,* and their scriptures known as *agams.*

Right Knowledge (*Samyak Jnana*):

Right perception or faith makes us realize the reality of life, and the seriousness of our purpose in life. Right knowledge is the true, correct, proper, and relevant knowledge of the reality, the tattvas.

Mainly one has to know the following:

Six Universal Entities (Substances) soul, matter, motion, rest, space, and time.

Nine *Tattavs* (Principles): *Jiva, Ajiva, Asrava, Bandh, Punya, Papa, Samvara, Nirjara,* and *Moksha.*

Philosophically, this is known as the theory of non-absolutism (*Anekantvada*) and calls for an attitude of openness. Our limitations of knowledge dictate a style of relativity. The style of *Syadvada* allows no room for assertions. This Jain theory of knowledge, incorporating the two principles of non-absolutism and relativity, has made an esteemed contribution toward liberalizing the mind of human being.

Right knowledge makes us examine in detail the matter brought into the mind by right conviction. Both are mental processes. Right knowledge must be free from three main defects: doubt, delusion, and indefiniteness.

Right Conduct (*Samyak Charitrya*):

Proper, correct, appropriate, and truly natural conduct of the living being (*soul*) is known as right conduct. The main purpose for a human being is to free himself from attachment (*raga*) and aversion (*dvesha*). That is to be free from all impure activities of thought, word, and deed.

This will attain the state of perfect equanimity.

Right faith and right knowledge are required for right conduct, and all are inter-dependent.

The trinity is necessary for a successful life. This threefold discipline helps us realize our own intrinsic purity. The three jewels must be cultivated collectively to ensure liberation. Individually, they are incomplete and insufficient because they are mutually dependent. In isolation, perception, knowledge or conduct causes conflicts or tensions and vitiates the environment. Collectively, the three jewels produce harmony, contentment, and blissfulness with the progressive march of the soul to higher planes.

Vows for Ultimate Freedom

Right conduct comprises ethical codes, rules, and disciplines which an aspirant is required to pursue for the ultimate freedom .All aspirants dedicate themselves to proper conduct through vows and sub-vows. Vows are at the heart of Jain morality and are undertaken with a full knowledge of their nature and a determination to carry them through. There are five (5) Great Vows for monks and nuns and twelve (12) vows for laypersons (house-holders).

Five Great Vows (*Maha-vratas*)

Right knowledge, right faith, and right conduct are the three most essentials for attaining liberation.

In order to acquire these, one must observe the five great vows:

1. Non-violence - *Ahimsa*
2. Truth - *Satya*
3. Non-stealing - *Achaurya or Asteya*
4. Celibacy/Chastity - *Brahmacharya*
5. Non-attachment/Non-possession - *Aparigraha*

Non-violence (Ahimsa):

Among these five vows, non-violence (*Ahimsa*) is the cardinal principle of Jainism and hence it is called the highest religious principle, or the cornerstone of Jainism.

Non-violence is the supreme religion (*Ahimsa parmo dharma*)

It is repeatedly said by all *Tirthankaras* in Jain literature "Do not injure, abuse, oppress, enslave, insult, torment, torture, or kill any creature or living being."

Lord Mahavir said, "If you kill someone, it is yourself you kill. If you overpower someone, it is yourself you overpower. If you torment some one, it is yourself you torment. If you harm someone, it is yourself you harm." A wise man knows this and so he does not kill, nor does he overpower or torment anyone

According to Jainism all living beings, irrespective of their size, shape, or different spiritual developments are equal. No living being has a right to harm, injure, or kill any other living being, including animals, insects, and plants. Every living being has a right to exist and it is necessary to live with every other living being in perfect harmony and peace.

Nonviolence is based on love and kindness for all living beings. Nonviolence in Jainism is not a negative virtue. It is based upon the positive quality of universal love and compassion. One who is actuated by this ideal cannot be indifferent to the suffering of others.

Violence of every type should be completely forbidden. Mental tortures by way of harsh words, actions, and any type of bodily injuries should also be avoided. Even thinking evil of some one is considered violence in Jainism.

Practically, it is impossible to survive without killing or injuring some of the smallest living beings. Some lives are killed even when we breathe, drink water, or eat food. Therefore, Jainism says that minimum killing of the lowest form of life should be our ideal for survival.

In the universe, there are different forms of life, such as, human beings, animals, insects, plants, bacteria, and even smaller lives which cannot be seen even through the microscopes. Jainism has classified all the living beings according to their senses as follows:

1. five senses - human, animals, birds, heavenly, hellish beings
2. four senses - flies, bees, etc.
3. three senses - ants, lice, etc.
4. two senses - worms, leaches, etc.
5. one sense - vegetables, water, air, earth, fire etc.

The five sense are, touch, taste, smell, sight, and hearing.

It is more painful if a life of the higher forms (more than one sense) is taken. All non-vegetarian food is made by killing a living being with two or more senses. Therefore, Jainism preaches strict vegetarianism, and prohibits non-vegetarian foods.

Jainism explains that violence is not defined by actual harm, for this may be unintentional. It is the intention to harm, the absence of compassion, and the ignorance that makes an action violent. Without violent thought there can be no violent actions.

Non-violence is to be observed in action, speech, and thought. One should not be violent, ask others to do so, or approve of such an activity.

Truth (*Satya*):

Anger, greed, fear, jokes, etc. are the breeding grounds of untruth. To speak the truth requires moral courage. Only those who have conquered greed, fear, anger, jealousy, ego, frivolity, etc., can speak the truth. Jainism insists that one should not only refrain from falsehood, but should always speak the truth which should be wholesome and pleasant.

One should remain silent if the truth causes pain, hurt, anger, or death of any living being.

Truth is to be observed in speech, mind, and deed. One should not utter an untruth, ask others to do so, or approve of such activities.

Non-stealing (*Achaurya or Asteya*):

Stealing consists of taking another's property without his consent, or by unjust or immoral methods. Further, one should not take anything which does not belong to him. It does not entitle one to take away a thing which may be lying unattended or unclaimed. One should observe this vow very strictly, and should not touch even a worthless thing which does not belong to him.

When accepting alms, help, or aid one should not take more then what is minimum needed. To take more than one's need is also considered theft in Jainism.

The vow of non-stealing insists that one should be totally honest in action, thought, and speech. One should not steal, ask others to do so, or approve of such activities.

Celibacy / Chastity (*Brahmacharya*):

Total abstinence from sensual pleasure is called celibacy. Sensual pleasure is an infatuating force which sets aside all virtues and reason at the time of indulgence. This vow of controlling sensuality is very difficult to observe in its subtle form. One may refrain from physical indulgence but may still think of the pleasures of sensualism, which is prohibited in Jainism.

Monks are required to observe this vow strictly and completely. They should not enjoy sensual pleasures, ask others to do the same, nor approve of it.

For householders, what is required is 'chastity'. Under this vow, a householder must not have sensual relationship with anybody but one's own lawfully wedded spouse. Even with one's own spouse, excessive indulgence of all kinds of sensual pleasure need be avoided. There are several rules laid down for observing this vow for householders.

Non-attachment / Non-possession (*Aparigraha*):

Jainism believes that the more worldly wealth a person possesses, the more he is likely to commit sin to acquire the possession, and in a long run he may be more unhappy. The worldly wealth creates attachments which will continuously result in greed, jealousy, selfishness, ego, hatred, violence, etc.

Lord Mahavir has said that wants and desires have no end, and only the sky is the limit for them.

Attachments to worldly objects results in the bondage to the cycle of birth and death. Therefore, one who desires spiritual liberation should withdraw from all attachments to pleasing objects of all the five senses.

Monks observe this vow by giving up attachments to all things such as:

- Material things: Wealth, property, grains, house, books, clothes, etc.
- Relationships: Father, mother, spouse, sons, daughters, friends, enemies, other monks, disciples, etc.
- Feelings: Pleasure and painful feelings towards touch, taste, smell, sight, and hearing objects. They have the equanimity towards

music and noise, good and bad smells, soft and hard objects for touch, beautiful and dirty sights, etc.

They do not eat food for taste but for survival with the intention to destroy his *karma* with the help of this body. Non-possession and non-attachment are to be observed in speech, mind, and deed. One should not possess, ask others to do so, or approve of such activities.

Jainism has laid down and described in much detail these five great vows for the path of liberation. These are to be observed strictly and entirely by the monks and nuns. Partial observance is laid down for the householders with additional seven vows.

Twelve Vows Of Layperson

The five great vows (*Maha-vratas*) can be adopted by monks who are very keen about the uplift of their souls and ready to sacrifice all worldly enjoyments and family ties.

For those who want to remain in family life and for whom complete avoidance of five principle sins are difficult, Jain ethics specifies the following twelve vows to be carried out by the householder.

Of these twelve vows, the first five are main vows of limited nature (*Anuvratas*). They are somewhat easier in comparison with great vows (*Maha-vratas*). The great vows are for the monks.

The next three vows are known as merit vows (*Guna-vratas*), so called because they enhance and purify the effect of the five main vows and raise their value manifold. It also governs the external conduct of an individual.

The last four are called disciplinary vows (*Shikhsa-vratas*). They are intended to encourage the person in the performance of their religious duties. They reflect the purity of one's heart. They govern one's internal life and are expressed in a life that is marked by charity. They are preparatory to the discipline of an ascetic's life.

Three merit vows (*Gunavrats*) and four disciplinary vows (*Shikhsa-vratas*) together are known as Seven vows of virtuous conduct (*Shilas*).

A person may adopt these vows, according to his individual capacity and circumstances with the intent to adopt ultimately as a great vows.

The layperson should be very careful while observing and following these limited vows. These vows being limited or restricted vows may still leave great scope for the commitment of sins and possession of property.

The twelve vows are as follows:

Five Main Vows of Limited Nature (*Anuvratas*):

1. Non-violence Anuvrat - *Ahimsa Anuvrat (Sthula Pranatipat Viraman)*

2. Truthfulness Anuvrat - *Satya Anuvrat (Sthula Mrisavada Viraman)*

3. Non-stealing Anuvrat - *Achaurya Anuvrat (Sthula Adattadana Viraman)*

4. Chastity Anuvrat - *Bhramacharya Anuvrat (Sthula Maithuna Viraman)*

5. Non-attachment Anuvrat- *Aparigraha Anuvrat (Sthula Parigraha Viraman)*

Three Merit Vows (*Guna-vrats*):

6. Dik Vrata - Limited area of activity vow

7. Bhoga-Upbhoga Vrata - Limited use of consumable and non-consumable items vow

8. Anartha-danda Vrata - Avoidance of purposeless sins vow

Four Disciplinary Vows (*Siksha-vratas*):

9. *Samayik Vrata* - Meditation vow of limited duration

10. *Desavakasika Vrata* - Activity vow of limiting space

11. *Pausadha Vrata* - Ascetic's life Vow of limited duration

12. *Atithi Samvibhaga Vrata* - Limited charity vow

1. Non-violence *Anuvrat* (*Ahimsa Anuvrat*):

In this vow, a person must not intentionally hurt any living being (plants,animals,humans etc.) or their feeling either by thought, word or deed, himself, or through others, or by approving such an act committed by somebody else.

Intention in this case applies selfish motive, sheer pleasure and even avoidable negligence.

He may use force, if necessary, in the defense of his country, society, family, life, property, religious institute.

His agricultural, industrial, occupational living activities do also involve injury to life, but it should be as minimum as possible, through carefulness and due precaution.

Four stages of violence are described:

■ Premeditated Violence to attack someone knowingly

■ Defensive Violence to commit intentional violence in defense of one's own life

■ Vocational Violence to incur violence in the execution of one's means of livelihood

■ Common Violence to commit violence in the performance of daily activities

Premeditated violence is prohibited for all. A householder is permitted to incur violence defensively and vocationally provided he maintains complete detachment. Common violence is accepted for survival, but even here, one should be careful in preparing food, cleaning house, etc. This explains the Jain's practices of filtering drinking water, vegetarianism, not eating meals at night, and abstinence from alcohol.

Nonviolence is the foundation of Jain ethics.

Lord Mahavir says: `one should not injure, subjugate, enslave, torture or kill any living being including animals, insects, plants, and vegetables.'

This is the essence of religion. It embraces the welfare of all animals. It is the basis of all stages of knowledge and the source of all rules of conduct. The scriptures analyze the spiritual and practical aspects of no-nviolence and discuss the subject negatively and positively.

2. Truthfulness Anuvrat (*Satya Anuvrat*):

The second of the five limited vows is Truth. It is more than abstaining from falsehood.

It is seeing the world in its real form and adapting to that reality. The vow of truth puts a person in touch with his inner strength and inner capacities.

In this vow, a person avoids lies, such as giving false evidence, denying the property of others entrusted to him, avoid cheating others etc. The vow is to be followed in thought, action, and speech, and by doing it himself or by getting it done through others.

He should not speak the truth, if it harms others or hurts their feelings. He should, under these circumstances, keep silence.

3. Non-stealing (*Achaurya / Asteya*) Anuvrat:

In this vow, a person must not steal, rob, or misappropriate others' goods and property. He also must not cheat and use illegal means in acquiring worldly things, nor through others or by approving such an act committed by others.

4. Chastity (*Bhramacharya*) Anuvrat:

The basic intent of this vow is to conquer passion and to prevent the waste of energy. Positively stated, the vow is meant to impart the sense of serenity to the soul.

In this vow, the householder must not have a sensual relationship with anybody but one's own lawfully wedded spouse. Even with one's own spouse, excessive indulgence of all kinds of sensual pleasure need be avoided.

5. Non-possession / Non-attachment (*Aparigraha*) Anuvrat:

Non-possession is the fifth limited vow. As long as a person does not know the richness of joy and peace that comes from within, he tries to fill his empty and insecure existence with the clutter of material acquisitions.

Lord Mahavir said: Security born of material things is a delusion. To remove this delusion, one takes the vow of non-possession and realizes the perfection of the soul.

One must impose a limit on one's needs, acquisitions, and possessions such as land, real estate, goods, other valuables, animals, money, etc. The surplus should be used for the common good. One must also limit the every day usage of number of food items, or articles and their quantity.

This Jain principle of limited possession for householders helps in equitable distribution of wealth, comforts, etc., in the society. Thus Jainism helps in establishing socialism, economic stability, and welfare in the world.

Non-possession, like non-violence, affirms the oneness of all life and is beneficial to an individual in his spiritual growth and to the society for the redistribution of wealth.

6. *Dik Vrata* - Limited Area of *Activity* Vow

This vow limits one's worldly activities to certain area in all the ten directions; north, south, east, west, north-east, north-west, south-east, south-west, above and below. He gives up committing sins in any place outside the limited areas. This vow provides a space limit to the commitments of sins not restricted by the limited vows of non-violence. Thus outside the limited area, the limited vows assumes the status of full vow (*Maha-vratas*).

7. *Bhoga-Upbhoga Vrata* - Limited use of Consumable/Non-consumable items vow

Generally one commits the sin by one's use or enjoyment of consumable (*Bhoga*) and non-consumable (*Upbhoga*) things.

Consumable (*Bhoga*) means enjoyment of an object which can only be used once, such as food, drink, fruits and flowers.

Non-consumable (*Upabhoga*) means enjoyment of an object which can be used several times, such as furniture, cloths, ornaments, buildings etc.

One should, therefore, limit the use of these two items in accordance with his own need and capacity by taking this vow.

This vow provides the time limit to the commitments of sins not restricted by Aparigraha Anuvrata

8. *Anartha-danda Vrata* - Avoidance of Purposeless Sins Vow

One must not commit unnecessary or purposeless sin or moral offense as defined below. Thinking, talking, or preaching evil or ill of others.

Doing inconsiderate or useless acts such as walking on the grass unnecessarily.

Manufacturing or supplying arms for attack.

Reading or listening, improper literature, or carelessness in ordinary behavior.

Thus this vow is of great practical importance. It makes life more vigilant and sin-proof.

9. *Samayik Vrata* - Limited Meditation Vow

Meditation of the soul and its relationship with nature is known as Samayik.

By giving up affection and aversion (*Rag* and *Dvesha*), observing equanimity in all objects, thinking evil of no one, and being at peace with the world, one should practice this vow of meditation (*Samayik*).

This vow consists in sitting down at one place for at least 48 minutes concentrating one's mind on religious activities like reading religious books, praying, or meditating. This vow may be repeated many times in a day. It is to be observed by mind, body, and speech.

The meditation of 48 minutes makes a person realize the importance of a life long vow to avoid all sinful activities and is a stepping stone to a life of full renunciation.

10. *Desavakasika Vrata* - Limited Duration of Activity Vow

This vow sets the new limit within the limitations already set by Dik Vrata and Bhoga-Upbhoga Vrata. The general life long limitation of doing business in certain areas and the use of articles are further restricted for a particular days time of the week.

This means that one shall not, during a certain period of time, do any activity, business, or travel beyond a certain city, street, house or have anything to do with the enjoyment of objects beyond that limit.

11. *Pausadha Vrata* - Limited Ascetic's Life Vow

This vow requires to live the life of a monk for a day. During this time one should retire to a secluded place, renounce all sinful activities, abstain in seeking pleasure from all objects of the senses, observe due restraint of body, speech and mind. A person follows five great vows (Mahavratas) completely during this time. He passes his time in spiritual contemplation, perform meditation (Samayik), engage in self study, and worship Gods (Arihants and Siddhas).

This vow promotes and nourishes one's religious life and provides training for ascetic life.

12. *Atithi Samvibhaga Vrata* - Limited Charity Vow

One should give food, clothes, medicine, and other articles of its own possession to monks nuns, and a pious person. The food offered should be pure and with reverence.

One should not prepare any foods specially for monks because monks are not allowed to have such foods. Donating of one's own food and articles to monks and others, provides an inner satisfaction and raises one's consciousness to higher level. It also saves him from acquiring of more sins if he would have used the same for his nourishment, comfort and pleasure.

Peaceful Death:

In the final days of life, a householder observes peaceful death. The house-holder can attain a peaceful death (*Sallekhana*) if he truly follows the above twelve vows. The peaceful death is characterized by non-attachment to the worldly objects and by a suppression of the passions at the time of death. The last thought should be of a calm renunciation of the body, and this thought should ever be present long before death supervenes.

Conclusion:

By performing these twelve vows, a lay follower may live a righteous life and advance towards a fuller and more perfect life, and conquer desire.

While earning wealth, supporting family, and taking up arms to protect himself, his family, his country, etc. against intruder, he is taught self restraint, love and enmity. On one hand, he is debarred from doing any harm to himself, to his family, to his country, or to humanity by his reckless conduct. On the other hand, by giving up attachments he gradually prepares himself for the life of ascetics.

If one goes deeper into the rules laid down, he will find that practice of limiting the number of things to be kept or enjoyed by himself eliminates the danger of concentration of wealth at one point, which will help to minimize poverty and crime in the society. Thus limiting the desires of individuals, results in a ideal society.

RULEL OF CONDUCT
Five Samitis(rules of conduct) and Three Guptis (rules of avoidance of misconduct)

Besides the five great vows for ascetics and twelve vows for laypeople, Jainism lays great emphasis on observance of five rules of conducts (*Samitis*) and three rules of avoidance of misconduct (*Guptis*).

A person must be careful in walking, sitting, standing, and lying down. He must speak only gentle, sweet, and righteous speech. He must be careful in placing and removing articles of his use. He must be clean and should not make himself instrumental in the growth or death of germs and insects.

Five *Samitis* (Rules of conduct)

1. *Iriya Samiti* - regulation of walking. One should walk carefully looking forward about six feet distance so as not to cause the pain or death of any living being.

2. *Bhasa Samiti* - regulation of speaking. One should avoid the eight faults of speech during conversation. The eight faults are anger, pride, deceit, greed, laughter, fear, gossip, and slander. Always use sinless and concise speech.

3. *Esnna Samiti* - regulation of begging. Monks should search and obtain pure foods and other articles necessary for use, and to use the same in a faultless manner.

4. *Adana Nikshepana Samiti* - regulation of taking or keeping. One should lay down or take up an article of use very carefully so as not to endanger the life of small creatures and insects.

5. *Utsarga Samiti* - regulation of disposal. One should dispose of waste things, such as mucus, urine, stools, etc. in a solitary and out of the way place in a proper manner so as not to cause any inconvenience to anybody by becoming a source of nuisance, insanitation, or contamination. This waste helps the growth of germs, and is also the indirect cause of their death.

Three *Guptis* (Avoidance of misconduct)

1. *Mana Gupti* - regulation of mind. One should guard one's mind from impure thoughts such as anger, hate, curse, greed, jealous, ego, etc. Always be forgiving and devote the mind to pious meditation.

2. *Vachana Gupti* - regulation of speech. One should guard his speech so that it might not utter harmful, harsh, careless, foul, senseless, embarrassing, or bad language.

3. *Kaya Gupti* - regulation of bodily activity. One should guard movement of his body, so as not to hurt others, walking with an eye on the path so as not to harm, or kill an innocent life such as ants, bugs, etc. One should not day dream while doing any activity. Develop decent behavior and manners.

Thus *Samitis* purify the actions and make them faultless, while Guptis are prohibitions against sinful activities of mind, speech, and body. Both are equally necessary for the spiritual uplift of soul. Collectively all eight virtues are known as *Ashta Pravachan Mata.*

THOUGHT PROCESS

Twelve *Bhavnas* (Reflections or Thoughts)

Jain religion puts a significant emphasis on the thought process of a human being. A person's behavior and his actions are the reflection of his internal thoughts, day in and day out. It is not the action but intention behind the action that results in the accumulation of Karma.

One should be very careful about his thoughts, how he thinks, and the subject matter of his thought.

To make room for pure thoughts, and to drive out the evil ones, Jainism recommends to meditate the following *twelve thoughts or Bhavnas.*

The twelve *Bhavnas* are the subject matter of one's meditation, and how to occupy one's mind with useful, religious, beneficial, peaceful, harmless, spiritually advancing Karma . They are designed to serve as aids to spiritual progress and detachment, and to lead the aspirants from the realm of desire to the path of renunciation. These *Bhavnas* are also called *Anuprekshas,* longings, thoughts, aspirations.

1. *Anitya Bhavna* - Impermanence of the world

2. *Asarana Bhavna* - No one provides protection

3. *Samsara Bhavna* - No permanent relationship in universe

4. *Ekatva Bhavna* - Solitude of the soul

5. *Anyatva Bhavna* - Separateness

6. *Asuci Bhavna* - Impureness of the body

7. *Asrava Bhavna* - Influx of karma

8. *Samvara Bhavna* - Stoppage of influx of karma

9. *Nirjara Bhavna* - Shedding of karma

10. *Loka Bhavna* - Transitory of universe

11. *Bodhi-durlabha Bhavna* - Unattainability of right faith, knowledge, and conduct

12. *Dharma Bhavna* - Unattainability of true preceptor, scriptures, and religion

1. *Anitya Bhavna* - Impermanence of the world

Under this reflection, one thinks that in this world every thing such as life, youth, wealth, property, etc. are transient or subject to alteration. Nothing in the universe is permanent, even though the whole universe is constant.

Spiritual values are therefore worth striving for as soul's ultimate freedom and stability. This will help to break all earthly attachments

2. *Asarana Bhavna* - No one provides protection

Under this reflection, one thinks that he is helpless against death, old age, and disease. The only way he can conquer death and disease is by destroying all his karma. The soul is his own savior, and to achieve total freedom and enlightenment, one takes refuge to the true path and to the five best personalities. They are *Arihanta, Siddha, Acharya, Upadhyay* and *Sadhus*. The refuge to others are due to delusion, and must be avoided.

3. *Samsara Bhavna* - No permanent relationship in universe

Under this reflection, one thinks that the soul transmigrates from one life to the other in any of the four forms, human, animal, hellish, and heavenly.

The continual cycle of birth, life, and death is full of pain and miseries, and has not yet ended. There are no permanent worldly relations like father, mother, friend, foe, etc. It is we who establish these relations and live accordingly.

This kind of thought will help minimize or stop any attachments to anybody, other living beings, or objects. The soul must achieve ultimate freedom from it, which is liberation or *Moksha*.

4. *Ekatva Bhavna* - Solitude of the soul

Under this reflection, one thinks that the soul is solitaire, and lonely in existence. The soul assumes birth alone, and departs alone from the life form. The soul is responsible for its own actions and karmas. The soul will enjoy the fruits, and suffer bad consequences of its own action alone. Such thoughts will stimulate his efforts to get rid of karmas by his own initiative and will lead religious life.

5. *Anyatva Bhavna* - Separateness

Under this reflection, one thinks that soul is separate from any other objects or living beings of the world. Even his body is not his. At the time of death, soul leaves the body behind. The body is matter, while the soul is all consciousness.

The soul therefore should not develop attachment for worldly objects, and other living beings. He should not allow himself to be controlled by desires, greed, and urges of the body.

6. *Asuci Bhavna* - Impureness of the body

Under this reflection, one thinks about the constituent element of one's body. It is made of impure things like blood, bones, flesh, etc. It also generates impure things like perspiration, urine, stool, etc.

The soul, which resides within the body, is unattached to the body. It is alone and pure. The body ultimately becomes nonexistent, but the soul is eternal. Therefore emotional attachments to the body is useless.

7. *Asrava Bhavna* - Influx of karma

Under this reflection, one thinks about karma streaming into the soul. Every time he enjoys or suffers through the senses (touch, taste, smell, sight, and hearing) he makes his karma increase. This thought will make him more careful, and will try to stop the influx of karmas

8. *Samvara Bhavna* - Stoppage of influx of karma

Under this reflection, one thinks about stopping evil thoughts, and becomes absorbed in achieving spiritual knowledge, meditation, etc. This prevents the influx of karma.

9. *Nirjara Bhavna* - Shedding of *karma*

Under this reflection, one thinks about the evil consequences of karma, and striving to destroy the previously acquired *karma* by austerity and meditation.

10. *Loka Bhavna* - Transitory of universe

Under this reflection, one thinks about the real nature of this universe. Judging from the standpoint of substance, it is eternal but from the standpoint of modification it is transitory.

Thus all objects of the world come into existence and perish. This thought makes him understand the true nature of reality, which is necessary for right knowledge.

11. *Bodhi-durlabha Bhavna*- Unattainability of right faith, knowledge, and conduct

Under this reflection, one thinks that it is very difficult for the transmigrating soul to acquire right faith, right knowledge, and right conduct in this world. Therefore, when one's has the opportunity to be a religious person, take the advantage of it to develop right religious talent. This thought will strengthen one's effort to attain them, and live accordingly.

12. *Dharma Bhavna*- Unattainability of true preceptor, scriptures, and religion

Under this reflection, one thinks that the true preceptor, scriptures, and religion are excellent shelters in this world full of agony. All other things lead to misery and suffering.

FOUR VIRTUES

Besides the twelve *Bhavnas* described above Jainism has laid great importance on the following four Bhavnas or virtues. They are mentioned here for clarification.

- Amity, love, and friendship - *Maitri*
- Appreciation, respect and joy - *Pramoda*
- Compassion - *Karuna*
- Equanimity and tolerance - *Madhyastha*

JAIN GODS

Jainism believes that universe and all its substances or entities are eternal. It has no beginning or end with respect to time. There is no need of some one to create or manage the affairs of the universe. Universe in run own its own accord by its own cosmic laws. Hence Jainism does not believe in God as a creator, survivor, and destroyer of the universe.

However Jainism does believe in God. When a living being destroys all his *karmas,* he possesses perfect knowledge, vision, power, and bliss. He becomes omniscient and omnipotent. This living being is a God of Jain religion. Hence

Jains do not believe in one God. Gods in Jain religion are innumerable and the number is continuously increasing as more living beings attain liberation. Every living being has a potential to become God of the Jain religion.

While travelling on the path of spiritual progress, a person destroys all eight types of his *karmas* in the following sequence.

First *Mohaniya* (delusion), then *Jnana-varaniya* (knowledge), *Darasna-varaniya* (vision), and *Antaraya* (natural qualities) all three together.

Lastly the remaining four namely *Nama* (body), *Ayu* (life span), *Gotra* (social standing), and *Vedniya* (pleasure and pain of the body). He then attains liberation.

The first four *karmas* are called *Ghati karmas* because they obscure the natural qualities of the soul. The last four *karmas* are known as *Aghati karmas* because they are related to the body of the soul. Once a person destroys all *Ghati karmas,* automatically he will destroy all his *Aghati karmas* at the end of his present life. No fall back can occur.

A person who destroys all eight types of *karmas* is called *Siddha*. A person who destroys only four *Ghati karmas* is called *Arihanta* (*Tirthankara, Jina* etc). Both *Arihantas* and *Siddhas* are classified as Gods in Jainism.

Arihanta:

When a person destroys his *Ghati karmas,* he attains *keval-jnana.* He has regained the original attributes of his soul which are perfect knowledge, vision, power, and bliss. He is omniscient of the past, present and future forms of all entities (living and non-living beings) of the universe. He is still a human being. He preaches the religion and remains in the state of blissful condition for the rest of his life. He is known as an *Arihant.*

Arihantas have two categories:
- *Tirthankara*
- *Ordinary-kevali*

Tirthankara:

Immediately after attaining keval-jnana, if a person establishes the four-fold religious order of *monks, nuns, sravaks* (male laypeople), sravikas (female laypeople) is known as *Tirthankara.*

He preaches the Jain philosophy, religion, ethics, etc. to his followers.

Twenty-four *Tirthankaras* are born during this descending part of the time cycle (*Avasarpini Kaal*) of this region (*Bharat Kshetra*) of the universe. No two Tirthankaras have lived at the same time in this region. Generally a *Tirthankara* is born when the religion is at its depression state. He revives the same philosophy and religion at that time. Sometimes he gives a different form to the religion depending upon the time, place, and human behavior.

For example, Lord Mahavir preached five great vows, while Lord Parshva preached four great vows. The vow of celibacy was included in the non-possession category during Parshav's time.

Tirthankaras are also known as *Jina* or *Nirgrantha.*

Jina means one who has conquered his inner passions like desire and hatred.

Nirgrantha means one who has gotten rid of all attachments

Ordinary-kevali

The only difference between *Tirthankara* and ordinary-*kevali* is that the latter does not establish the religious order. He remains in the state of perfect blissful condition for the rest of his life after attaining *Keval-jnan*.

In the religious scriptures the name *Arihantas* and *Tirthankaras* are interchangeably used because ordinary-*kevalis* do not play a significant role in the religious order.

Siddha

All *Tirthankaras* and ordinary-*kevalis* destroy their remaining *Aghati karmas,* and attain liberation at the end of their present life. Now they are known as *Siddhas*. They are totally free. They do not possess body. They are free from the birth and death cycle. They do not feel pleasure and pain, or joy and sorrow. They live in an ever lasting blissful condition at the top of *Lokakas* known as *Moksha*. All *Siddhas* possess the same quality of soul, and their attributes are same. However, they still maintain their unique identity.

For Example, Lord Mahavir's soul as a *siddha* has a different form than the soul of Lord Bahubali.

Both *Arihants (Tirthankaras* and ordinary-*kevalis*) and *Siddhas* are considered Gods of Jain religion.

JAIN SCRIPTURES

Lord Mahavira's preaching were orally compiled into many texts (scriptures) by his immediate disciples. These scriptures are known as *Jain Agam* or *Agam Sutras*. The *Agam Sutras* teach great reverence for all forms of life, strict codes of vegetarianism, asceticism, nonviolence, and opposition to war. The scriptures were not documented in any form but were memorized by ascetics and orally passed on to future generations of ascetics.

In the course of time, many of the *Agam Sutras* were not remembered, some were modified, and new *Sutras* were added. About one thousand years after Lord Mahavir's *nirvan* (death) the memorized *Agam Sutras* were recorded on leafy papers *(Tadpatris)*. Swetambar Jains have accepted these *Sutras* as an authentic version of Lord Mahavira's teaching while *Digambar* Jains did not accept them as authentic. *Digambars* follow two main texts *(Shatkhand Agam and Kasay Pahud)* and four *Anuyogs* (consist of about 20 texts) written by great Acharyas (scholars) from 100 to 800 AD

JAIN PILGRIMAGES
Sravanabelagola - Bahubali (Karnataka)

One of the most important Jain pilgrimage sites is the monolithic statue of Bahubali at Sravanabelagola in the southern state of Karnataka. Wedged between two rocky hills, Indragiri and Chandragiri, Sravanabelgola literally translated means 'white pond of the ascetic'. The pond referred to is the temple tank located at the foot of Indragiri and the ascetic is the *Tirthankar* Gomateshwara or Bhagwan Bahubali. According to Jaina literature, he was the son of Vrishadeva, the *Aditirthankara,* the founder of the Jain faith. Prince Bahubali renounced his kingdom to perform penance and attained *Kevala jnana* or absolute knowledge. The history of Sravanabelagola goes back to the third century BC when after renouncing his kingdom, Chandragupta Maurya settled here with sage Bhadrabahu. Around 983 A.C., Chamundarya, a general and minister of the Ganga king Ramachamalla had the 17 metre high statue of Lord Gomateshwara erected at Sravanabelagola. Both the Chandragiri and Indragiri hills have *bastis* or Jain temples.

A special time to visit this site is during the *Mahamastakabhishekha* festival held every twelve years when the statue of Bahubali is anointed with offerings of milk, curd, honey, rice, coins, etc. It is indeed a grand sight to behold-tons and tons of offerings are poured over the head of the serene statue by eager devotees and yet the huge figure still does not get wet completely.

Dilwara Temple, Mount Abu (Rajasthan)

Jains from all over the world congregate at Mount Abu in Rajasthan, specifically at the Mount Abu in Rajasthan, specifically at the Dilwara Temple which is one of the finest examples of Jain art and architecture. The plain marble exteriors do not prepare the visitor for richly embellished interiors. Episodes from different Jain legends are intricately carved in marble and so life-like and delicate are the sculptures that it is difficult to believe they are indeed carved out of stone. Legend has it that the marble used in the temple sprang out of the earth some thousand years ago. For Jains, Mount Abu is the pivot of the Jain world.

Palitana (Gujarat)

There are many popular Jain pilgrimage sites in Gujarat. Palitana is an important temple town and lies at the foot of the sacred Shatrunjaya Hill. To the south of the town, the Shatrunjaya River flows by, lending immense beauty and serenity to this holy spot. As many as 863 beautiful marble temples built over as many as span of 900 years dominate the landscape-a sight to fill any pilgrim's heart with delight. An air of devotion and spirituality permeates the town with pilgrims preparing for the ritual four-kilometer (3,572 steps) climb up the hill. For those who cannot climb up, chair slings are available. The temples of Girnar also hold a special appeal for Jain pilgrims. The Girnar Hill which rises to a height to more than 600 metres is sacred to the Jains and there are as many as 16 exquisite temples adorning the hill sides. These marble shrines are visited by thousands of Jains every year.

Digambara Jain Temple, Delhi

The Digambara Jain temple is the oldest and most important Jain temple in Delhi. Located at the eastern end of Chandni Chowk, it has detailed carvings and excellent gilded paintings. Jains coming to Delhi from different parts of the country and abroad make it a point to visit this temple which is an oasis of peace in the bustling marketplace. South of the Jain temple is the Jain Bird hospital which tends to injured and sick birds and which epitomizes the Jain belief that all life is sacred.

Other Jain pilgrimages in India

There are many other important Jain temples all over India. The temple in the fort of Jaisalmer where countless feet have polished the yellow Jaisalmer stone into gold, making the whole temple glow with a strange radiance in the afternoon sun. Ranakpur is yet another important pilgrim site. To visit the Jain pilgrim sites is to see yet another facet of this fascinating religion. It is an experience filled with great spiritual and aesthetic satisfaction. In contrast to the austere practices, most Jain temples are expressions of immense beauty and are often very extravagant in their use of carvings, both of figures and decorative motifs. This richness in terms of iconography is evident in other Jain aesthetic traditions such as manuscript illustrations, pato embroidery and paintings on cloth.

JAINISM

PRAYER OF JAIN RELIGION:

Every day Jains bow their heads and say their universal prayer, the *Navkar-mantra*. All good work and events start with this prayer of salutation and worship.

Namo Arihantanam:	- I bow to the enlightened souls
Namo Siddhanam:	- I bow to the liberated souls
Namo Ayariyanam:	- I bow to religious leaders
Namo Uvajjayanam:	- I bow to religious teachers
Namo Loe Savva Sahunam:	I bow to all saints and sages everywhere in the world.
Eso Panch Namukkaro:	These five salutations are capable of
Savva Pava Panasano:	destroying all the sins and this is Mangalancha Savvesin the first happiness among all forms
Padhamam Havai Mangalam:	of happiness .

In the above prayer, Jains do not ask for any favours or material benefits from their Gods, the *Tirthankaras* or from monks and nuns. They do not pray to a specific *Tirthankara* or monk by name. By saluting them, Jains receive the inspiration from the five benevolent for the right path of true happiness and total freedom from the misery of life.

VEGETARIANISM

Vegetarianism is a way of life for a Jain, taking its origin in the concept of compassion for living beings, *Jiva Daya*. The practice of vegetarianism is seen as an instrument for the practice of non-violence and peaceful, cooperative coexistence. Jains are strict vegetarians, consuming only one-sensed beings, primarily from the plant kingdom. While the Jain diet does, of course, involve harm to plants, it is regarded as a means of survival which involves the bare minimum amount of violence towards living beings. (Many forms of plant material, including roots and certain fruits, are also excluded from the Jain diet due to the greater number of living beings they contain owing to the environment in which they develop.)

JAIN SECTS

Jains have two main sects, whose origins can be traced back to the fourth century BC. The more numerous *Svetambaras* - the 'white clad' - largely settled in eastern and western India, separated from the *Digambaras* - or 'sky -clad'-who often go naked. The *Digambaras* may well have been forced to move south by drought and famine in the northern region of the Deccan and they are now concentrated in the south of India.

The two Jain sects differ chiefly on the nature of proper ascetic practices. The *Svetambara* monks wear white robes and carry a staff, some wooden pots and a woollen mop for sweeping the path in front of them, wool being the softest material available and the least likely to hurt any living thing swept away. The highest level of *Digambara* monks will go completely naked, although the lower levels will wear a covering over their genitalia. They carry a water pot made of a gourd and peacock feathers to sweep the ground before they sit down

WOMEN IN JAIN ORDER

Women have been accorded equal status in the Jain religion. In fact, there were more women in the order of Lord Mahavir than men. The scriptures record many tributes to exceptional women. The care of women, especially in critical situations, is given a higher priority than that of men. Mothers of the *Tirthankaras* are given special honour through communal worship. Legends abound in which women of high spiritual merit such as Brahmi, Sundari, Mallikumari, and Rajimati have come to the aid of men. Women have been recognized for their exceptional contributions in the field of education, culture and religion.

JAIN WEDDING

A typical Jain marriage initiates with *"Vagdana"* - wherein the parents of the bride and groom declare the intention to marry them after which the *"Pradana"* takes place where the bride is gifted with ornaments. Then the mandap and the vedi are made ready - *"Mandapa-vedi-Pratishtha"* and also the ornament is installed in a ceremony called *"Torana Pratishtha"*.

The *"Vara Ghoda"* is taken out wherein the groom rides the horse. Upon reaching the destination the *"Torana Vidhi"* - rites of welcoming - is performed which includes *"Gotra Occhara"* - reciting of the genealogies or *gotra*. Then the bride and groom are allowed to take a look at each other's faces in a ceremony called *"Paraspara Mukh Avalokana"* after which the *"Varmala"* - garlanding - ceremony takes place and vows are taken in "Vara Pratijna". Then the couple goes round the fire in *"Agni Pradakshina"* and the bride's father gives her away in *"Kanyadaan"*.

Thereafter comes the *"Deva Shastra Guru Puja"* wherein the Jina, Scriptures and Gurus are worshipped. The knot is then tied between the bride and groom's dresses in *"Granthi Bandhana"* after which the *"Panigrahana"* ceremony takes place where the groom holds the bride's hand and takes seven steps - *"Sapta Padi"*. The couple then seeks *"Ashirvada"* - blessings - groom the elders present after which the the bride comes to her own new house which is called *"Sva Graha Aagamana"*.

Lastly suitable donations are made to the temples, institutes in *"Jina Grahe Dhan Arpana"*.

JAIN RITUALS
Birth
Priyodhbhav Sanskar

Ten days of cleansing or Sutak are observed after delivery. During this period no rituals are performed. But in the temple the priest recites mantras and receives offerings on behalf of the new-born.

Namkaran Sanskar

This is the naming ceremony. It is done on the eleventh, thirteenth or twenty-ninth day after the birth of a child. For Namkaran the name is selected from the 1008 Jinasahasranam for the boys and names of the girls are selected from famous women of the Puranas. The priest, chanting mantras declares the name and then the child is blessed.

Marriage (Described above)
Death

The Jains cremate the dead as soon as possible. A suitable place in the crematorium without any living organisms like grass or insects is selected so as not to harm them. The body is placed on a platform of wood . The eldest son of the deceased does the last rites. The mortal remains are collected in bags and the place is thoroughly cleansed. The remains are not immersed in rivers as they can pollute the water. Instead a hole is dug in the earth ; the remains are placed in the hole; and salt is sprinkled all over, so that the remains dissolve easily.

The Jains believe that the dead soul would be reborn immediately. So for them death is a festival or *Mahotsav*. Loud wailing and observing anniversaries are not part of the Jain tradition.

GLOSSARY OF JAIN TERMS

Acharya/ji: A Sadhu who is learned, is master of scriptures, and is head of a Sangh.

Aghati : The four types of Karmas, whose effect on soul are much milder than the other four.

Anuvrat: A vow for laypersons that is not as strict as a Mahavrat

Arihant: Conqueror of internal enemies, such as anger, pride, deceit, greed, jealousy, hatred, intrigue, passions, etc.

Atma: Soul

Beindriya: Lives with two senses, namely touch and taste.

Charitra : Conduct, or behavior, without any hatred or attachment. A pure soul is completely free from Attachments and hatreds.

Chauvisantho: A prayer to the twenty four Tirthankars of this Kaal in Bharat Kshetra.

Choindriya: Lives with four senses, namely touch, taste, smell, and sight.

Darshan: Perception. A pure soul has infinite perception.

Darshanavaraniya: A Ghati Karma that obscures the capacity of soul of perceiving everything.

Ganadhar/ji: The first (principal) disciples of Tirthankars. Mahavir had eleven.

Ghati : The four types of Karmas, whose effects are much stronger than the other four.

Gnan: Knowledge.

Gnanavaraniya: A Ghati Karma that obscures the capacity of soul of knowing everything.

Gunavrat: Three vows that enhance the five Anuvrats.

Gupti: Self-controls over Mind, Speech, and Body.

Jina/Jineshwar: Another word for Tirthankars,

Karma: A deed, good or bad. .

Kevaldarshan Infinite perception: After acquiring it, the cycle of births and deaths is broken forever.

Kevaldarshi: One who has Kevaldarshan.

Kevalgnan Infinite knowledge

Kevali/gnani One who has Kevalgnan.

Mahavrat A vow that is much stricter than an Anuvrat.

Moksha The state of liberation for a soul.

Muktishila The topmost area of universe. After death, a liberated soul rises to it, and never comes back

Muni One who keeps Maun (silence). He only observes, without praising or complaining.

Navkar A prayer consisting of nine lines, the most meaningful of all the prayers.

Panchendriya Lives with five senses, namely touch, taste, smell, sight, and hearing.

Poshadh A day when a householder lives like a Muni.

Pratikraman Going back to the original virtues (of soul) -peace, compassion, forgiveness, even-temperament, , etc

Sadhu A man who has given up family life and worldly comforts

Sadhvi/ji A female Sadhu / Monk

Sangh Fourfold society, as founded by a Tirthankar, consisting of male and female Sadhus and householders.

Shikshavrat Four vows, which prepare a house-holder for the eventual Muni life.

Shravak/ji Male householder, following Jainism.

Shravika Female householder

Siddha One who has achieved liberation from cycle of births and deaths

Tapa Penance, or austerities. Intended to destroy the Karmas.

Teindriya Lives with three senses, namely touch, taste, and smell.

Tirthankar One who after attaining keval-jnana establishes the four-fold religious order of Sadhus, Sadhvis, Shravaks, and Sharavikas.

Upadhyay/ji A Sadhu who has mastered and teaches religious scriptures.

Vandana Act of bowing, or offering salutations

Vrat Vow.

JAIN POPULATION

Almost all estimates for the world population of the followers of Jainism are under 5 million. This religion is almost entirely confined to India and to ethnic Jains. Its importance historically and philosophically far outstrips its relatively small number of adherents. Some Jains have emigrated to other countries, such as the United States and Canada. According to 2001 census, Jain population in India is 4.2 million (0.40% of Indian population).

Source: www.adherents.com

JAIN SAYINGS

In happiness and suffering, in joy and grief, we should regard all creatures as we regard our own self.

—**Lord Mahavir**

First is knowledge, then compassion; that is how the disciplined live. How would an ignorant discriminate between good and evil?

—**Dashvaikalik Sutra**

Non-violence is the highest religion

—**Lord Mahavir**